INDIA'S WATER SECURITY CHALLENGES

CHALLENGES

MYTHS , REALITY AND MEASURES

INDIA'S WATER SECURITY CHALLENGES

MYTHS , REALITY AND MEASURES

by

Colonel Vishal Murada

(Established 1870)

United Service Institution of India

New Delhi

Vij Books India Pvt Ltd

New Delhi (India)

Published by

Vij Books India Pvt Ltd
(Publishers, Distributors & Importers)
2/19, Ansari Road
Delhi – 110 002
Phones: 91-11-43596460, 91-11-47340674
Fax: 91-11-47340674
e-mail: vijbooks@rediffmail.com

ISBN (Pb)   : 9789385563423 (2017)

Contents

Figures

List of Tables

FOREWORD

The issues of water are as old as mankind itself; in fact it is ironic that the Earth is an inhabited planet essentially due to the presence of water. I am sure many readers will agree with the striking conclusion of Hungarian-born Nobel laureate physicist, Dénes Gábor: "Until today man has fought nature. From now on man has to fight his own nature." The world is increasingly turning its attention to the issue of water scarcity. Many countries face water scarcity as a fundamental challenge to their economic and social development; by 2030 over a third of the world population will be living in river basins that will have to cope with significant water stress, including many of the countries and regions that drive global economic growth. It is known that with population growth and economic development, the demand on water increases; so does competition among the economic sectors for water resources.

The Twenty First century foresees a bleak picture for future generations. The ever-expanding water demand of the world's growing population and economy, combined with the impacts of climate change, are already making water scarcity a reality in many parts of the world. Also, the transboundary component of the water agenda is a serious issue that demands urgent and adequate measures. The significance of the ratification of the 1997 UN Convention on the Law of the Non-Navigational Uses of International Watercourses and the adoption of the Resolution on the Law of Transboundary Aquifers by consensus cannot be lost on us. Globally, in just 20 years, demand for water will be 40 percent higher than it is today, and more than 50 percent higher in the most rapidly developing countries. Historic rates of supply expansion and efficiency improvement will close only a fraction of this gap. Unless local, national and global communities come together and dramatically improve the way we envision and manage water, there will be many more hungry villages and degraded environments—and economic development itself will be put at risk in many countries.

Due to its geographical disposition India is probably one of the most vulnerable to climate change. The demand for water has tripled at a time when the supply of water is inefficient with socio-economic diversities. India is exposed to climate change on multiple fronts. Immediate planning and preparation is therefore critical in designing our adaptation strategies. Over the next few decades, 2 billion human beings will be added to the global population amid dramatically changing climatic conditions, and this will necessitate significant changes in the way we manage our waters. The detailed inputs in this book highlight the inter-linked issues that must be addressed to find a global solution to this spiraling criticality. Water Security in India therefore, needs an immediate and holistic focus. Water must therefore be treated as a high political priority that is integrated into other policy areas. Cooperation is vital, across geographical, political boundaries and also between sectors.

15 Mar 2016
               Lt Gen PK Singh, PVSM, AVSM (Retd)
               Director,
               United Service Institution of India

ABBREVIATIONS

BCM	Billion Cubic Metres
FAO	Food and Agriculture Organization of the United Nations
GBM	Ganges-Brahmaputra-Meghna
GEF	Global Environment Facility
GOI	Government of India
GWP	Global Water Partnership
ICID	International Commission on Irrigation and Drainage
ICWR	India-Nepal Joint Committee on Water Resources
ILC	International Law Commission
IPCC	Intergovernmental Panel on Climate Change
IUCN	International Union for Conservation of Nature
IWRM	Integrated Water Resources Management
IWT	Indus Water Treaty
JCWR	Joint Committee on Water Resources
JCE	Joint Committee of Experts
JGE	Joint Group of Experts
JMP	Joint Monitoring Programme
MDG	Millennium Development Goals
MAF	Million Acre Feet
MHa	Million Hectares
NAPCC	National Action Plan of Climate Change
NCIWRD	National Commission for Integrated Water Resource Development
NE	Neutral Expert

NHPC	National Hydro Power Corporation
PIC	Permanent Indus Commission
POK	Pakistan Occupied Kashmir
ROR	Run-of-River Projects
SADC	Southern African Development Community
SDG	Sustainable Development Goals
SIWI	Stockholm International Water Institute
TWM	Transboundary Water Management
UN	United Nations
UNDP	United Nations Development Programme
UNECE	United Nations Economic Commission for Europe
UNEP	United Nations Environment Programme
UNESCAP	United Nations Economic and Social Commission for Asia and the Pacific
UNESCO	United Nations Educational, Scientific and Cultural Organization
UNGA	United Nations General Assembly
UNHCR	United Nations High Commissioner for Refugees
UNICEF	United Nations Children's Fund
UNISDR	United Nations International Strategy for Disaster Reduction
UNSC	United Nations Security Council
UNU	United Nations University
UNU-EHS	United Nations University – Institute for Environment and Human Security
UNU-INWEH	United Nations University – Institute for Water, Environment and Health
UNW-DPC	UN-Water Decade Programme on Capacity Development
WHO	World Health Organization
WWAP	World Water Assessment Programme
WWF	World Wildlife Fund

CHAPTER -1: WATER CONUNDRUM

"The wars of this century have been on oil, and the wars of the next century will be on water ... unless we change the way we manage water."

Ismail Serageldin,

Former Vice President, World Bank

Introduction

The water on the surface of the Earth is naturally organised within river basins which are the primary entities of the fresh water. Over the last century the world's population has tripled, the global demand for water has increased by seven times and the irrigated areas by six times. Agriculture is the world's greatest water consumer. Global water resources are decreasing due to increasing water pollution. A time when the world's usable water resources arc lesser than the demand made on them is foreseen. This development is leading to a growing shortage of water resources and thus to a worldwide water crisis that can be expected to be experienced virtually everywhere[1].

Figure 1: Global Per Capita Water Availability: 2025

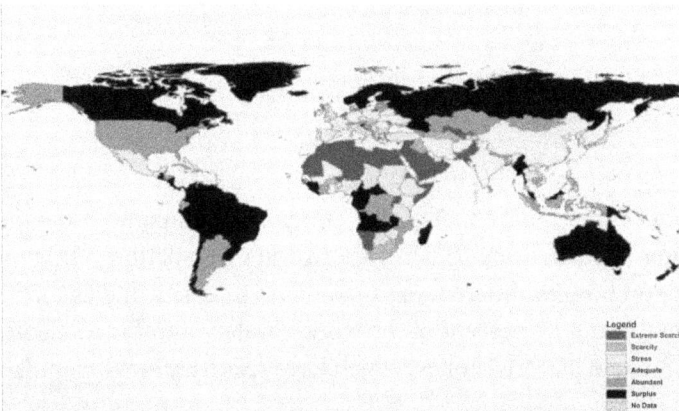

Of all the natural resources on which the modern world depends, water is the most critical. There are replacements for oil, but there is no substitute for water[2]. It is essential to produce virtually all the goods in the marketplace, from food to industrial products, as well as to produce electricity, to refine oil and gas, and to mine coal and uranium. Put simply, water scarcity and rapid economic advance cannot go hand in hand[3.] Yet water scarcity now affects more than two-fifths of the people on Earth, and by 2025 two-thirds of the global population is likely to be living in water-scarce or water-stressed conditions.[4] Water-scarce nations face very tough choices and serious socioeconomic consequences. The world's available fresh water supply is also distributed extremely unevenly around the globe. Internationally shared basins supply 60 % of global freshwater supply, and are focal points for interstate conflict and, as importantly, cooperation.

Figure 2: Water Stress Per Basin

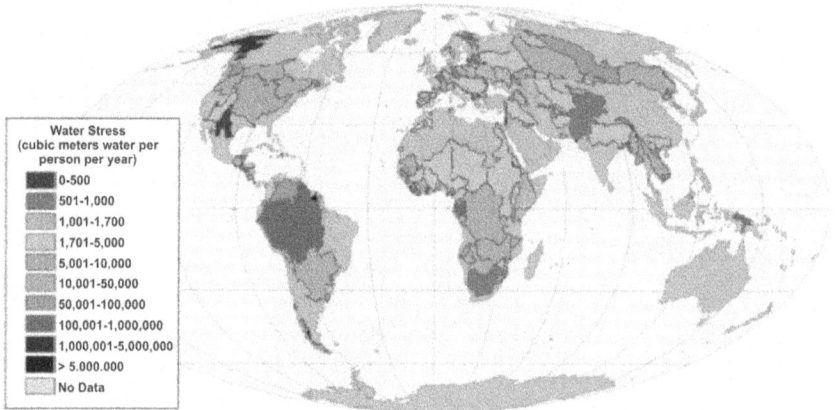

About three-quarters of global annual rainfall comes down in areas containing less than one-third of the world's population[5]. This disparity is a function both of differences in population density and available water resources. About 80 percent of the world's water runoff is concentrated in Northern and equatorial zones, which have relatively small populations.

Figure 3: International River Basins

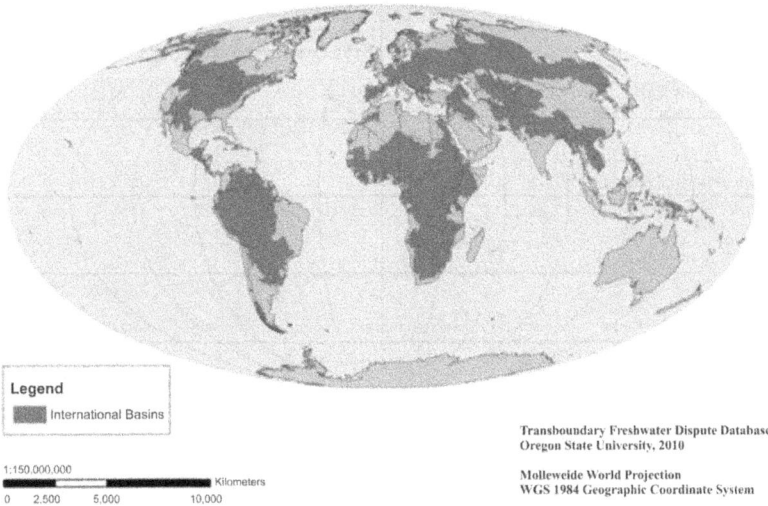

Legend
International Basins

Transboundary Freshwater Dispute Database
Oregon State University, 2010

1:150,000,000
0   2,500   5,000   10,000   Kilometers

Molleweide World Projection
WGS 1984 Geographic Coordinate System

Demands for freshwater will continue to increase significantly over the coming decades to meet the needs of growing populations and economies, changing lifestyles and evolving consumption patterns, greatly amplifying existing pressures on limited natural resources and on ecosystems.

Figure 4: Population Density per River Basins

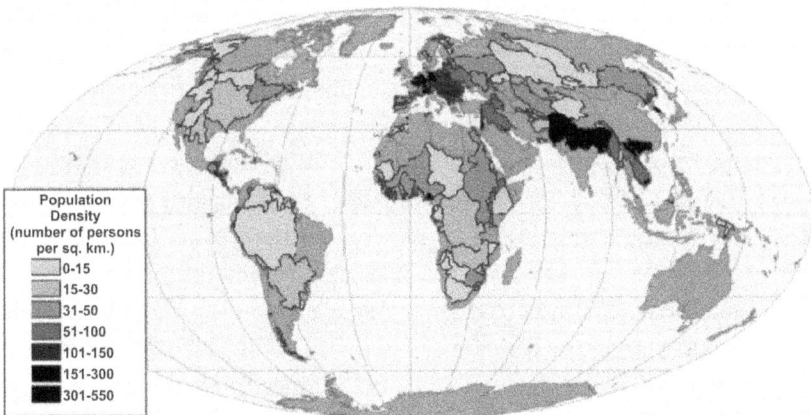

Population Density
(number of persons per sq. km.)
0-15
15-30
31-50
51-100
101-150
151-300
301-550

Demands for freshwater will continue to increase significantly over the coming decades to meet the needs of growing populations and economies, changing lifestyles and evolving consumption patterns, greatly amplifying existing pressures on limited natural resources and on ecosystems. The resulting challenges will be most acute in countries undergoing accelerated transformation and rapid economic growth, or those in which a large segment of the population lacks access to modern services[6].

Figure 5: Average Annual Runoff

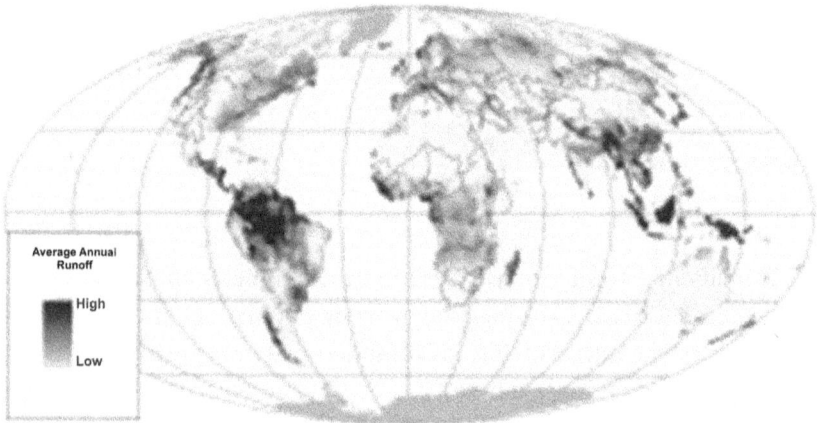

Water has emerged as a key issue that will determine if Asia heads toward greater cooperation or greater competition. Asia is the world's driest continent, with availability of freshwater less than half the global annual average of 6,380 m[3] per inhabitant. Asia's rivers, lakes and aquifers give it, per capita, less than one-tenth the water of South America or Australia and New Zealand, less than one-fourth of North America, almost one-third of Europe, and moderately less than Africa[7]. Yet the world's fastest-growing demand for water is in Asia, which now serves as the locomotive of the world economy. Today, the most dynamic Asian economies, including China, India, Indonesia, South Korea and Vietnam, are all in or close to being in conditions of water stress. Yet Asia continues to draw on tomorrow's water to meet today's needs[8]. Worse still, Asia has one of the lowest levels of water efficiency and productivity in the world. Against this background, it is no exaggeration to say that the water crisis threatens Asia's economic and political rise and its environmental sustainability. Experts contend that, although Asia is relatively well-endowed with water resources, many of the continent's countries will in the near future experience water shortages for all or part of the year (Asian Development Bank, 1999).

In developed and developing countries alike, fierce competition among water users is rising as people demand more and more from limited water resources. Tensions are particularly severe in places that face population pressures, rapid urbanisation, and urgent development needs. Transboundary waters pose enormous challenges for achieving water security. Where water systems, such as river or lake basins and aquifer systems, are shared across internal or external political boundaries, water-related challenges are compounded by the need to ensure coordination and dialogue between sovereign states, each with its own set of varied and sometimes competing interests (GWP, 2013).

The increasing diversity of water use, as well as the rapid growth in demand, coupled with the decreasing water resources and the international character of water resources across the globe have increased tensions over utilisation of water. Added to these problems are the changes to water resources expected through global climate change.

Global Water Issues

Years of rapid population growth and increasing per capita consumption have squeezed the world's freshwater resources. As global population has grown to nearly 6.1 billion today (and continues to grow by about 78 million people each year), the demand for fresh water in some areas exceeds nature's capacity to provide it. A growing number of countries are expected to face water shortages in the near future—shortages that will be fuelled by problems both on the demand side (population growth, urbanisation and development) and on the supply side (inadequate water supplies, management and poor policies). The total volume of water on Earth is about 1.4 billion km^3. The volume of freshwater resources is around 35 million km^3, or about 2.5 percent of the total volume. According to the United Nations Educational, Scientific and Cultural Organisation (UNESCO)[9] estimates, the total volume of water on earth is about 1.4 billion km3, which is enough to cover the earth with a layer of 3 km depth. However, World's oceans cover about three-fourths of earth's surface while the fresh water constitutes a very small proportion of this enormous quantity available on the earth. It is only about 35 million km3 or 2.5% of the total volume. Of these, 24 million km3 or 68.9% is in the form of ice and permanent snow cover in mountainous regions, and in the Antarctic and Arctic regions and another 29.9% is present as ground water (shallow and deep groundwater basins up to 2,000 metres). The rest 0.3% is available in lakes, rivers (0.3%) and 0.9% in soil moisture, swamp water and permafrost atmosphere. A detailed analysis by the Office of Director National Intelligence, USA, 2012 gives a graphic representation of the actual freshwater available (Figure) .

Figure 6: EARTH'S WATER: THE ACTUAL AVAILABILITY

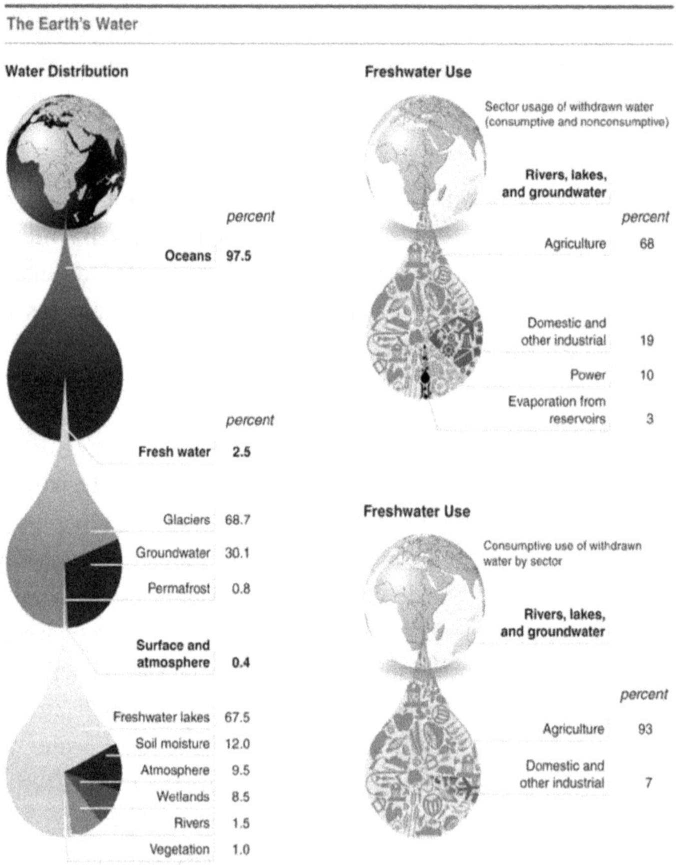

The Earth's Water

Water Distribution

	percent
Oceans	97.5

	percent
Fresh water	2.5

Glaciers	68.7
Groundwater	30.1
Permafrost	0.8
Surface and atmosphere	0.4

Freshwater lakes	67.5
Soil moisture	12.0
Atmosphere	9.5
Wetlands	8.5
Rivers	1.5
Vegetation	1.0

Freshwater Use

Sector usage of withdrawn water (consumptive and nonconsumptive)

Rivers, lakes, and groundwater

	percent
Agriculture	68
Domestic and other industrial	19
Power	10
Evaporation from reservoirs	3

Freshwater Use

Consumptive use of withdrawn water by sector

Rivers, lakes, and groundwater

	percent
Agriculture	93
Domestic and other industrial	7

Note: When humans use water, they effect the quantity, timing, or quality of water available to other users. Water for human use typically involves withdrawing water from lakes, rivers, or groundwater and either consuming it so that it reenters the atmospheric part of the hydrological cycle or returning it to the hydrological basin. When irrigated crops use water, it is consumptive use—it becomes unavailable for use elsewhere in the basin. In contrast, releasing water from a dam to drive hydroelectric turbines is generally a nonconsumptive use because the water is available for downstream users but not necessarily at the appropriate time. Withdrawals by a city for domestic and industrial use are mainly nonconsumptive, but if the returning water is inadequately treated, the quality of the water downstream is affected.

Source: Multiple, as quoted by World Bank, 2010.

Water Security: It's Varied Dimensions

Water security is defined '*as the capacity of a population to safeguard sustainable access to adequate quantities of acceptable quality water for sustaining livelihoods, human well-being, and socio-economic development, for ensuring protection against water-borne pollution and water-related disasters, and for preserving ecosystems in a climate of peace and political stability*'.[10]

This definition implies that water is managed sustainably throughout the water cycle and is done so through an inter-disciplinary focus, so that it contributes to socio-economic development and reinforces societal resilience to environmental impacts and water-borne diseases without compromising the present and future health of populations and ecosystems. Achieving water security requires allocation among users to be fair, efficient and transparent; that water to satisfy basic human needs is accessible to all at an affordable cost to the user; that water throughout the water cycle is collected and treated to prevent pollution and disease; and that fair, accessible and effective mechanisms exist to manage or address disputes or conflicts that may arise.

The term "water security" offers a common frame-work and a platform for communication. A mutually agreed-upon definition, especially across the UN system, will guide how water security is to be achieved, and provide a shared understanding of the concept and its various complex dimensions. It facilitates the incorporation of water security issues in the international development dialogue, particularly in the formulation of Sustainable Development Goals (SDGs).[11] Uncertainties about the definition of "water security" restrict the use of the term in the context of inter-national, regional, and national processes. This potentially places water issues at a disadvantage when compared to other interests, such as food security or energy security, in similar forums. In such settings, more effort will be required to articulate water issues, often in more complicated and incomplete ways.

Water conflicts are becoming prevalent at all levels. The issues based on this responsive affair are going to conclude the future scenario as practised in the past. Conflicts over water are primeval that the idea is incorporated into language, the word 'rivals' is derived from the Latin 'rivalis', meaning 'the one using the same stream as another.'

The term water security facilitates capturing the dynamic dimensions of water and water - related issues and offers a holistic outlook for addressing water challenges. A broad understanding highlights the various dimensions of the term. Approaching water issues under the umbrella of water security captures most interests in water and offers a means for considering these issues holistically, as many issues are closely interrelated and have multiple causes, impacts, and solutions across sectors. Water security encapsulates complex and interconnected challenges and highlights water's centrality for achieving a sense of security, sustainability, development and human well-being, from the local to the international level. Many factors contribute to water security and range from biophysical to infrastructural, institutional, political, social and financial, many of which lie outside the water realm. Water security, therefore, lies at the centre of many security areas, each of which is intricately linked to water (Zeitoun, 2011). Addressing water security, therefore, requires interdisciplinary collaboration across sectors, communities and political borders, so that the potential for competition or conflicts over water resources, between sectors and between water users or states, is adequately managed (Wouters *et al.*)

A number of important global drivers are significantly affecting water resources, increasing the risks and vulnerabilities to human security. As per the assessment by UNESCO in the document The 10 Drivers of Water Security 2010-2050 are as follows[12]:-

- ➢ Agiculture
- ➢ Climate Change
- ➢ Demography
- ➢ Economy_and_Security
- ➢ Ethics_society_and_culture
- ➢ Governance_and_Institutions
- ➢ Infrastructure
- ➢ Politics
- ➢ Technology
- ➢ Water Resources and Ecosystem

Governance And Water Security

Good governance is a prerequisite to achieving water security, as the international community has long and repeatedly recognized. One of the few definitions of global water governance comes from a 2008 study that defines it as "the development and implementation of norms, principles, rules, incentives, informative tools, and infrastructure to promote a change in the behaviour of actors at the global level in the area of water governance" (Pahl-Wostl et al. 2008, 422). Early water governance efforts emphasized the local and regional scales, in part because water challenges were largely perceived as local issues.

There is growing recognition that the scope and complexity of water-related challenges extend beyond national and regional boundaries and therefore cannot be adequately addressed solely by national or regional policies alone. Over the past sixty years, a number of efforts have sought to address the many challenges facing the water sector. Earlier efforts to address these challenges were almost entirely based on developing large-scale physical infrastructure, such as dams and reservoirs, to produce new water supplies. Over years it is seen that water crisis is essentially a crisis of governance and societies are facing a number of social, economic and political challenges on how to govern water more effectively" (UN 2003b, 370).

As water security has social, humanitarian, economic, legal and environmental dimensions, it requires an equally wide range of capacities and expertise that go beyond the immediate management of available water resources. In particular, capacity development at the institutional level is of great importance, as it sets the framework for capitalizing on human capacities and coordinating multi-sectoral policies. Poor governance mechanisms, expressed through weak legislative and institutional arrangements, under investment, poorly enforced legislation and accountability mechanisms and corruption, hamper efforts to achieve water security (International Freshwater Conference, Bonn 2001; World Water Forum, Istanbul 2009; World Water Forum, Marseille 2012).

Governance mechanisms necessary for water security include operating capacity, transparency, participation, accountability, and access to legal recourse. It comprises formal and informal instruments—including global governmental and nongovernmental organisations, regimes, actors, frameworks, and agreements — created to balance interests and meet global water challenges that span national and regional boundaries .Good water governance relies on well-designed, empowered institutions to enact and enforce legislative and policy instruments and are conducive to the attainment of predetermined social, economic and environmental goals associated with water security. Governance may be expressed through different organisational structures and arranged according to local conditions, capacities and agreed domestic and international policy goals[13].

Governance structures must take into account power groups and local arrangements when designing systems aimed at improving water security in an efficient and sustainable manner. Water governance is an evolving process that requires continuous refinement as it responds to new challenges, information, experiences, and problems. Achieving water security requires institutional and regulatory support, capacity for change, adaptive management structures, new forms of relationships, and multi-layered models capable of integrating complex natural and social dimensions. A number of international instruments have been under development for the last two decades . Financing is essential for good water governance, with the private sector poised to play a key role in this regard. Global business has already put water on its agenda in recognition of the importance of reliable water supplies and healthy living conditions and the associated need to manage business risks. A large number of organisations exist to address water challenges at various scales—particularly the United Nations system, multilateral lending institutions, and regional basin organisations—all working on different aspects of water management. UN-Water, however, has several deficiencies. In particular, it "does not have a strong mandate," nor does it make centralized policies (Pahl-Wostl et al. 2008, 427). UN-Water also has its own areas of focus (water and climate change, water quality, water supply and sanitation, and transboundary water), which fail to address the full range of water-related challenges.

A number of countries have been working to ratify existing framework water conventions and implement related guidelines and best practices; some examples of relevant instruments include the following:-

- The 1997 UN Convention on the Law of the Non-Navigational Uses of International Watercourses. This convention has since been ratified by the thirty fifth signatory, Vietnam in may 2014 and the treaty is deemed ratified since August 2014[14]; (Appendix 1)

- The 1992 UNECE Convention on the Protection and Use of Transboundary Watercourses and International Lakes, It provides an intergovernmental platform for the day-to-day development and advancement of transboundary cooperation. Initially negotiated as a regional instrument, it turned into a universally available legal framework for transboundary water cooperation, following the entry into force of amendments in February 2013, opening it to all UN Member States. It is expected that countries outside the ECE region will be able to join the Convention as of early 2015[15].

- The 2008 ILC Draft Articles on the Law of Transboundary Aquifers, The 63rd session of the UN General Assembly adopted the Resolution A/RES/63/124 on the Law of Transboundary Aquifers by consensus in December 2008. All 19 articles of the Law of Transboundary Aquifers, prepared by UNESCO's International Hydrological Programme (IHP) and the UN International Law Commission, have been endorsed by the UN General Assembly in New York. The resolution encourages the States concerned 'to make appropriate bilateral or regional arrangements for the proper management of their transboundary aquifers, taking into account the provisions of these draft articles', which are annexed to the resolution. These provisions include cooperation among States to prevent, reduce and control pollution of shared aquifers[16].

- The 63rd session of the UN General Assembly adopted the Resolution on the Law of Transboundary Aquifers by consensus in December . It includes 19 articles of the Law of Transboundary Aquifers, prepared by UNESCO's International Hydrological Programme (IHP) and the UN International Law Commission which have been endorsed by the UN General Assembly .[17]

- Climate change has been recognized by the UN Security Council for its security implications (United Nations Department of Public Information, 2011), with water being the medium through which climate change will have the most effects. Similarly, by including water security on its agenda, the UN Security Council has formally recognized the direct implications of water on human security issues: either as a trigger, a potential target, a contributing factor or as contextual information. Such recognition acknowledges that water is in itself a security risk[18] that acknowledging water insecurity could act as a preventative measure for regional conflicts and tensions; and that water security could contribute to achieving increased regional peace and security in the long term.

Opportunity With Contemporary Events

For India, as also most rapidly developing nations, it is an opportune time for deliberate analysis and decided action as the 1997 UN Convention on the Law of the Non-navigational Uses of International Watercourses (which sets rules on shared water resources to establish an international water law) (Appendix 1) has come into force. The ratification process was completed after the thirty fifth signatory (Vietnam) ratified the convention[19] . As per the report by the International Water Law Project the 35th ratification was received on 19 May 2014. Accordingly, the Convention entered into force on 17 August 2014, 90 days after that 35th ratification was deposited. In addition to the 35 ratifications to the Convention, there are an additional 3 nations that had signed but not yet ratified the treaty[20]. On 02 January 2015, the "State of Palestine" acceded to 1997 UN Convention on the Law of the Non-navigational Uses of International Watercourses, making it the 36th Party to the instrument. The position of various nation states varies as the convention impacts different countries differently it reflects in their stance towards the Convention.(Appendix 2). China, in rejecting the 1997 UN Watercourse Convention earlier , placed on record its assertion of absolute territorial sovereignty over the waters within its borders stating that "The text did not reflect the principle of territorial sovereignty of a watercourse state. Such a state had indisputable sovereignty over a watercourse which flowed through its territory." India too stands amongst the non signatories and must ensure it's national interests are safeguarded before being a signatory to the convention. India abstained from signing the Convention on account of certain reservations; which are mentioned below[21]:

- Article 3, which deals with Watercourse Agreements, provides that 'an agreement may be entered into with respect to an entire international watercourse or any part thereof or a particular project, programme or use except in so far as the agreement adversely affects, to a significant extent, the use by one or more other watercourse States of the waters of the watercourse, without their express consent'. Regarding this Article, India believes that a Framework Convention should not be prescriptive but should leave states free to evolve and implement mutually agreeable terms in relation to specific international watercourses. Thus Article 3 fails adequately to reflect the principle of freedom, autonomy and the right of states to conclude international agreements without being fettered by the UN Framework Convention.

- Article 5 on Equitable and Reasonable Utilisation and Participation is not clear and unambiguous especially as the term "sustainable utilisation" has been imposed on the principle of optimal utilisation without defining what the former implies in the given context. Article 5 is, therefore, vague and difficult to implement.

- Article 32 dealing with non-discrimination presupposes political and economic regional integration of states, as say within the European Union. Otherwise, prescribing national treatment for non-nationals claiming recompense for alleged transboundary injury will be unimplementable.

- Article 33 pertaining to the settlement of disputes mandates an element of compulsion in setting up fact-finding commissions. India believes that the parties should be left free to choose any acceptable procedure for securing an amicable settlement through mutual consent.

Another major global event in 2014 was the announcement by USA and China in November 2014 that both countries will curb their greenhouse gas emissions over the next two decades. The significance of U.S. President Barack Obama and Chinese President Xi Jinping announcement in November 2014 is critical[22]. At The United Nations climate-change negotiations in Lima in 2014, a quietly negotiated bilateral agreement between the world's two largest emitters and economies, which would see Chinese emissions peak by 2030 and the rate of US emissions reductions double by 2025 is of significance as a significant change from their earlier stance, as also a welcome precedence. The two countries had in the past blocked progress at the United Nations Framework Convention on Climate Change (UNFCCC) over fundamental disagreements about historical responsibility for emissions and in deciding who should bear the financial responsibility for adapting and decarbonising developing countries' economies. In 2014, the EU also committed to reducing carbon-dioxide emissions by 40% from 1990 levels by 2030. These emission cuts are not deep enough to avoid exceeding the 2°C increase from the present temperatures of the earth, but they represent a significant change in tone and are an indication of momentum and cooperation from key players in the negotiations. The Lima agreement commits all countries to emissions reductions, representing an important move away from traditionally entrenched positions. Responsibility for cutting emissions had previously been placed at the door of rich countries, reflecting a historical division between richer, developed countries (Annex I) and poorer, developing countries (Non-Annex I). The Annexes were defined in 1997 as part of the Kyoto Protocol, and the circumstances of many countries classed as 'developing' at that time (including China) have changed dramatically in the intervening years. As a result, the principle of only requiring cuts from Annex I countries while allowing Non-Annex I nations unrestricted emissions as they pursue economic growth has become increasingly strained. Any Paris deal will include national plans for emissions reductions referred to as Intended Nationally Determined Contributions (INDCs). These will outline pledges for action that each country is expected to make, determined according to their capabilities. Richer countries are expected to make these INDCs public by 31 March 2015, with other countries following in June. India, will perforce, have to put forth the figures as INDCs after a thorough and detailed analysis in harmony with policy implications. The impact on future use of water, fuel, technologies and resultant pollution etc will be significant. It has to be so calibrated that it adequately supports the progressive economic and development trajectory that India is predicted to follow in the coming decades. The public review process that will follow is intended to allow scrutiny of the plans for their ambition and achievability, and to allow a calculation of whether planned contributions are sufficient to limit warming to the Lima Call for Climate Action's stated goal of 2°C above pre-industrial temperatures by 2100 – the internationally accepted target to avoid 'dangerous' climate change[23]. The conference in Lima was intended to make progress on these issues ahead of Paris. However, reasons for caution remain. Despite optimism following the historic US–China agreement, it did not eliminate the oppositional dynamic between the two countries, who still disagree on whether the deal to be struck in Paris should be legally binding for developed countries and how transparent the review process should be for INDCs. UN climate talks in Geneva in February 2015 have enabled the preparation of a formal draft negotiating text for the summit in Paris in December 2015. The document, which runs to 86 pages, builds on negotiations in Peru 2014. The Swiss meeting set out to create a draft for consideration at the Paris talks. The aim is to have a new global climate agreement in place by the end of 2015[24].

China and India have traditionally headed a group calling for developing countries to have the right to emit and for industrialised nations to fund developing countries' adaptation and transition to clean energy systems, and the decarbonisation of their economies. Industrialised nations, headed by the US, have resisted these initiatives, pointing out that China and India are the world's first- and third-largest emitters respectively, and must commit to reducing emissions if the 2°C target is to be met.

India's position in the negotiations has become more critical, since China's decision to commit to its own emissions-reduction targets has removed a key excuse for inaction. India must, therefore, ensure her own security of national Interests before committing to similar targets as it has yet to create the basic infrastructure and development objectives to ensure its economic progress in the decades ahead. India's National Water Policy, 2012[25] suitably mentions the aspect of climate change but the effective translation of the policy into meaningful and yet dynamic action will largely impact the future generation of Indians.

The Era of Water Shortages

Hydrologists consider a country to be under *water stress* when its annual water supplies drop to between 1,000 and 1,700 cubic meters per person. The most widely cited measure for water resources management is Malin Falkenmarks (1989) Water Stress Index. This index divides the volume of available water resources for each country by its population. In turn, countries face *water scarcity* when their annual water supplies drop below 1,000 cubic meters per person. Once a country enters the water-scarce category, it faces severe constraints on food production, economic development, and protection of natural ecosystems. There is clear evidence that groundwater supplies are diminishing, with an estimated 20% of the world's aquifers being over-exploited, some massively so (Gleeson et al., 2012). Globally, the rate of groundwater abstraction is increasing by 1% to 2% per year (WWAP, 2012), adding to water stress in several areas (Figure 2.4) and compromising the availability of groundwater to serve as a buffer against local supply shortages.

Figure 7: Water Stress of Aquifers

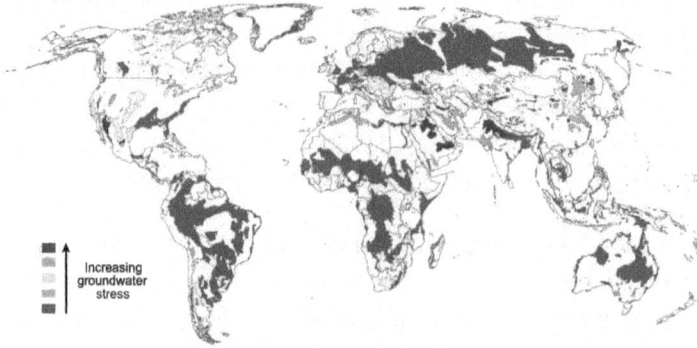

Source: Gleeson et al. (2012, fig. 1, as appears in Nature News, http://www.nature.com/news/demand-for-water-outstrips-supply-1.11143#/ref-link-1)

While data on precipitation , which can be measured with relative ease , is generally available for most countries, river runoff and groundwater levels are generally much more difficult and costly to monitor[26]. As a result, trends regarding changes in the overall availability of freshwater supplies are difficult to determine in all but a few places in the world. However, it is clear that several countries face varying degrees of water scarcity, stress or vulnerability. Global water demand (in terms of water withdrawals) is projected to increase by some 55% by 2050, mainly because of growing demands from manufacturing (400%), thermal electricity generation (140%) and domestic use (130%). As a result, freshwater availability will be increasingly strained over this time period, and more than 40% of the global population is projected to be living in areas of severe water stress through 2050. There is clear evidence that groundwater supplies are diminishing, with an estimated 20% of the world's aquifers being over-exploited[27]. Deterioration of wetlands worldwide is reducing the capacity of ecosystems to purify water.

More and more countries are facing water stress and scarcity as their populations grow, urbanisation accelerates, and water consumption increases. Thirty-one countries (with a combined population of close to half a billion) faced water stress or scarcity as of 1995. The number of people estimated to live in water-short countries increased by nearly 125 million between 1990 and 1995. By 2025, 50 countries and more than 3.3 billion people will face water stress or scarcity. By 2050, the number of countries afflicted with water stress or scarcity will rise to 54, and their populations to 4 billion people—40 percent of the projected global population of 9.4 billion. The majority of these countries—40 of them—are in the Near East, North Africa, and sub-Saharan Africa (Gardner-Outlaw & Engelman, 1997; UNFPA, 1997). It is no coincidence that nearly all countries with looming water shortages also suffer from rapid population growth rates. The rapid increase in world population by about 80 million a year is escalating pressure on freshwater demands of about 64 billion cubic metres a year[28]. Besides, population pressure, jumpy-urbanisation, and climatic anomalies are amalgam the problems associated with water scarcity.

Figure 8 : Future demand for Water : 2030

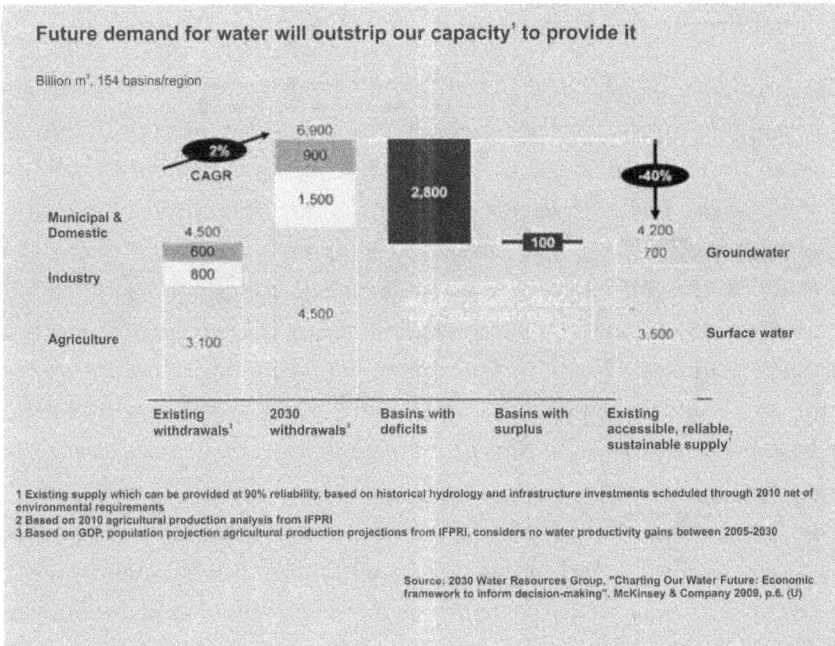

There is no more water on earth now than there was 2,000 years ago, when the population was less than 3 percent of its current size. Fresh water's per capita availability has been falling for centuries and stood at 7,044 cubic meters in 2000 (World Resources, 2000). The supply of fresh water per capita is one-third lower now than it was as recently as 1970, a direct result of the nearly 2 billion dropping more precipitously in recent years as the globe's population growth has exploded. Unsurprisingly, the availability of fresh water has also fallen, from 17,000 cubic meters per person people added to the planet since. The global demand for water is expected to grow significantly for all major water use sectors, with the largest proportion of this growth occurring in countries with developing or emerging economies[29]. However, quantifying potential increases in water demand is extremely difficult, as 'there are major uncertainties about the amount of water required to meet the [growing] demand for food, energy and other human uses, and to sustain ecosystems' (WWAP, 2012, p. 2).

Global Freshwater Distribution

The world's available fresh water supply is also distributed extremely unevenly around the globe. About three-quarters of global annual rainfall comes down in areas containing less than one-third of the world's population [30]. Some 70 percent of the earth's surface is covered by oceans. On the less than 30 percent covered by land, more than 84 percent of the world's population lives on the driest half[31]. More than half the global runoff occurs in Asia (31 percent) and South America (25 percent). '*Runoff*' is defined as water originating as precipitation on land that then runs off the land into rivers, streams, and lakes, eventually reaching the ocean, inland seas, or aquifers. That portion of the runoff that can be used year after year by human beings is known as '*stable runoff*' (Hinrichsen, Robey & Upadhyay, 1998). While North America has the most fresh water available (at over 19,000 cubic meters per capita as estimated in 1990), Asia has only 4,700 cubic meters of fresh water per capita (Population Reference Bureau, 1998). This disparity is a function both of differences in population density and available water resources. (Figure)

Figure 9: Water Availability As per Continents

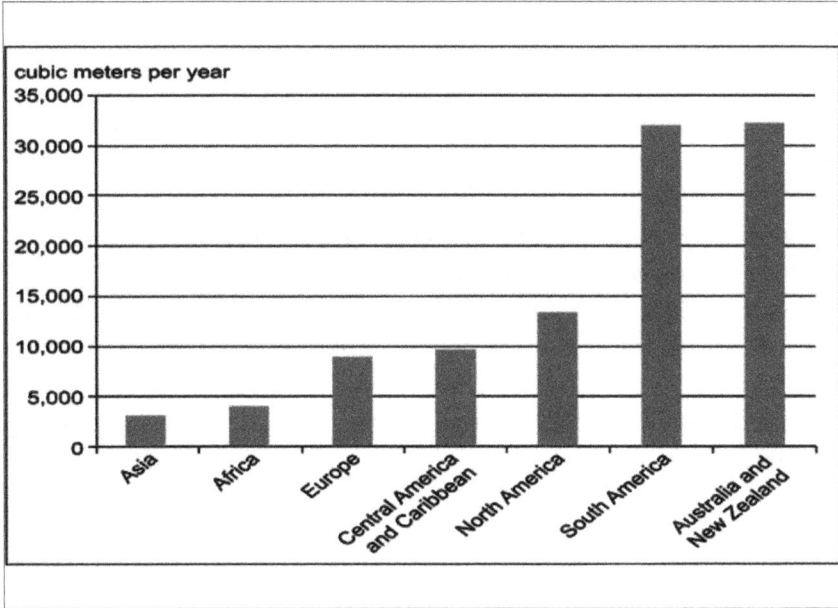

cubic meters per year

The Amazon Basin alone, a vast region with less than 10 million people, accounts for 20 percent of the global average runoff each year. In Africa, the Congo River and its tributaries account for 30 percent of the entire continent's annual runoff; but the Congo's area contains only 10 percent of Africa's population. Even more dramatic water disparities hold at the country level. Ranging from 46,000 cubic meters per person in Brazil to only 75 cubic meters per person in Kuwait (Gardner-Outlaw & Engelman, 1997). There are also striking differences in water availability within countries. In Mexico, for instance, less than 10 percent of the land area provides more than half of the national rainwater runoff every year. Despite the fact that 90 percent of Mexico is chronically water-short and arid, its total per capita water availability in 1990 was over 4,000 cubic meters. Such a figure is grossly misleading as a measure of actual water availability for most Mexicans. In addition, freshwater supplies throughout much of the developing world comes in the form of seasonal rains. Because rains often run off too quickly for efficient use (as during Asia's monsoons), some developing countries can use no more than 20 percent of their potentially available water resources. India, for instance, gets 90 percent of its rainfall during the summer monsoon season. Measures adopted to mitigate this problem generally are by altering natural supply systems. As water-short societies have done for centuries, many countries resort to certain measures to overcome such shortages.

To make up for this imbalance, humans have extensively re-engineered the global hydrological system, erecting dams, drilling wells, creating irrigation systems, and other water works. To move water from where it occurs in nature to where people want it. This infrastructure ensures water supplies for human consumption, sanitation, agriculture, industry, energy production, and other uses. With the aim of storing water for future use. Dams have emerged over the last 50 years as the major strategy for such alteration But in many cases such interventions are also proving unsustainable in the long run, exhausting underground aquifers and interrupting sediment flows and nutrient cycles in surface waters, among other repercussions.

Water Usage

The amount of precipitation falling on land is almost 110 000 km³ per year. Almost two-thirds of this amount evaporates from the ground or transpires from vegetation (forest, rangeland, cropland). The remaining 40 000 km³ per year is converted to surface runoff (feeding rivers and lakes) and groundwater (feeding aquifers)[32]. These are called renewable freshwater resources. Part of this water is being removed from these rivers or aquifers by installing infrastructure. This removal of water is called water withdrawal. Most of the withdrawn water is returned to the environment some period of time later, after it has been used. The quality of the returned water may be less than the quality when it was originally removed.

People use water for agriculture, industry, and domestic (municipal) purposes. As population grows, requirements for basic personal use rise proportionately. Rising living standards, which bring such amenities as running water to homes, dramatically increase per capita water consumption. Increasing agricultural and industrial water consumption also reflects changing living standards.

Figure 10: Global Water Use

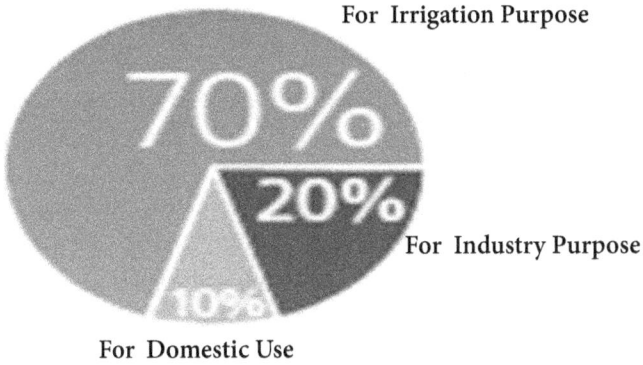

For Irrigation Purpose

70%

20%

For Industry Purpose

10%

For Domestic Use

Figure 11: Irrigated Areas: 1995

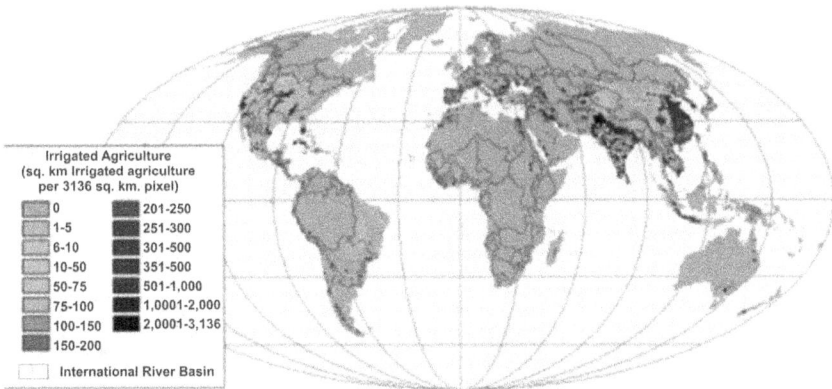

Irrigated Agriculture
(sq. km Irrigated agriculture
per 3136 sq. km. pixel)

0	201-250
1-5	251-300
6-10	301-500
10-50	351-500
50-75	501-1,000
75-100	1,0001-2,000
100-150	2,0001-3,136
150-200	

International River Basin

Data source: Irrigated agriculture- Döll and Siebert (2000), Siebert and Döll (2001).

In Asia as a whole, competition among water users is also increasing. Almost 84 per-cent of the water withdrawal in the region is used for agricultural purposes, compared to 71 percent for the world. The Indian subcontinent (92 percent) and Eastern Asia (77 percent) have the world's highest level of regional water withdrawal for agriculture (World Resources Report, 1998). The two regions together represent about 82 percent of the total irrigated area in Asia. More and more water is demanded from all sectors. In Malaysia, for instance, the annual water demand for the domestic and industrial sectors has been expanding at the rate of 12 percent due to the rapid population increase and the rapid growth of industries. By 2020, the domestic and industrial sectors are expected to be the main water users in the country (Malaysian Water Partnership, 2000). This is also true in Thailand, the Philippines, and other Asian countries.

Water- Food- Energy Nexus

Water, energy and food are linked in a vicious loop where each aspect is increasing the demand for the other. Security concerns form a critical nexus for understanding and addressing development challenges. The complex interlinkages between water and energy systems requires a more systematic approach that takes into account the multiple interactions and relationships between domains, and explores strategic complementarities and potential synergies across all sectors. Water, energy and food are strategic resources sharing many comparable attributes: there are billions of people without access to them; there is rapidly growing global demand for each of them; each faces resource constraints; each depends upon healthy ecosystems; each is a global good with trade implications; each has different regional availability and variations in supply and demand; and each operates in supply and demand; and each operates in heavily regulated markets (Bazilian *et al.*, 2011) (Figure). Food, Energy and water planning must be better integrated to optimise investments and avoid inefficiencies. Water is crucial for energy. Water is used in the extractive industries for producing fuels such as coal, uranium, oil and gas. Water is an input for energy crops such as corn and sugar cane for ethanol and biomass for fuel pellets. Water is also crucial for cooling purposes in most power plants and the driving force for hydroelectric and steam turbines.

Many of the external pressures that drive the increasing demands for water also play influential roles in the growing demand for energy. Both are fundamentally driven by as also drive social development and economic growth, and both are strongly influenced by economic forces, increasing living standards, technological development and government policy. Progressive energy access programmes, accelerated urbanisation and rapid economic development in some developing countries have provided access to modern energy services for hundreds of millions of people over the past two decades, especially in China and India. However, nearly one-fifth of the global population, close to 1.3 billion people, did not have access to electricity in 2010, and roughly 2.6 billion people relied on the traditional use of biomass for cooking (IEA, 2012a). Globally, electricity demand is expected to grow by roughly 70% by 2035. This growth will be almost entirely in non-OECD countries, with China and India accounting for more than half that growth. the greatest increases in the power generation mix in both OECD and non-OECD countries.

Figure 12: The Water- Food- Energy Nexus

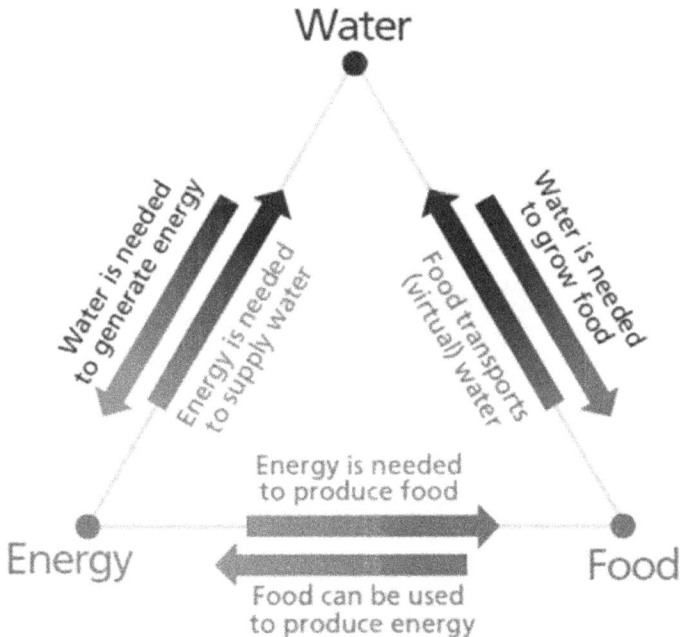

Adapted from: Water - A Global Innovation Outlook Report, IBM, 2009

Adapted from: Water - A Global Innovation Outlook Report, IBM, 2009

In developing countries, relative water use by the power sector is generally lower, and by the agriculture sector is generally higher. But developing regions today still use far less water per capita than do developed regions. In Africa, for example, annual water withdrawals average only 17 cubic meters of water per capita. In Asia, the figure is 31 cubic meters (Clarke, 1991). In spite of the uncertainties, coal is expected to remain the backbone fuel for electricity generation globally through to 2035. However, with energy (and thermal power in particular) expected to be the fastest growing water demand sector over the next few decades, it is imperative that the water implications of energy options such as thermal power are taken into consideration. The IEA's *World Energy Outlook 2012* estimates global water withdrawals for energy production in 2010 at 583 billion m³ (representing some 15% of the world's total withdrawals), of which 66 billion m³ was consumed (IEA, 2012*a*). By 2035, withdrawals would increase by 20%, whereas consumption would increase by 85%, driven by a shift towards higher efficiency power plants with more advanced cooling systems (that reduce withdrawals but increase consumption) and due to increased production of biofuel.

Figure 13:

World electricity generation by source of energy as a percentage of world electricity generation, 2011

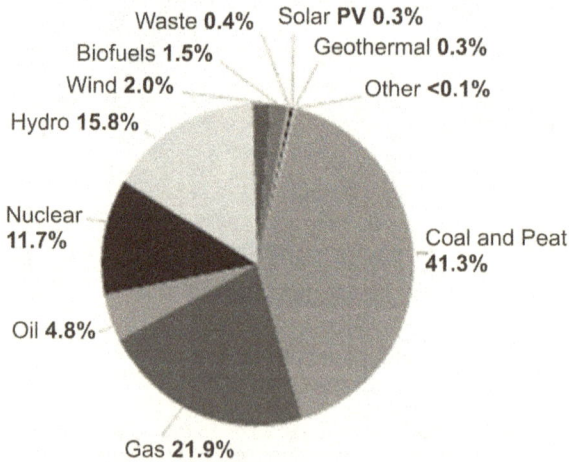

Waste **0.4%**   Solar **PV 0.3%**
Biofuels **1.5%**   Geothermal **0.3%**
Wind **2.0%**   Other **<0.1%**
Hydro **15.8%**
Nuclear **11.7%**   Coal and Peat **41.3%**
Oil **4.8%**
Gas **21.9%**

Note: PV, solar photovoltaic.
Source: WWAP, from data in IEA (2013).

Water is an input for producing agricultural goods in the fields and along the entire agrifood supply chain. Energy is required to produce and distribute water and food: to pump water from groundwater or surface water sources, to power tractors and irrigation machinery, and to process and transport agricultural goods. Agriculture is currently the largest user of water at the global level, accounting for 70% of total withdrawal. The food production and supply chain accounts for about 30% of total global energy consumption (FAO, 2011*b*). There are many synergies and trade-offs between water and energy use and food production. In this way, water, food and energy are fundamental to the functioning of society, closely interlinked and associated with deep security concerns and development areas. Adopting a holistic approach towards the water-energy-food security nexus can help reduce the potential for conflicts and tensions. The increasing interdependencies of water, food and energy may raise security concerns and create flashpoints for instability. The linkages between these three strategic resources make them central to achieving security, with their securitisation increasingly being recognized in global dialogues (The Water, Energy and Food Security Nexus, Bonn 2011; Food Security in Dry Lands Conference, Qatar 2012 ; International Water Summit, Abu Dhabi 2013). Using water to irrigate crops might promote food production but it can also reduce river flows and hydropower potential. Growing bioenergy crops under irrigated agriculture can increase overall water withdrawals and jeopardize food security. Converting surface irrigation into high efficiency pressurized irrigation may save water but may also result in higher energy use. Recognizing these synergies and balancing these trade-offs is central to jointly ensuring water, energy and food security.

Hydroelectricity is currently the largest renewable source for power generation in the world, meeting 16% of global electricity needs in 2010 (IEA, 2012a). The recent rate of growth in electricity generation from additional hydro capacities has been similar to that of all other renewables combined[33] (IEA, 2012*b*). Hydroelectricity generation is one way to help meet future energy demands. Multi-purpose dams can provide energy as well as water for irrigation and flood management. However, water demand for energy production can be in conflict with water demand for agriculture. The benefits of hydropower generation do not always flow to the people who depend on rivers for their livelihoods (WCD, 2000). Developed countries use a greater portion of this energy for processing and transport; in developing countries, cooking consumes the highest share. In the context of *thermal power generation*, there is an increasing potential for serious conflict between power, other water users and environmental considerations[34].

Water of acceptable quality and in adequate quantity is needed to meet food production demands. At the same time, food production and supply have a negative impact on the sustainability and quality of water resources. Specialized crops and livestock products often require more water (and in most cases more energy) to produce and lead to higher levels of water pollution. In the pursuit of food security, technological advancements in the agricultural sector could have significant impacts, both positive and negative, on water demand, supply and quality. Without improved efficiencies, agricultural water consumption is expected to increase by about 20% globally by 2050 (WWAP, 2012). Domestic and industrial water demands are also expected to increase, especially in cities and countries undergoing accelerated economic growth and social development.

Developing economies pose a critical challenge in the water-food-energy security nexus affecting economic, social, and political stability as well as raising issues of equity. Emerging economies are characterised by common challenges such as population growth, increasing rates of urbanisation, large investment needs in infrastructure development, the emergence of new consumers, and the impacts of climate change on freshwater availability. These challenges will place additional stress on water resources, with serious consequences for water, energy and food sectors in these countries, especially at the local level. The convergence of drivers on the water-food-energy nexus threatens water security, posing risks for public health, political stability, and continued economic growth in many developing regions of the world, with Asia being a notable example. As population growth and urbanisation rates in the region rise, stress on water resources in Asia is rapidly intensifying. For multiple reasons, already as many as 635 million people in Asia lack access to safe water, and 1.9 billion people lack access to effective sanitation (JMP, 2012). Strong income growth is also leading to changes in diets, favouring foods such as meat, which use more water inputs. Demand for energy is also expected to increase, particularly in China and India, where projections for water, energy and food in those countries suggest a sharp increase to keep up with demand and growth. Ensuring a secure supply of water, food and energy is essential given Asia Pacific's growing population, increasing demands, and increasingly scarce water and land resources.

Water demand for energy will certainly increase as energy demand is expected to increase by more than one-third in the period 2010–2035, with countries outside the Organisation for Economic Co-operation and Development (OECD) accounting for 90% of demand (IEA, 2012a). In the absence of new policies (i.e. the Baseline Scenario), freshwater availability will be increasingly strained through 2050, with 2.3 billion more people than today (in total more than 40% of the global population) projected to be living in areas subjected to severe water stress, especially in North and South Africa and South and Central Asia. Global water demand in terms of water withdrawals is projected to increase by some 55% due to growing demands from manufacturing (400%), thermal electricity generation (140%) and domestic use (130%) (OECD, 2012a) without including environmental flows.

Demand for food, water, and energy will grow by approximately 35, 40, and 50 percent respectively owing to an increase in the global population and the consumption patterns of an expanding middle class[35]. Many countries probably won't have the wherewithal to avoid food and water shortages without massive help from outside. Tackling problems pertaining to one commodity won't be possible without affecting supply and demand for the others. Agriculture is highly dependent on accessibility to adequate sources of water as well as on energy-rich fertilizers. Hydropower is a significant source of energy for some regions while new sources of energy—such as biofuels—threaten to exacerbate the potential for food shortages. There is as much scope for negative tradeoffs as there is the potential for positive synergies. Agricultural productivity in Africa, particularly, will require a sea change to avoid shortages. Energy efficiency improvements can bring direct savings through technological or behavioural changes, or indirect savings through co-benefits derived from the adoption of agroecological farming practices. For both large and small systems, any means of avoiding food wastage should be encouraged and can result in considerable savings in the energy, land and water used to produce this food that no one consumes. Knowledge-based precision irrigation, which provides reliable and flexible water application, along with deficit irrigation and wastewater reuse, will be a major platform for sustainable crop production intensification (FAO, 2011*d*). Mechanical irrigation systems should be designed to use water as efficiently as possible. Crops often take up only half of the irrigation water applied (FAO, 2011*d*), so there is clearly potential to improve water use efficiency, which would also result in less demand for electricity or diesel fuel for pumping. The global community is well aware of food, energy and water challenges, but has so far addressed them in isolation, within sectoral boundaries. At the country level, fragmented sectoral responsibilities, lack of coordination, and inconsistencies between laws and regulatory frameworks may lead to misaligned incentives. If water, energy and food security are to be simultaneously achieved, decision-makers, including those responsible for only a single sector, need to consider broader influences and cross-sectoral impacts. They must strive for innovative policies and integrated institutions. Water development and management programmes, if planned properly, can serve multiple functions, from contributing to energy and food production to helping communities adapt to climate change.

Population

Global population is projected to reach 9.3 billion in 2050 (UNDESA, 2012). Population growth leads to increased water demand, reflecting growing needs for drinking water, health and sanitation, as well as for energy, food and other goods and services that require water for their production and delivery. Urban areas of the world, particularly those in developing countries, are expected to absorb all this population growth, at the same time drawing in some of the rural population[36]. This intense urbanisation will increase demand for water supply, sanitation services and electricity for domestic purposes. Consumer demand and increasing standards of living are driving increased demand for water, most notably by middle income households in developing and emerging economies through their greater demand for food, energy and other goods, the production of which can require significant quantities of water.

Figure 14: Link Between Population and Fresh Water Demand

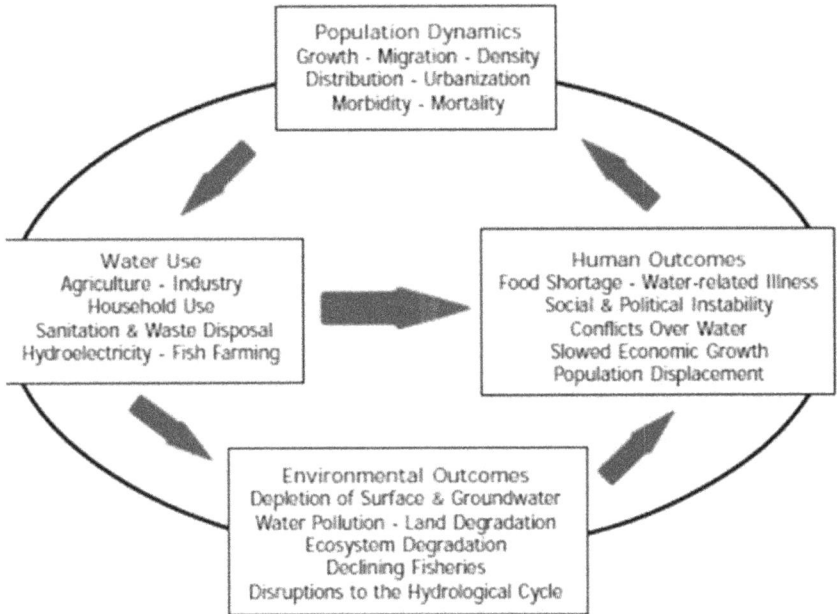

Source: IUCN et al. (1996)

The IWMI, estimates that 1.2 billion people—nearly 20 percent of the world's population—live in areas of physical water scarcity, where water withdrawals for agriculture, industry, and domestic purposes exceed 75 percent of river flows. An additional 500 million people live in areas approaching physical scarcity. Another 1.6 billion people live in areas of economic water scarcity, where water is available but human capacity or financial resources limit access[37]. In these areas, adequate infrastructure may not be available or, if water is available, its distribution may be inequitable (IWMI 2007). Numerous human activities—such as untimely water use, pollution, insufficient or poorly maintained infrastructure, and inadequate management systems—can result in or exacerbate water scarcity. As noted by the United Nations, there are adequate water resources to meet our needs, but water "is distributed unevenly and too much of it is wasted, polluted and unsustainably managed" (UN 2012b).

Figure 15: Population Density Per River Basin

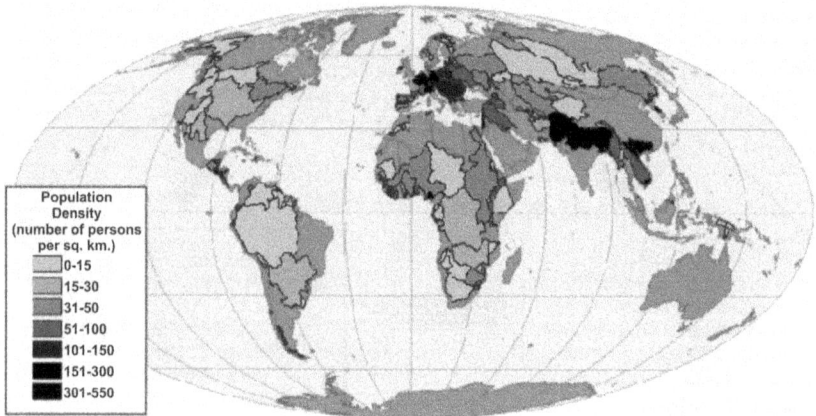

Population Density (number of persons per sq. km.)
- 0-15
- 15-30
- 31-50
- 51-100
- 101-150
- 151-300
- 301-550

While population growth rates are slowing in most developing countries, absolute numbers of people added each year remain near historic highs. As a result of projected population growth, global per capita availability of fresh water is likely to be no more than 5,100 cubic meters in the year 2025 (Gardner-Outlaw & Engelman, 1997). China and India, the world's first and second most populous countries, respectively, provide examples of how even modest population growth rates can translate into large absolute numbers because of an already-enormous population base. China's population growth rate in 2000 was only 0.9 percent—but, with China's total population at over 1.2 billion, even this small growth rate translates into an additional 12 million people each year. Similarly, India's population growth rate of about 1.8 percent means that about 18 million people a year will be added to its current population of one billion. The world's annual population growth of 78 million a year (as of 2000) implies an increased demand for fresh water on the order of 64 billion cubic meters a year—an amount equivalent to the entire annual flow rate of the Rhine River, assuming countries continue to withdraw water at current rates (Clarke, 1991).

Figure 16: Total Renewable Water Resources: 2011

Total renewable water resources, 2011 (m³ per capita per year)

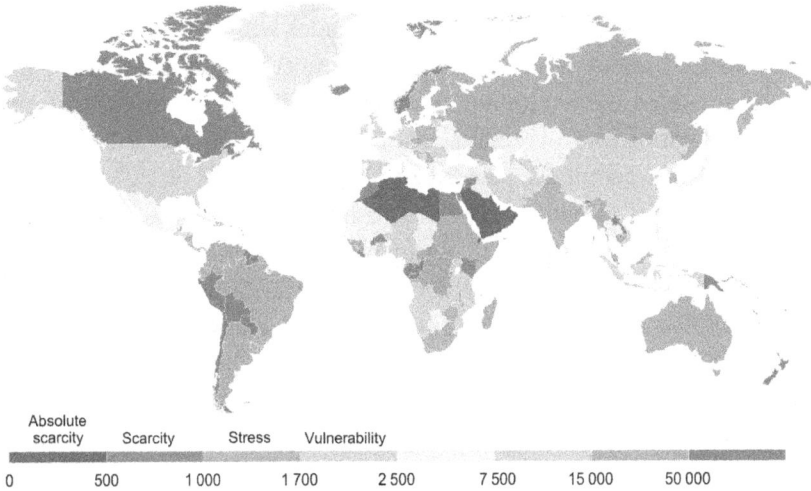

Rapid population growth not only makes it increasingly difficult to provide adequate supplies of fresh water; it can also strain resources for proper sanitation, housing, health care, education, employment, and food supplies. Agriculture currently uses 11% of the world's land surface, and irrigated agriculture uses 70% of all water withdrawals on a global scale. Rainfed agriculture is the predominant agricultural production system around the world. Water scarcity and decreasing availability of water for agriculture constrain irrigated production overall, and particularly in the most hydrologically stressed areas and countries. As many key food production systems depend on groundwater, declining aquifer levels and the depletion of non-renewable groundwater put local and global food production at risk.

Urbanisation

Cities are home to just over 50% of the global population, but they consume 60% to 80% of the commercial energy and emit about 75% of the pollutants (IEA, 2008b; UNEP, 2011b). More than half of humanity currently lives in cities, and this proportion is expected to grow rapidly. Between 2011 and 2050, it is estimated that the world's population will increase by 2.3 billion, while the urban population will increase by 2.6 billion (UNDESA, 2012). This means that urban areas will absorb all the population growth over the next four decades while the rural population will start to decrease in about a decade. Almost all of this increase will be in cities located in developing countries, while the urban population in developed countries will remain close to constant. Between 2010 and 2015, almost 200,000 people are projected to be added to the world's cities every day; 91% of this growth is expected to take place in cities of developing countries (UN-Habitat, 2012). As many of the rapidly growing cities in developing countries – particularly in Africa, South Asia and China – already face problems related to water and energy, and have limited capacity to overcome these problems, such cities will be major hotspots for water and energy crises in the future. Cities are complex systems that use inputs such as water, energy, food, materials and nutrients, much of which is imported from outside, and produce outputs such as waste, wastewater and emissions that pollute the surrounding environment. Growing urban populations and their increasing affluence generally lead to higher energy and water consumption for domestic use. Cities not only consume large amounts of water, their high concentration of industry, transport systems and buildings also demands large amounts of energy.

Water supply and wastewater management are significant consumers of energy in the urban context. A survey of water and wastewater management in 71 Indian cities found that electricity is the single highest cost for water utilities. In some cities, such as Jodhpur, where water is pumped and transported from the Indira Gandhi Canal more than 200 km away, electricity cost is as high as 77% of the total operating cost (Narain, 2012). As cities continue to grow, they will have to go further or dig deeper to obtain water, which will further increase demand for energy, particularly in developing countries where energy is already in short supply and in many cases expensive.

Water Security and Human Rights

Recognition of the human right to safe drinking water and sanitation is an important step towards ensuring water security at the individual and community levels. Since the adoption of the UN resolutions on the human right to water and sanitation (United Nations General Assembly, 2010; United Nations General Assembly Human Rights Council, 2010b), an increasing number of states have explicitly integrated this right into national policy and/or legislation through new strategies, laws, and constitutional amendments (Boyd, 2012). Water is best placed within this broader definition of security and acts as a central link across the range of securities, including political, health, economic, personal, food, energy, and environmental, among others (cf. Zeitoun, 2011). This movement has fostered a new focus and emphasis on addressing the concerns of those who have traditionally been vulnerable, marginalized or left behind.

It is critical to retain this focus for further policy discussion between stakeholders and across sectors, and in the development of programmes that make possible the full realization of the rights of individuals and communities. Water is required for ensuring securities are met, from access to water supply at the individual or community level, to the peaceful sharing and management of transboundary water resources across political boundaries (cf. Ministerial Declaration of The Hague on Water Security in the 21st Century)[38]. The integration of these human rights also emphasizes the role of water and sanitation in ensuring water security, two areas identified as major bottlenecks for the progressive realization of universal access.. The formal recognition of a human right to water and sanitation will not in itself alter the realities on the ground, such as water scarcity, polluted wells and rivers, poor governance, a lack of investments in infrastructure, or the prevalence of inequalities. Water security can therefore reduce the potential for conflicts and tensions, contributing to significant social, development, economic and environmental benefits on a larger scale, as well as to the realization of states' international obligations.

Important issues such as shifting demographics, population growth, increasing urbanisation and migration, and changing consumption patterns will result in increased demand for water resources. In addition a changing hydrological cycle due to human influences such as deforestation, land-use changes and the effects of climate change will have an impact on the water cycle and water availability. To add to it increasing demands and competition for water resources across sectors, such as food, energy, industry and the environment, will put a strain on water resources. Finally, safe wastewater treatment and re-use will need to be managed so as to prevent pollution and contamination and protect the quality of precious water resources. Multi-disciplinary approaches and cross-sectoral policies are needed to address water issues under-lying human security. The cross-sectoral nature of water means it is critical to ensure that each sector's reasonable demands for water can be satisfied in a way that will also satisfy critical elements of human security. Integrated, cross-sectoral policies, coordinated decision-making and enforceable legal instruments and institutional mechanisms are needed to ensure that water acts as a linking factor to achieving security and that competition between sectors for limited water resources can be adequately managed.

Climate Change

Climate change impacts will have direct consequences for water security, which will vary according to geographic location (Figure). Rising concentrations of greenhouse gases resulting from human activities are causing large-scale changes to Earth's climate. These climatic changes will have major implications for global water resources[39]. As temperatures rise, the flows of water in the hydrologic cycle will accelerate. In short, climate change will intensify the water cycle, altering water availability, timing, quality, and demand.

The Intergovernmental Panel on Climate Change (IPCC) points towards a great vulnerability of freshwater resources as a result of climate change, with severe consequences for economic, social and ecological systems (IPCC, 2008; IPCC, 2012). Indeed, all of the major international and national assessments of climate change have concluded that freshwater systems are among the most vulnerable, presenting risk for all sectors of society (Compagnucci et al. 2001; SEG 2007; Kundzewicz et al. 2007; Bates et al. 2008; USGCRP 2013). The latest Intergovernmental Panel on Climate Change (IPCC) report (2014)[40] predicts that the Himalayan glaciers could lose between a third and half of their mass by 2100[41]. Having revised previous predictions, which suggested total glacial melt in the Himalayas by 2035, the latest IPCC report still recognises the problem as a high priority issue.

Figure 17: Climate Change and Water Resources

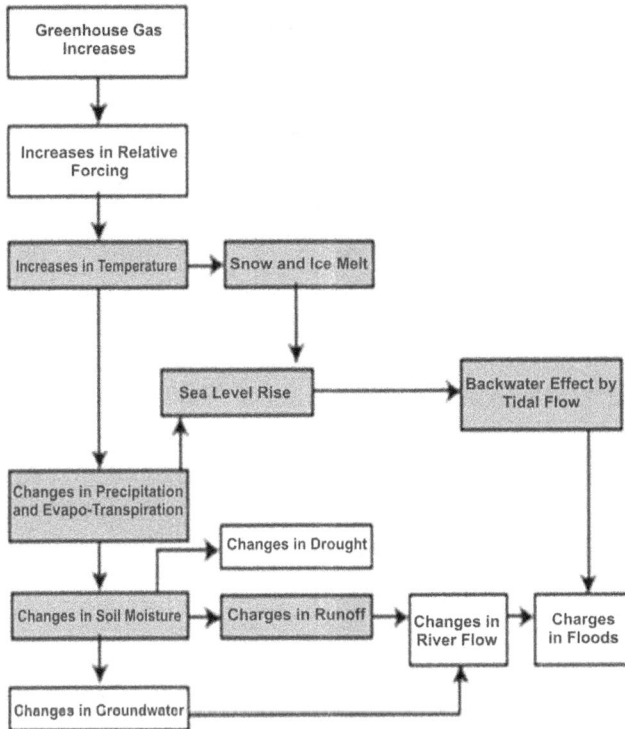

Source: M. Monirul Qader Mirza and Q.K. Ahmad, eds,. Climate Changes and Water Resources in South Asia London: Taylor & Francis Group, 2005).

According to the IPCC an average surface temperature increase of 1.8 degrees Celsius from 2006, will result in glacial shrinkage of up to 45 per cent by 2100; with an increase of 3.7 degrees, the reduction would be closer to 68 per cent. Other studies have found that in the last three to four decades, warming in the Himalayas has been more than the average of 0.75 per cent over the last century. Some have confirmed that it is warming five to six times faster than the global average. Climate change is also affecting the Asian monsoon. Official studies show the monsoon is erratic in four out of every 10 years. Simulated tests predict that climate change will result in increased monsoonal precipitation over South Asia, East Asia and the Western Pacific Ocean[42]. Increased precipitation, along with increased glacial melting, could potentially have devastating consequences; as witnessed in Pakistan in 2010 and In Jammu and Kashmir in September 2014 when a fifth of Pakistan's total land area was affected by flooding and large losses to life and property were seen in Jammu and Kashmir. The height of the Himalayan mountain range has contributed to the development of the monsoonal rainfall pattern. Changes in the mountain region due to glacial melting could therefore have a direct impact on the monsoon. The monsoon is extremely important for the farmers of the region, who rely on its rains for food production. In India alone, monsoonal rainfall contributes 85 per cent of the country's annual rainfall. Changes to monsoonal rainfall patterns could affect agricultural productivity and thus reduce food security. Over the long-term, glacial shrinkage will reduce water supplies in dry seasons, creating increased variability in water availability. The region can expect to experience shorter, more intense, rainfall and lengthier drought periods. The fertile plains of the Ganga, Indus and Brahmaputra depend on the rivers flowing from the glaciers. Reduced water availability and lengthier drought periods will diminish regional agricultural productivity. Rainfall contributes 59 per cent of the flow of the Indus River and 85 per cent of this is received during the monsoon[43]. There is, therefore, a need to make water storage a priority. Moreover, with declining monsoonal periods, aquifers are less likely to receive the water required to replenish groundwater supply.

Climate change will worsen the outlook for the availability of these critical resources. Climate change analysis suggests that the severity of existing weather patterns will intensify, with wet areas getting wetter and dry and arid areas becoming more so. The effect on water security will differ regionally and will depend upon a number of factors, including geographic location and features, conditions of water availability and utilisation, demographic changes, existing management and allocation systems, legal frame-works for water management, existing governance structures and institutions, and the resilience of ecosystems. The IPCC (2012) expects an increased incidence of droughts due to decreasing trends in precipitation in some areas, while others will see an increasing incidence of floods and other extreme events such as cyclones due to increasing trends in precipitation intensity. Much of the decline in precipitation will occur in the Middle East and Northern Africa as well as Western Central Asia, Southern Europe, Southern Africa, and the US Southwest[44]. The world is not headed into dire scarcities, but policymakers and their private sector collaborators will need to be proactive to avoid such a future. Similarly, increased risk of water supplies or increased risk of sea-level rise will follow the melting of glaciers, while increased temperature and saltwater intrusion from rising sea levels will compromise water quality. Rainfall variability alone could push more than 12 million people into absolute poverty (World Bank, 2006), while climate change could increase global malnutrition by up to 25% by 2080 (Fischer *et al.*, 2002).

As per estimated modelling assessments by IIPC, 2014 freshwater-related risks of climate change increase significantly with increasing greenhouse gas concentrations, The fraction of global population experiencing water scarcity and the fraction affected by major river floods increase with the level of warming in the 21st century. In presently dry regions, drought frequency are *likely to* increase by the end of the 21st century. In contrast, water resources are projected to increase at high latitudes[45]. Climate change is projected to reduce raw water quality and pose risks to drinking water quality even with conventional treatment, due to interacting factors: increased temperature; increased sediment, nutrient, and pollutant loadings from heavy rainfall; increased concentration of pollutants during droughts; and disruption of treatment facilities during floods.

The population and assets projected to be exposed to coastal risks as well as human pressures on coastal ecosystems will increase significantly in the coming decades due to population growth, economic development, and urbanisation. The relative costs of coastal adaptation vary strongly among and within regions and countries for the 21st century. Some low-lying developing countries and small island states are expected to face very high impacts .

In 2012, a report by the UN Environment Program's global environmental alert service identified that a lack of reliable and consistent data was impeding the gathering of scientific knowledge on the state of the Himalayan glaciers. Uncertainty surrounding the effects of climate change on the glaciers, as well as the constitution of the glaciers themselves, makes it difficult to identify the most effective ways to counteract the effects. Temperature increase and glacial melt will provide more water in the short-term. Predictions indicate that the quantity of run-off water from melting glaciers will rise until at least 2050. Coupled with increased precipitation, more run-off water will lead to increased flooding events.[46]

Changes in the hydrological cycle will threaten existing water infrastructure, making societies more vulnerable to extreme water-related events and resulting in increased insecurity. Poor and marginalized communities can be even more affected, yet have much less capacity to adequately cope due to under-lying factors such as environmental mismanagement, rapid and unplanned urbanisation in hazardous areas, and failed governance (IPCC, 2012).Ensuring water security in the face of climate change can be achieved through appropriate adaptation measures. Climate change impacts, combined with social, political and governance factors, will generate new or exacerbate existing water insecurities as availability, supply and demand of freshwater resources are increasingly affected (UN-Water, 2010).

Water Pollution

Ecosystems and Pollution . In 1996, the world's human population used an estimated 54 percent of all the fresh water contained in rivers, lakes, and aquifers (Postel et al., 1996). This percentage is conservatively projected (merely using population growth estimates) to climb to at least 70 percent by 2025. The figure will be more if per capita consumption continues to rise (Postel et al., 1996). By the year 2025, when the world is expected to have about eight billion people, more than 70 percent of all accessible fresh water could be used by humanity (Postel et al., 1996).

Water Pollution. Water pollution has become a major problem for both developed and developing countries. When coupled with the enormous quantities of water withdrawn for human use, water pollution has reduced the capacity of waterways to assimilate or flush pollutants from the hydrological system. Water engineers like to say that "the solution to pollution is dilution." In today's world of mounting pollution, this saying has taken on new and frightening connotations. Roughly 450 cubic km of wastewater are discharged globally into rivers, streams, and lakes every year. Another 6,000 cubic km of clean water are needed to dilute and transport this dirty water before it can be used again (Shiklomanov, 1997). This amount equals about two-thirds of the world's total available runoff. Hydrologist M. I. L'Vovich has estimated that, if current trends continue, the world's entire stable river flow would soon be needed for pollutant transport and dilution (FAO, 1990). Industrialized countries in Europe and North America face enormous water pollution problems. Over 90 percent of Europe's rivers have elevated nitrate concentrations, mostly from agrochemicals; and five percent have concentrations 200 times greater than background levels found in unpolluted rivers (WHO, 1992). Over half of Europe's lakes are eutrophied, the result of an overdose of nutrients from agriculture and municipalities (WHO, 1992). Groundwater pollution in Europe is also worsening.

Developing Countries. Pollution is a vexing problem wherever populations are growing rapidly, development demands are great, and governments cannot afford to invest in proper sanitation and waste treatment facilities. In developing countries on average, 90 to 95 percent of all domestic sewage and 75 percent of all industrial waste on average is discharged into surface waters without any treatment whatsoever (Carty, 1991). Consider the following examples:-

(a) All of India's 14 major rivers are badly polluted. Together they transport 50 million cubic meters of untreated sewage into India's coastal waters every year. India's capital, New Delhi, dumps 200 million litres of raw sewage and 20 million litres of industrial wastes into the Yamuna River every day as it passes through the city on its way to the Ganges (Harrison, 1992).

(b) Thailand and Malaysia have such heavy water pollution that their rivers often contain 30 to 100 times more pathogens, heavy metals, and poisons from industry and agriculture than government standards permit (Niemczynowicz, 1996).

(c) 80 percent of China's 50,000 km of major rivers are so filled with pollution and sediment that they can no longer support fish life. In 1992, China's industries discharged 36 billion metric tons of untreated or partially treated effluents into rivers, streams, and coastal waters.

(d) The Tiete River, which passes through Greater Sao Paulo, Brazil, receives 300 metric tons of untreated effluents from 1,200 industries every day. The river contains high concentrations of heavy metals, such as lead and cadmium. The city also dumps some 1,000 metric tons of sewage a day into its waters. Only 12 percent of the sewage receives any treatment (WHO, 1992).

Industrial And Municipal Pollutants. Recent decades have seen an enormous increase in pollution of many kinds from industry and municipalities. Industrial pollutants (such as wastes from chemical plants) are often dumped directly into waterways. Oils and salts are washed off city streets, while others (such as heavy metals and organochlorines) are leached from municipal and industrial dumpsites. Secondary pollutants such as sulphur dioxide and oxides of nitrogen combine in the atmosphere to form acid rain, with pervasive effects on both freshwater and terrestrial ecosystems. Acid rain lowers the pH of rivers and streams. Unless buffered by calcium (i.e., limestone), acidified waters cause many acid-sensitive fish, like salmon and trout, to die off. Once in soil, acids can release heavy metals, such as lead, mercury, and cadmium, which can then percolate into watercourses.

Agricultural Pollution. Agricultural activity is the world's largest polluter. In virtually every country where farmers use them, agricultural fertilizers and pesticides have contaminated groundwater aquifers and surface waters. What little water trickles back into rivers and streams after irrigation is often severely degraded by excess nutrients, higher salinity, more pathogens, more sediments, and less dissolved oxygen.

Water Quality

While most water assessments emphasize water quantity, water quality is also critical for satisfying basic human and environmental needs. The quality of the world's water is under increasing threat as a result of population growth, expanding industrial and agricultural activities, and climate change. Poor water quality threatens human and ecosystem health, increases water treatment costs, and reduces the availability of safe water for drinking and other uses (Palaniappan et al. 2010).

Many countries do not have standards to control water pollution adequately, nor do they have the capacity to enforce existing pollution standards. Increasingly, international development agencies such as the World Bank are urging developing countries to devote more attention and funds to improving water quality. Pollution is pervasive throughout the world. Few developing or industrialized countries have paid adequate attention to safeguarding water quality and to controlling water pollution. But the developed world must also spend more money on cleaning up its degraded waterways. Without clean water, future economic development will stall.

Some Measures Adopted

Integrated Water Resources Management (IWRM). Considering the multi faceted , cross sectoral nature of water ,there is an urgent requirement for a considered adaptation to IWRM. The comprehensive integrated approach to water resources management is almost a century old today (White, 1998). A methodology to consider water holistically, to avoid a fragmented approach of managing water resources across sectors, and to ensure wide participation in decision making. By definition as given by the Global Water Partnership (GWP, 2000)[47] it is :-

> *'A process which promotes the coordinated development and management of water, land and related resources, in order to maximize the resultant economic and social welfare in an equitable manner without compromising the sustainability of vital ecosystems'.*

It was formalized following the concept's inclusion under Agenda 21 (UNCED, 1992) and incorporation of ideas from the 1992 Dublin conference (ICWE, 1992). It was meant to enable the establishment of an overall water policy and laws which use the basin as the scale of management, establish water rights, use water pricing in allocation, and include participation in decision making (Shah & van Koppen, 2006). Water management must be responsive to the needs and demands of a growing diversity of central, state and municipal institutions, user groups, the private sector, NGOs and other appropriate bodies. Concentration of authorities into one, or fewer, water institutions could increase bias, reduce transparency and proper scrutiny of their activities[48]. Various critiques to the model have been raised over the years to the extent of criticizing IWRM in becoming end in itself rather than a means[49] to solve specific challenges, thereby diverting resources from practical problems and sometimes undermining alternative, functioning systems and shutting out alternative thinking on pragmatic solutions to water problems[50]. Assessments of various feedbacks and surveys have substantiated the fact that the creation of formal, national policy related to IWRM not only will improve water outcomes but is required for better water outcomes. IWRM has become a necessary condition. The IWRM, tends to encourage river-basin planning based on IWRM and the creation of river-basin organisations, support decentralization of decision making, transferable water rights, cost recovery and pricing, to create a national water policy , supporting legal and regulatory framework, adopt the polluter-pays principle, decentralize decision making, and have participation in irrigation decision making through water user associations and participation of farmers in agricultural water use through participatory irrigation management.

Yet there is a view by IWRM proponents that while the specific concepts such as formal national water laws, basin-scale planning and water pricing are associated with IWRM. IWRM is actually a process without formulas and should be very context specific. The IWRM does attempt to put the Dublin Principles into practice, emphasizing the ideas of integration, decentralization, participation, and economic and financial sustainability, and with the basin as the unit for decision making. As Biswas (2004, p. 251) noted and as still seems to hold, "Because of the current popularity of the concept, some people have continued to do what they were doing in the past, but under the currently fashionable label of IWRM in order to attract additional funds or to obtain greater national and international acceptance and visibility." Even with access to state of the art tools, the existing segmentation of institutions responsible for water resources planning and management often severely inhibits optimal management for the majority of the population. Furthermore, there are many barriers to the use of climate forecasts by water managers such as low forecast skill, lack of interpretation and demonstrated applications, low geographic resolution, inadequate links to climate variability related impacts, and institutional aversion to incorporating new tools into decision making (Callahan et al., 1999). This situation poses difficulties for effective regional, national, and international water resources management. Moreover, the situation becomes even more complicated by the looming climate change which, in the longer term, has the potential to decrease the availability of natural water resources in many areas of the world due to probable changes in the rainfall distribution and the increase in temperature (Xu and Singh, 2004). As a result, in many river basins around the world, local decision makers have insufficient knowledge of exactly how much water is available and the risks to its future availability (Xu and Singh, 2004).

The balanced approach of IWRM suggests that the integrated water resources management should be constantly evolved and strengthened. The capacity building for the integrated water resources management should be strengthened. The participation of stakeholders in water resources management should be enhanced. Effective public participation and supervision mechanisms should be established.. The integrated water resources management combining river basin management and local administration management can be achieved by unified planning, distribution and monitoring of water resources in river basins. The establishment of participatory, democratic consultation and joint decision-making mechanisms. Further improvements can be achieved by some vital yet basic actions like the integration of urban and rural water supply by means of strengthening the integrated management at local, district and state levels. Combining the assessment, planning, distribution, regulation, conservation and protection of urban and rural water resources, coordinating the construction of water source areas, flood control, drainage, supply and demand, conservation, discharge, recycle, sewage treatment and reuse are amongst the many options that could be implemented .

Desalination. Some countries have so little fresh water available that they must resort to the costly conversion of sea water into fresh water. Without desalination, the Arab states of the Persian Gulf could not support a number anywhere close to their current populations. Desalination is the most energy intensive water treatment technology. The energy cost of treating low salinity seawater is about ten times greater than a typical freshwater source and about double the energy cost of treating wastewater for reuse (Pearce, 2012). Desalination is therefore an appropriate option only when there are no other sources or the cost of energy for transporting water is very high. However, the desalination industry is working on reducing energy costs. The International Desalination Association has a goal of achieving a 20% energy reduction by 2015, and some companies have started to experiment with using renewable energy for desalination. At present, desalination is far too expensive and impractical for widespread use. Despite falling prices—the costs of desalination are down to US$1.00-to-$1.60 per cubic meter—the technology is highly energy intensive and beyond the reach of most poor water-short countries, not to mention land-locked countries. Three oil-rich Arab states— Saudi Arabia, Kuwait, and the United Arab Emirates—accounted for close to half the world's 1993 desalination capacity (Gleick, 2000). These countries are, in effect, turning oil into water.

Water Security and Transboundary Water Management

Transboundary waters pose enormous challenges for achieving water security. Where water systems, such as river or lake basins and aquifer systems, are shared across internal or external political boundaries, water-related challenges are compounded by the need to ensure coordination and dialogue between sovereign states, each with its own set of varied and sometimes competing interests (GWP, 2013). Around the world, there are some 276 major transboundary watersheds, crossing the territories of 148 countries and covering nearly half of the earth's land surface[51] More than 300 transboundary aquifers have also been identified, most of which are located across two or more countries (Puri and Aureli, 2009)[52]. Transboundary water management and cooperation within and across states on the development and protection of transboundary water resources are essential in the context of water security. Trans-boundary water management (TWM)[53] cuts across many sectors and disciplines, including international water law, water resources management and ecosystem protection, food and energy security, peace and political stability, human rights, international relations, and regional development and integration.

Figure 18: Transboundary Waters

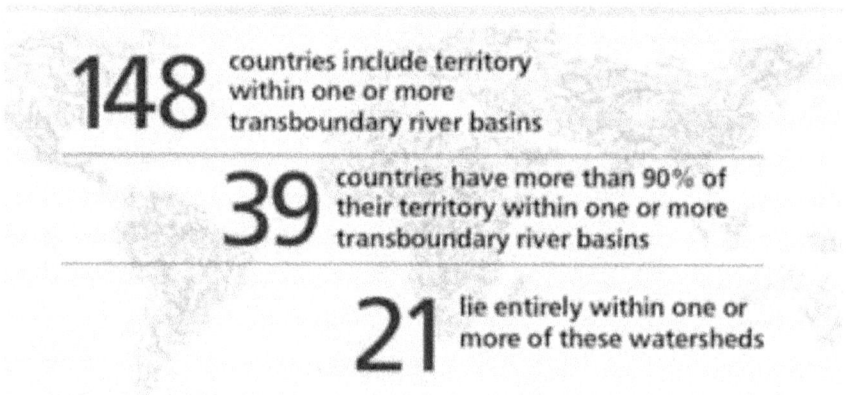

148 countries include territory within one or more transboundary river basins

39 countries have more than 90% of their territory within one or more transboundary river basins

21 lie entirely within one or more of these watersheds

Figure 19: Number of Agreements Per River Basin

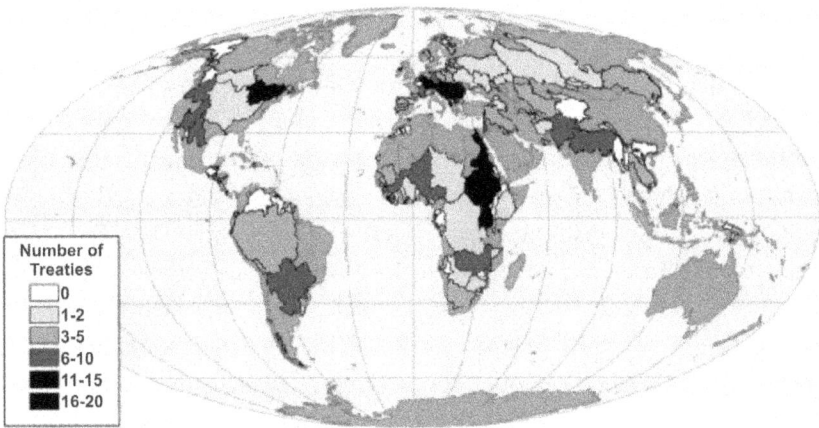

Number of Treaties
0
1-2
3-5
6-10
11-15
16-20

Data source: Treaties- Wolf (1999b).

Figure 20: Sectorial Distributions of 145 Water Agreements on Transboundary Water Resources

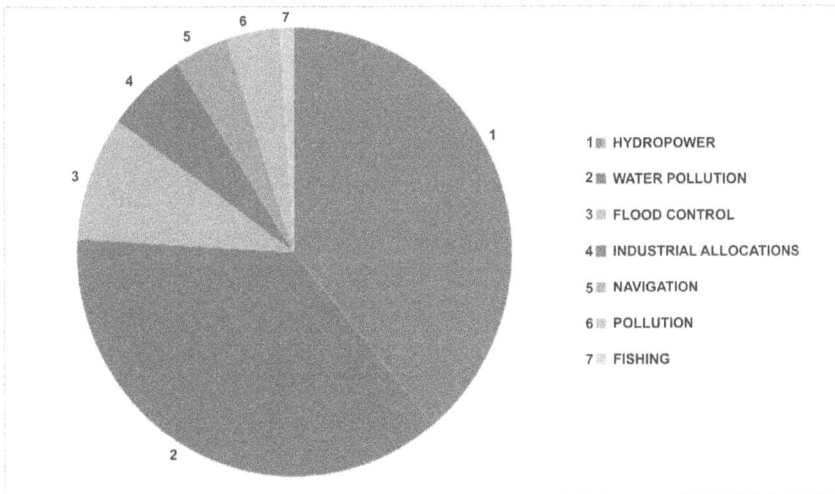

1 HYDROPOWER
2 WATER POLLUTION
3 FLOOD CONTROL
4 INDUSTRIAL ALLOCATIONS
5 NAVIGATION
6 POLLUTION
7 FISHING

Source: Uttam K Sinha : Prospects And Challenges Of Hydro Diplomacy In Water Scarce Regions 13 Feb 2012. https://www.youtube.com/watch?v=jtPvtcK48UA

The role of transboundary aquifers and management issues needs to be included in both national and inter-national water legal systems. While aquifers contribute significantly to a global river basin's water availability, their collaborative governance across sectors and political borders has largely been overlooked, hampering efforts to achieve water security. Given the particular characteristics of transboundary aquifers and their greater vulnerability to contamination, exploitation, and the impending impacts from climate change, increased attention is needed to ensure that these resources are protected and sustainably and equitably managed (Cooley and Gleick, 2011). "Without ongoing dialogue and cooperation, unilateral development measures, such as hydropower development and water extractions, can lead to significant impacts on neighbouring countries sharing the same basin[54] (Wolf, 2007). Achieving transboundary water security can stimulate regional cooperation, especially when supported by international instruments. While historically trans-boundary water cooperation has been difficult, several examples from across the globe demonstrate that shared waters provide opportunities for cooperation across nations and support political dialogue on broader issues such as economic integration and sustainable development. International watercourses, particularly when supported by international instruments such as the 1997 UN Watercourses Convention and the 1992 UNECE Convention, can help to alleviate increased incidents of water insecurity as a result of the pursuit of sovereign interests that may threaten regional peace and security.

While aquifers contribute significantly to a global river basin's water availability, their collaborative governance across sectors and political borders has largely been overlooked, hampering efforts to achieve water security. Given the particular characteristics of transboundary aquifers and their greater vulnerability to contamination, exploitation, and the impending impacts from climate change, increased attention is needed to ensure that these resources are protected and sustainably and equitably managed (Cooley and Gleick, 2011).The role of transboundary aquifers and management issues needs to be included in both national and inter-national water legal systems.

Existing interstate relationships, evolving demographic trends, economic growth, climate change, and human efforts to manage fresh water availability will determine the quantity and quality of available water supplies in the coming decades. The interplay of these factors makes water availability both a human security and national security issue. Water and resource stresses interact with a host of other factors adding to the risk of conflict. People, groups, and countries rarely fight over these resources directly, but resource stress causes various forms of social dislocation that make violence more likely.

Governing institutions in the developing world often fail to understand water challenges or make the necessary difficult political and economic decisions to correct deficiencies in water quality and quantity for human consumption, agriculture, or industry. Water planners frequently lack adequate, accurate data for effective policymaking. Knowledge of water balances in specific tributaries, replenishment rates for shared aquifers, or water demands in particular communities may be either unavailable or scattered among multiple entities across multiple countries. Similarly, responsibilities for different aspects of climate, water, and development policies are typically divided, with different institutions and authorities serving different constituencies and objectives. Such institutions are often not trusted by the population as many view state agencies as alien or corrupt. In many water stressed countries, the state faces multiple crises.

Role of Non-State Actors. The role of non state actors is becoming increasingly important in the process of transboundary water cooperation. Non-state actors, such as community groups in border areas, individual and community rights holders, and water users, have largely been absent from the formal TWM process The experience, knowledge and expertise of such actors can add legitimacy to decision-making, and provide valuable perspectives to the potential impacts on ecosystems and livelihoods. Their participation is essential to ensuring buy-in and effective implementation of joint development projects between states. Similarly, sub-national entities can have an important role in transboundary water management when supported by their governments, contributing to the establishment of trust among one another, leading to greater technical cooperation and paving the way for coordination and cooperation over shared waters once institutions are established.

Endnotes

1   Don Hinrichsen and Henrylito Tacio The Coming Freshwater Crisis Is Already Here. http://www.wilsoncenter.org/sites/default/files/popwawa2. pdfhttp://www.wilsoncenter.org/sites/default/files/popwawa2.pdf

2   Asia's Worsening Water Crisis- Posted on March 17, 2012. Brahma Chellaney.: http://chellaney.net/2012/03/17/asias-worsening-water-crisis/. *Survival* | vol. 54 no. 2 | April–May 2012 | pp. 143–156, DOI: 10.1080/00396338.2012.672806

3   There are a variety of definitions of water scarcity and water stress. The most common define water stress as per capita water available for human use below 1,700 m³ per year, water scarcity below 1,000 m³ per year, and absolute scarcity below 500 m³ per year. See Amber Brown and Marty D. Matlock, *A Review of Water Scarcity Indices and Methodologies*, White Paper 106 (Tempe, AZ: The Sustainability Consortium, 2011),http://www.sustainabilityconsortium. org/wp-content/themes/sustainability/assets/pdf/whitepapers/2011_Brown_ Matlock_Water-Availability-Assessment-Indices-and-Methodologies-Lit-Review.pdf

4   'Coping with Water: Q&A with FAO Director-General Dr. Jacques Diouf', UN Food and Agriculture Organization, 22 March 2007

5   Water Security and the Global Water Agenda- A UN - Water Analytical Report.2013. http://www.unwater.org/downloads/watersecurity_analytical brief.pdf

6   WWAP (United Nations World Water Assessment Programme). 2014. *The United Nations World Water Development Report 2014: Water and Energy*. Paris, UNESCO. http://www.unesco.org/new/en/natural-sciences/ environment/water/wwap/wwdr/2014-water-and-energy/

7   UN Food and Agriculture Organization, 'Freshwater Availability: Precipitation and Internal Renewable Water Resources (IRWR)', Aquastat online table, http://www.fao.org/nr/water/2011

8   UN Economic and Social Commission for Asia and the Pacific, *The State of theEnvironment in Asia and the Pacific 2005* (Bangkok: UN Economic and Social Commission for Asia and the Pacific, 2006), pp. 57–8.

9   Igor A. Shiklomanov, State Hydrological Institute (SHL. St. Petersburg) and United Nations Educational, Scientific and Cultural Organisation (UNESCO, Paris), 1999.

10 *This definition of water security is based on the one provided in UNESCO's International Hydrological Programme's (IHP) Strategic Plan of the Eighth Phase (see UNESCO-IHP, 2012a), endorsed at the 20ᵗʰ Session of the UNESCO-IHP Intergovernmental Council (UNESCO-IHP, 2012b: Resolution XX-5).*

11 Ibid,5

12 Exploring alternative futures of the World Water System. Building a second generation of World Water Scenarios. Prepared for the United Nations World Water Assessment Programme UN WWAP, 2010. http://www.unesco.org/new/en/natural-sciences/environment/water/wwap/world-water-scenarios/phase-1/

13 Ibid,5

14 International Water Law Project (IWLP), Status of the Watercourses Convention, http://www.internationalwaterlaw.org/documents/intldocs/watercourse_status.html

15 United Nation Economic Commission for Europe; http://www.unece.org/env/water/

16 Natural sciences, UNESCO http://www.unesco.org/water/news/transboundary _aquifers.shtml

17 UN General Assembly adopts resolution on the Law of Transboundary Aquifers. http://www.unesco.org/water/news/transboundary_aquifers.shtml

18 Sources: Adapted from the UN-Water Concept Note "Water Security – A Working Definition" [internal document, 4th Draft, 2011] and the Ministerial Declaration of The Hague on Water Security in the 21st Century, Second World Water Forum, 22 March, 2000

19 Ibid, 14

20 ibid

21 Theme Paper on Transboundary Waters, World Water Day 2009 , Central Water Commission , Government Of India Ministry Of Water Resources. http://www.cwc.nic.in/main/downloads/Theme%20Paper%20WWD-2009.pdf

22 An interview with Jennifer L. Turner on , U.S.- China Cooperation: The Significance of the Joint Agreement on Climate Change and Clean Energy, Wilson Center NOW; Dec 04, 2014 http://www.wilsoncenter.org/article/us-china-cooperation-the-significance-the-joint-agreement-climate-change-and-clean-energy

23 Lima climate accord: positive steps on the road to Paris, IISS Strategic Comments

24 BBC, News on Science and Environment, 13 February 2015, http://www.bbc.com/news/science-environment-31456369

25 India's National Water Policy, 2012; Government of India, Ministry of

Water Resources India, Pages 3 and 5 http://wrmin.nic.in/writereaddata/NationalWaterPolicy/NWP2012Eng6495132651.pdf

26 Ibid, 6

27 Ibid, 6

28 Fresh Water Futures: Imagining Responses to Demand Growth, Climate Change, and the Politics of Water Resource Management by 2040, Prepared by- The Stimson Center, www.stimson.org/images/uploads/.../StimsonCenterConfWaterReport.pdf

29 Ibid, 6

30 Ibid, 1

31 Ibid, 28

32 FAO http://www.fao.org/nr/water/aquastat/water_use/index.stm

33 Ibid, 6

34 Ibid, 6

35 Global Trends 2030 Alternative Worlds, NIC 2012-001; National Intelligence Council, http://www.dni.gov/files/documents/GlobalTrends_2030.pdf

36 Ibid,6

37 Heather Cooley, Newsha Ajami, Mai-Lan Ha, Veena Srinivasan, Jason Morrison, Kristina Donnelly, and Juliet Christian-Smith, *Global Water Governance in the Twenty-First Century.* http://worldwater.org/wp-content/uploads/sites/22/2013/07/ww8-ch1-us-water-policy.pdf

38 Ibid, 5

39 Ibid, 37

40 IPCC, 2014: Summary for policymakers. In: *Climate Change 2014: Impacts, Adaptation, and Vulnerability. Part A: Global and Sectoral Aspects. Contribution of Working Group II to the Fifth Assessment Report of the Intergovernmental Panel on Climate Change* [Field, C.B., V.R. Barros, D.J. Dokken, K.J. Mach, M.D. astrandrea, T.E. Bilir, M. Chatterjee, K.L. Ebi, Y.O. Estrada, R.C. Genova, B. Girma, E.S. Kissel, A.N. Levy, S. MacCracken, P.R. Mastrandrea, and L.L. White (eds.)]. Cambridge University Press, Cambridge, United Kingdom and New York, NY, USA, pp. 1-32.

41 Cécile Levacher, Strategic Analysis Paper, Future Direction International. 29 May 2014, Global Food and Water Security Research Programme *Climate Change in the Tibetan Plateau Region: Glacial Melt and Future Water Security*

42 World Climate Research Programme's Third Coupled Model Inter-comparison Project

43 Ibid, 40

44 Ibid,6

45 Ibid, 40

46 Ibid, 40

47 Asit K. Biswas (2008) Integrated Water Resources Management: Is It Working?, International Journal of Water Resources Development, 24:1, 5-22, DOI: 10.1080/07900620701871718, http://dx.doi.org/10.1080/07900620701871718

48 Ibid

49 This quotation was taken from the foreword to the Global Water Partnership's ToolBox Version 2. GWP ToolBox Version 2 is available at: http://www.gwp.org/Global/ToolBox/About/ToolBox/ToolBox%20(English).pdf.

50 Mark Giordano & Tushaar Shah (2014) 'From IWRM back to integrated water resources management', International Journal of Water Resources Development, 30:3, 364-376, DOI: 10.1080/07900627.2013.851521

51 A review of the evolution and state of transboundary freshwater treaties, 2013, Mark Giordano, Alena Drieschova, James A. Duncan, Yoshiko Sayama, Lucia De Stefano & Aaron T. Wolf. (http://www.transboundarywaters.orst.edu/publications/publications/Giordano%20et%20al.%20Treaty%20Update%20 4-13.pdf)

52 Aaron T.Wolf, SharedWaters: Conflict and Cooperation, 2007, http://www.transboundarywaters.orst.edu/publications/abst_docs/wolf_2007_shared_waters.pdf

53 ibid

54 There is a long history of water-related conflicts, as documented in The Pacific Institute's Water Conflict Chronology (see: http://worldwater.org/conflict.html).

CHAPTER 2 : INDIA'S WATER SITUATION

"I believe water will be the defining crisis of our century, the main vehicle through which climate change will be felt—from droughts, storms and floods to degrading water quality. We'll see major conflicts over water; water refugees. We inhabit a water planet and unless we protect, manage, and restore that resource, the future will be a very different place from the one we imagine today".

— *Alexandra Cousteau*

Background

Water on the earth is in motion through the hydrological cycle. The utilisation of water for most of the users i.e. human, animal or plant involve movement of water. The dynamic and renewable nature of the water resources and the recurrent need for its utilisation requires that water resources are measured in terms of its flow rates. Thus water resources have two facets. The dynamic resource, measured as flow is more relevant for most of developmental needs. The static or fixed nature of the reserve, involving the quantity of water, the length of area of the water bodies is also relevant for some activities like navigation.

India is a land of many rivers and mountains. Its geographical area of about 329 MHa (Million Hectares) is criss-crossed by a large number of small and big rivers, some of them figuring amongst the mighty rivers of the world[1]. A major part of India's population of 1,241492000 [2](2011) is rural and agriculturally oriented for whom the rivers are the source of their prosperity.

Rapid growth in it's economy and industrialisation has modified the demographic texture, which continues to progress towards an urban, industrialised and water guzzling nation. Although, India is not a water poor country, due to growing human population, severe neglect and over-exploitation of this resource, water is becoming a scarce commodity. India is more vulnerable because of the growing population and in-disciplined lifestyle. This calls for immediate attention by the stakeholders to make sustainable use of the available water resources[3].

Water is one of the most important renewable natural resources for supporting life. With the increasing population of India as well as its all-round development, the utilisation of water is also increasing at a fast pace. On an average, India receives annual precipitation (including snowfall) of about 4000 km³. However, there exist considerable spatial and temporal variations in the distribution of rainfall and hence in availability of water in time and space across the country. It is estimated that out of the 4000 km³ water, 1869 km³ is average annual potential flow in rivers available as water resource. Out of this total available water resource, only 1123 km³ is utilisable (690 km³ from surface water resources and 433 km³ from ground water resources). The water demand in the year 2000 was 634 km³ and it is likely to be 1093 km³ by the year 2025[4]. Due to rapid rise in population and growing economy of the country, there will be continuous increase in demand for water, and it will become scarce in the coming decades (Table-1).

Table-1: Water Availability Facts at a Glance

Area of the country as % of World Area	2.4%
Population as % of World Population	17.1%
Water as % of World Water	4%
Rank in per capita availability	132
Rank in water quality	122
Average annual rainfall	1160 mm (world average 1110 mm)
Range of distribution	150-11690 mm
Range Rainy days	5-150 days, Mostly during 15 days in 100 hrs
Range PET	1500-3500 mm
Per capita water availability (2010)	1588 m³

Water In India

India's constitution places water as a state subject. Each state manages water differently, with different bodies dealing with specific aspects of water management through various departments and ministries including agriculture, irrigation, hydropower, fisheries, rural development, flood control, supply and sanitation. Centrally there are national boards such as the National Water Development Agency and the Central Water Commission providing guidance and technical support to the states. The challenge facing government lies in better coordinated planning and assessing tradeoffs at the national level .It emphasises the need to recognize 'environmental flows' as necessary to maintain the ecological health of the river, improve water infrastructure for water security and ensure clean and safe water supply for all. However, it can be inferred from observed indicators and the growing number of social protests against water development projects that the water sector has not yet met its objective of inclusive and sustainable development. However, the ineffectiveness of policies as also, that of the process of policy-making is mainly due to the gap between policy and practice. Numerous NGOs have been working to promote community-based water management programmes in India to cover this void. The Indian states are without effective interstate water organisations. Water is essential for livelihood and has a pivotal role in socio-economic development of the country and for maintaining healthy ecosystems.

Improving transboundary water relations without ensuring domestic water security is not prudent, especially with the current zero-sum approach to water resources. For this governance to be effective, countries need to develop their own water governance capacity through transparent, coherent and cost-efficient policies, laws and institutions. Another issue that of 'Political Will' is a problem both in domestic water management and in transboundary water relations. Whether due to internal compulsions or poor understanding of the subject lack of political commitment has been responsible for numerous stalled cross-border projects, such as those between India and Nepal, Pakistan and even Bangladesh. The plethora of organisations and lack of synchronisation amongst them within India is a problem in water planning and management. India has been gradually developing it's water policy and by its implementation securing her water interests. The comprehensive National Water Policy, 2012 incorporates a large number of vital, essential and even desirable aspects[5] (Annexure 3)

National Water Policy. The National Water Policy 2012 has made considerable improvements from the policy document of 2002. A large number of shortcomings experienced earlier have been addressed. The water policy has taken into account the updated figures of demand and supply and incorporates numerous modern water management methods and conservation technologies. Though this is a promising development the process is ever evolving and must remain in harmony with ground realities and developments. It does partly factor the international dimensions of water sharing and on water cooperation with India's neighbours[6]. The river waters must be given greater importance in India's foreign policy priorities. Conflicting and converging interests, particularly the sharing/distribution issues of river waters are the more critical and immediate concern. Comprehensive water management of issues which are less immediate, mid term and longer-term must lead to the priority of focus. Multilateral and bilateral actions involving river-basin actors on water management issues should be an ongoing process. The essential structure of the new policy is comprehensive and does cover a wide range of issues and aspects very vital for water management. In the document these are broadly covered under the following heads:

- Preamble. Giving the Geopolitical Considerations.

- Water Framework Law.

- Uses of Water.

- Adaptation to Climate Change.

- Enhancing Water Available For Use.

- Demand Management and Water Use Efficiency.

- Water Pricing.

- Conservation of River Corridors, Water Bodies and Infrastructure.

- Project Planning and Implementation.

- Management of Flood and Drought.

- Water Supply and Sanitation.

- Institutional Arrangements.

- Trans-Boundary Rivers.

- Database and Information System.

- Research and Training Needs.

- Implementation of National Water Policy.

Factual Information

According to the international norms, a country can be categorized as 'water stressed' when water availability is less than 1700 m³ per capita per year whereas classified as 'water scarce' if it is less than 1000 m³ per capita per year[7]. In India, the availability of surface water in the years 1991 and 2001 were 2309 m³ and 1902 m³. However, it has been projected that per capita surface water availability is likely to be reduced to 1401 m³ and 1191 m³ by the years 2025 and 2050, respectively[8]. The per capita water availability in the year 2010 was 1588 m³ against 5200 m³ of the year 1951 in the country.

Table-2: India's Water Resources

Water Resource at a Glance	Quantity (km³)	Percentage
Annual precipitation (Including snowfall)	4000	100
Precipitation during monsoon	3000	75
Evaporation + Soil water	2131	53.3
Average annual potential flow in rivers	1869	46.7
Estimated utilisable water resources	1123	28.1
Surface water	690	17.3
Replenishable groundwater	433	10.8
Storage created of utilisable water	253.381	22.52

Water Resource at a Glance	Quantity (km³)	Percentage
Storage (under construction) of utilisable water	50.737	4.5
Projects under consideration[9]	107.54	
Estimated water need in 2050	1450	129
Estimated deficit	327	29
Interlinking can give us	200	17.8

(Source: Water Resources at a Glance 2011, CWC, New Delhi)

Water Availability

Water Resources Potential: The water resources potential of the country which occurs as natural run off in the rivers is about 1869 BCM as per the estimates of Central Water Commission (CWC), considering both surface and ground water into account. Of the major rivers, the river basin Ganga-Brahmaputra-Meghna is the largest in respect of catchment area of about 11 lakh sq km. The other major rivers with catchment area of about one lakh sq km or more are: Indus, Godavari, Krishna, Mahanadi and Narmada. Its share is 59% in total water resources potential of the various rivers. The estimated per capita availability of water works out to 1588 cubic metre (cu.m) as on March 2010[10]. Due to various constraints of topography, uneven distribution of resource over space and time, it has been estimated that only about 1111 BCM of total potential of 1869 BCM can be put to beneficial use, 690 BCM being due to surface water resources. Again about 40% of utilisable surface water resources are presently in Ganga – Brahmaputra - Meghna system.

Table 3: Per Capita Availability 2010: India

Sl No	River Basin	Average Water Resources Potential	Estimated Population in 2010 (Millions)	Per Capita Availability of Water in 2010 (Cubic Meters)
1	Indus (upto Border)	73.31	58.42	1255
2	Ganga	1110.62	549.94	2020
3	Godavari	110.54	75.30	1468
4	Krishna	78.12	84.78	921
5	Cauvery	21.36	40.85	523
6	Subermarekha*	12.37	13.10	944
7	Brahamani & Baitarni	28.48	13.66	2085
8	Mahanadi	66.88	37.09	1803
9	Pennar	6.32	13.53	467
10	Mahi	11.02	14.64	753
11	Sabarmati	3.81	14.64	260
12	Narmada	45.64	20.50	2227
13	Tapi	14.88	20.64	721
14	West Flowing Rivers	87.41	112.25	779
15	East Flowing Rivers	22.52	95.65	235
	Others	62.54	12.00	-
TOTAL		1869.35	1177	1588

Source: B. P. Directorate, CWC

1. Reassessment of Water Resources Potential of india March 1993, CWC.

2. Report of the Standing Sub-committee for assessment of availability and requirement of water for diverse uses in the country, August 2000.

* Note: Combining Subermarekha and other small rivers between Subermarekha and Baitarni.

Source: Water And Related Statistics, Water Resources Information System Directorate Information System Organisation, Water Planning & Projects Wing Central Water Commission, December 2010.

The distribution of water resources potential in the country shows that the national per capita annual availability of water at 1820 cu. m in 2001 was estimated at 1588 in 2010. The average availability in Ganga, Brahmaputra and Barak is estimated as at 2020 cu m while it was as low as 260 cu m in Sabarmati basin in 2000. Cauvery, Pennar, Sabarmati and East Flowing Rivers are some of the basins, which fall into this category out of which Pennar, Sabarmati and East Flowing rivers will face more acute water scarcity with per capita availability of water less than or around 500 cu m during 2010[11].

Water Bodies in India

Inland Water resources of the country are classified as rivers and canals; reservoirs; tanks and ponds; beels, oxbow lakes, derelict water; and brackish water. Other than rivers and canals, total water bodies cover an overall area of about 7 MHa. Of the rivers and canals, Uttar Pradesh occupies the first place with the total length of rivers and canals being 31.2 thousand km, which is about 17 percent of the total length of rivers and canals in the country. Other states following Uttar Pradesh are Jammu & Kashmir and Madhya Pradesh. Among the remaining forms of the inland water resources, tanks and ponds have maximum area (2.9 M.Ha.) followed by reservoirs (2.1 M.Ha.). Most of the area under tanks and ponds lics in Southern States of Andhra Pradesh, Karnataka and Tamil Nadu. These states along with West Bengal, Rajasthan and Uttar Pradesh, account for 62 percent of total area under tanks and ponds in the country. As far as reservoirs are concerned, major states like Andhra Pradesh, Gujarat, Karnataka, Madhya Pradesh, Maharashtra, Orissa, Rajasthan and Uttar Pradesh account for larger portion of area under reservoirs. More than 77 percent of area under beels, oxbow lakes and derelict water lies in the states of Orissa, Uttar Pradesh and Assam. Orissa ranks first as regards the total area of brackish water and is followed by Gujarat, Kerala and West Bengal[12].

The total area of inland water resources is, thus, unevenly distributed over the twelve states with five states namely Orissa, Andhra Pradesh, Gujarat, Karnataka and West Bengal accounting for more than half of the country's inland water bodies.

Table 4: Inland Water Resources: India

Name of the State	Rivers & Canals (Length in Km)	Water Bodies (Lakh ha)				
		Reservoirs	Tanks & Ponds	Flood plain Lakes & Derelict Water	Brackish Water	Total
Orissa	4500	2.56	1.14	1.8	4.3	9.80
Andhra Pradesh	11514	2.34	5.17	-	0.6	8.11
Karnataka	9000	4.4	2.9	-	0.1	7.40
Tamil Nadu	7420	5.7	0.56	0.07	0.6	6.93
West Bengal	2526	0.17	2.76	0.42	2.1	5.45
Kerala	3092	0.3	0.3	2.43	2.4	5.43
Uttar Pradesh	28500	1.38	1.61	1.33	-	4.32
Gujarat	3865	2.43	0.71	0.12	1	4.26
Maharashtra	16000	2.79	0.59	-	0.1	3.48
Arunachal Pradesh	2000	-	2.76	0.42	-	3.18
Rajasthan	5290	1.2	1.8	-	-	3.00
Madhya Pradesh	17088	2.27	0.6	-	-	2.87
Others incl UTs	84415	3.53	3.24	1.39	1.2	9.36
TOTAL	195210	29.07	24.14	7.98	12.4	73.59

Source: Department of Animal Husbandry, Dairying & Fisheries, Ministry of Agriculture

Rivers

India is blessed with many rivers. Twelve of them are classified as major rivers whose total catchment area is 252.8 million hectares (MHa). Of the major rivers, the Ganga - Brahmaputra Meghana system is the biggest with catchment area of about 110 MHa which is more than 43 percent of the catchment area of all the major rivers in the country. The other major rivers with catchment area more than 10 MHa are Indus (32.1 MHa.), Godavari (31.3 MHa.), Krishna, (25.9 MHa.) and Mahanadi (14.2 MHa). The catchment area of medium rivers is about 25 M.Ha and Subernarekha with 1.9 MHa. catchment area is the largest river among the medium rivers in the country. The rivers of India can be classified into four groups[13]:

> The Himalayan rivers (Ganges, Brahmaputra, Indus) are formed by melting snow and glaciers as well as rainfall and, therefore, have a continuous flow throughout the year. As these regions receive very heavy rainfall during the monsoon period, the rivers swell and cause frequent floods.

> The rivers of the Deccan plateau (with larger rivers such as Mahanadi, Godavari, Krishna, Pennar and Cauvery draining into the bay of Bengal in the east, and Narmada and Tapi draining into the Arabian sea in the west), making up most of the Southern-central part of the country, are rainfed and fluctuate in volume, many of them being non-perennial.

> The coastal rivers, especially on the west coast, south of the Tapi, are short with limited catchment areas, most of them being non-perennial.

> The rivers of the inland drainage basin in Western Rajasthan in the North-Western part of the country, towards the border with Pakistan, are ephemeral and drain towards the salt lakes such as the Sambhar, or are lost in the sands.

The rivers in India are divided into 20 River Basins, the basin wise availability of water differs considerably from basin to basin (Table 5) .

Table 5: Water Availability Basin Wise (Cubic Km/Year)

Sl. no	River Basin	Catchment Area (Sq. Km.)	Average Water Resources Potential	Utilisable Surface Water Resources
1	Indus (up to Border)	321289	73.31	46.0
2	Ganga- Brahmaputra-Meghna			
	a) Ganga	861452	525.02	250.0
	b) Brahmaputra	194413	537.24	24.0
	c) Barak & Others	41723	48.36	
3	Godavari	312812	110.54	76.3
4	Krishna	258948	78.12	58.0
5	Cauvery	81155	21.36	19.0
6	Subermarekha*	29196	12.37	6.8
7	Brahamani & Baitarni	51822	28.48	18.3
8	Mahanadi	141589	66.88	50.0
9	Pennar	55213	6.32	6.9
10	Mahi	34842	11.02	3.1
11	Sabarmati	21674	3.81	1.9
12	Narbada	98796	45.64	34.5
13	Tapi	65145	14.88	14.5
14	West Flowing Rivers From Tapi to Tadri	55940	87.41	11.9
15	West Flowing Rivers From Tadri to Kanyakumari	56177	113.53	24.3
16	East Flowing Rivers between Mahanadi & Pennar	86643	22.52	13.1
17	East Flowing Rivers between Pennar and Kanyakumari	100139	16.46	16.5
18	West Flowing Rivers of Kutch and Saurashtra including Luni	321851	15.10	15.0
19	Areas of Inland drainage in Rajasthan	-	negl.	-
20	Minor River Draining into Myanmar (Burma) & Bangladesh	36302	31.00	-
	Total		1869.37	690.1

*Note: Combining Subermarekha and other small rivers between Subermarekha and Baitarni.

Source: BP Directorate, CWC

The Impact of Development and Irrigation.

Groundwater irrigation is a key driver of future expansion of the irrigated area. Expanding groundwater irrigation, on the one hand, contributes to increasing gross irrigated area, crop yield and crop production. Uncontrolled pumping, on the other hand, contributes to physical water scarcities and groundwater-depletion-related environmental issues in some basins.

Figure 21 and 22 below shows how the degree of development and the groundwater abstraction ratio of the potentially utilisable water resources (PUWR) will change over the period 2000–2050. Many river basins will be physically water scarce by 2050[14]. These river basins will not have adequate freshwater resources for meeting the future development without affecting the environment or other water users. The degree of development of 10 river basins, home to 75% of the total population, will be well over 60% by 2050. These water-scarce basins would have developed much of the potentially utilisable water resources by the second quarter of this century. The water reallocation between different sectors in these basins would be a common exercise to meet the increasing demand. There is a likelihood of transfer of surface irrigation resources to domestic and industrial water uses. Increased groundwater irrigation is likely to have severe detrimental effects on many basins. Groundwater abstraction ratios of many basins are significantly high. Given the current level of recharge, groundwater use patterns of these basins are not sustainable.

Figure 21: India's Water Future 2025- 2050: Development

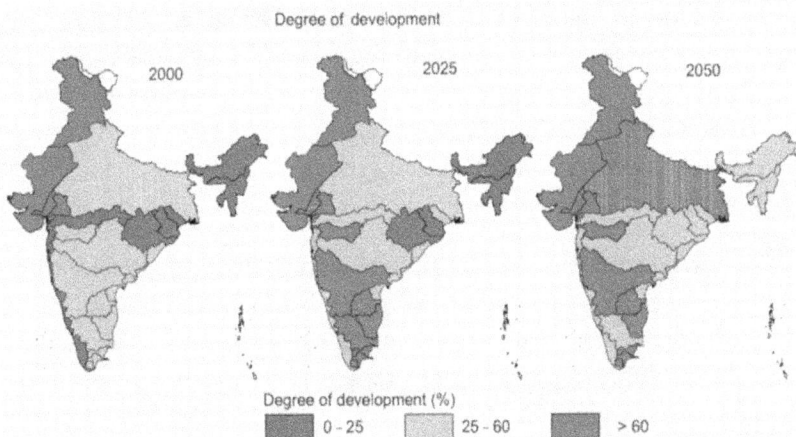

~ 63 ~

Figure 22: India's Water Future 2025- 2050: Groundwater Abstraction

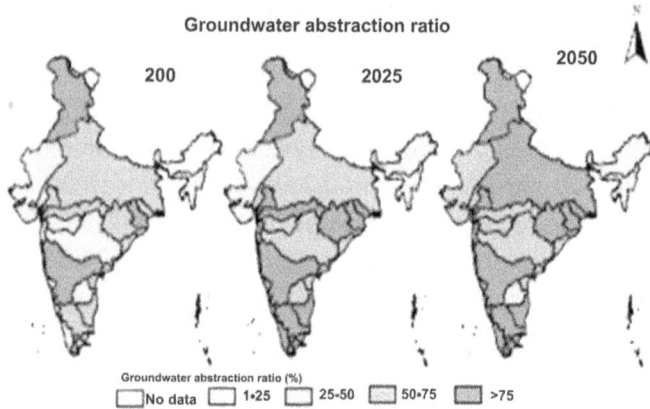

Water Storage

Surface Storage: A total storage capacity of about 253.4 BCM has been created in the country due to the major and medium irrigation projects since completed. The projects under construction will contribute to additional 51 BCM. Thus likely storage available will be 304.3 BCM once the projects under construction are completed against the total water availability of 1869 BCM in the river basins of the country. Maximum storage (taking into consideration of projects under construction) lies in the Ganga Basin followed by Krishna, Godavari and Narmada. Pennar is the leading basin in terms of storage capacities as percentage of average annual flow. The storage capacities as percentage of average annual flow exceed 50% for Tapi, Krishna and Narmada while for Ganga and Brahmaputra sub-basins the corresponding figures are 11 % and 0.5 % respectively. But if projects under consideration are also taken into account, Brahmaputra and Barak basin will occupy the second place after Ganga Basin.[15]

The storage capacities as percentage of average annual flow exceed 50% for Tapi, Krishna, West Flowing Rivers of Kutch and Saurashtra, Narmada, Brahmani and Baitarni basins while for Ganga basin and Brahmaputra - Barak Basin, the corresponding figures are 17 % and 9 % respectively. Major States like Andhra Pradesh, Gujarat, Karnataka, Madhya Pradesh, Maharashtra, Orissa and Uttar Pradesh together account for about 72 % of total live storage capacity in the country. The States of Arunachal Pradesh,

Orissa and Uttar Pradesh account for 72 % of the total storage of projects under consideration.

For a better perspective on the issue the details of 'Status of Live Storages Capacity of Reservoirs in India', 'Basin Wise   Live Storages Capacity of Major and Medium Irrigation Projects in India' and ' Basin-Wise Flows and Storage Potential in India' are shown in Figures 23, 24 and 25 below.

Figure 23: Status of Live Storages Capacity of Reservoirs: India

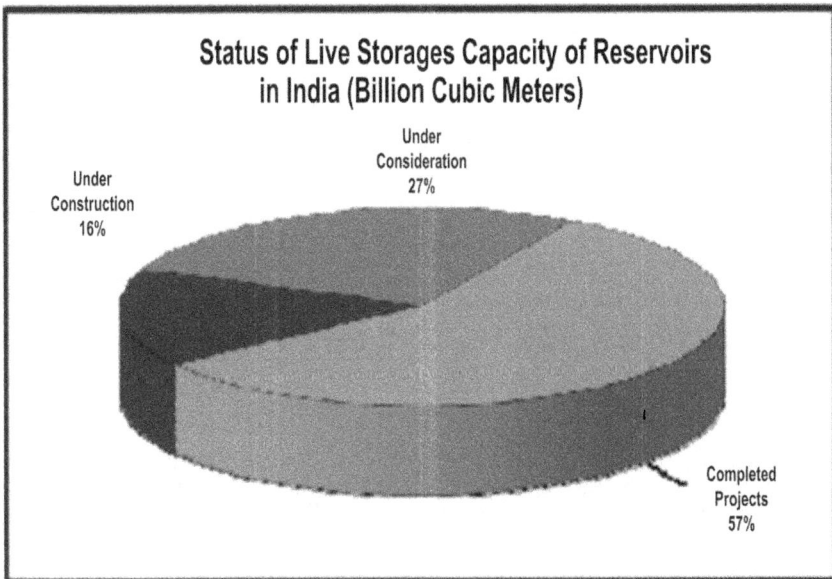

Source: Water And Related Statistics, Central Water Commission, December 2010.

Figure 24: Basin Wise Live Storages Capacity Major and Medium Irrigation Projects: India

| Sl. No. | Basin | Average Annual Flow | Live Storage Capacities | | | | Percentage of Likely Average Flow ((Col 6+ col 7)/ col 3) * 100 |
			Completed Project	Project Under Construction	Total	Project under Consideration	
(1)	(2)	(3)	(4)	(5)	(6)	(7)	(8)
1	Indus	73305.00	16285.90	282.53	16568.43	2576.39	26.12
2	A) Ganga	525023.00	42060.20	18600.18	60660.38	30083.92	17.28
	B) Brahmaputra & Barak	585597.00	2326.92	9353.64	11680.56	41262.88	9.04
3	Godavari	110540.00	25124.60	6250.79	31330.39	5841.16	33.63
4	Krishna	78124.00	41803.98	7743.54	49547.52	1127.84	64.87
5	Cauvery	21358.00	8597.20	269.82	8867.02	261.99	42.74
6	Pennar	6316.00	2649.40	2170.71	4820.11		76.32
7	EFR from Mahanadi to Godavari and Krishna to Pennar	22520.00	1601.44	1424.97	3026.41	945.29	17.64
8	EFR B/W Pennar and Kanyakumari	16458.00	1838.41	68.49	1906.90	-	-
9	Mahanadi	66879.00	12334.80	1873.00	14207.80	10094.20	36.34
10	Brahmani & Baitarni	28477.00	4648.09	875.60	5523.69	8721.19	50.02
11	Subermerekha	12368.00	672.02	1650.19	2322.21	1380.50	29.94
12	Sabarmati	3809.00	1306.77	60.77	1367.54	99.33	38.51
13	Mahi	11020.00	4722.60	261.43	4984.03	11.81	45.33
14	WFR of Kutch, Saurashtra including Luni	15098.00	4726.92	797.23	5524.15	2849.06	55.46
15	Narmada	45639.00	16979.50	6625.10	23604.60	465.73	52.74
16	Tapi	14879.00	9408.37	847.42	10255.79	286.92	70.86
17	WFR from Tapi to Tadri	87411.00	11268.03	3464.38	14732.41	81.69	16.95
18	WFR from Tadri to Kanyakumari	113532.00	10236.16	1317.54	11553.70	1453.31	11.46
19	Area of Inland Drainage of Rajasthan	-	-	-	0.00	-	-
20	Minor River Basins Draining into Myanmar and Bangladesh	31000.00	312.00		312.00	1.47	1.01
	Grand Total in BCM	1869.35	218.90	63.89	282.80	107.54	20.88

Source: 1. Central Water Commission (WM, Directorate), 2. ISO, CWC for Col.8
Note: Projects having a live storage capacity of 10 M.Cum and above only are included. An additional live storage capacity of 6.241 BCM (approx) is estimated to be created through medium projects each having capacity of less than 10 MCM thus making a total live storage capacity of 225.14 BCM in completed projects.
EFR: East Flowing Rivers, WFR: West Flowing Rivers, BCM: Billion Cubic Meters, MCM: Million Cubic Meters

Figure 25: Basin Wise Flows and Storage Potential: India

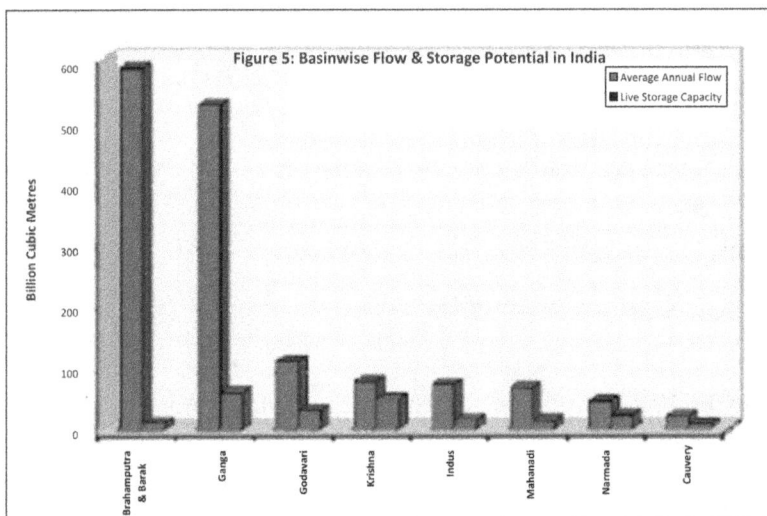

SOURCE: Water And Related Statistics, Central Water Commission, December 2010.

Rainfall: The annual precipitation including snowfall, which is the main source of water in the country, is estimated to be of the order of 4000 BCM. The two main sources of water in India are rainfall and glacial snowmelt in the Himalayas about 80 percent of the river flow occurs during the four to five months of the southwest monsoon season. India has an annual average precipitation of 1170 mm and about 80 percent of the total area of the country experiences annual rainfall of 750 mm or more. Owing to the large spatial and temporal variability in the rainfall, water resources distribution is highly skewed in space and time[16]. Rainfall in India is dependent in differing degrees on the South-West and North-East monsoons, on shallow cyclonic depressions and disturbances and on violent local storms which form regions where cool humid winds the sea meet hot dry winds from the land and occasionally reach cyclonic dimension. The rainfall in India shows great variations, unequal seasonal distribution, still more unequal geographical distribution and the frequent departures from the normal. A summary of rainfall in the country has been given in Table below:-

Table 6 : Volume of Rainfall in India

Year	2001	2002	2003	2004	2005	2006	2007	2008	2009	2010	2011
Total Rainfall (mm)	1110	930	1234	1086	1215	1161	1181	1117	954	1213	1116
Total Volume of Rainfall (BCM)	3648	3200	4057	3570	3996	3819	3882	3674	3136	3989	3669

SOURCE: Water And Related Statistics, Central Water Commission, December 2010.

The two main sources of water in India are rainfall and glacial snowmelt in the Himalayas. Although snow and glaciers are poor producers of freshwater, they are good distributors as they yield at the time of need, in the hot season. Indeed, about 80 percent of the river flow occurs during the four to five months of the southwest monsoon season.

Ground Water

Groundwater is a critical resource in India, accounting for over 65% of irrigation water and 85% of drinking water supplies.[17] However, on current trends it is estimated that 60% of groundwater sources will be in a critical state of degradation within the next twenty years.[18] Total annual replenishable ground water potential of the country has been estimated as 431 BCM. The break-up of annual replenishable ground water resources by State with share 2.5% or more have been presented in Table below:-

Table 7 : Annual Replenishable Ground Water Resources in India

State	Annual Replenishment Ground Water Resources	
	BCM / Year	%
Andhra Pradesh	33.83	7.8
Assam	30.35	7.0
Bihar	28.63	6.6
Chhatisgarh	12.22	2.8
Gujarat	18.43	4.3
Karnataka	16.81	3.9
Madhya Pradesh	33.95	7.9
Maharashtra	35.73	8.3
Orissa	17.78	4.1
Punjab	22.56	5.2
Rajasthan	11.86	2.8
Tamil Nadu	22.94	5.3
Uttar Pradesh	75.25	17.5
West Bengal	30.50	7.1
Others	40.19	9.3
Total	431.02	100.0

Source: Central Ground Water Board, Min. of Water Resources

14 States comprise 91% of ground water potential. Among the States, Uttar Pradesh ranks first (17.5%) in terms of share of replenishable ground water resources followed by Maharashtra (8.3%), Madhya Pradesh (7.9%), Andhra Pradesh (7.8%), West Bengal (7.1%) and Assam (7.0%).

In the most seriously affected North-Western states, recent satellite measurements indicate an average decline of 33 cm per year from 2002 to 2008.[19] Local observations of annual water table decline exceeding 4 metres are common throughout India.[20] In India, however, it would seem almost impossible for the national government to manage the estimated 25 million groundwater extraction structures already in existence[21]; this is particularly the case given that India's government institutions require significant strengthening and responsibility for groundwater management which is fragmented throughout different official departments[22]. What's more, India's state governments have primary jurisdiction over groundwater usage and, in many cases, state agencies are even more poorly equipped.

Groundwater contributes more than 79% of the total ultimate potential through minor irrigation. Uttar Pradesh and Bihar are two largest states in term of potential due to Major and Medium Irrigation Projects. These two states along with Madhya Pradesh, Andhra Pradesh and Maharashtra account for about 54% of the total ultimate potential of Major and Medium Irrigation in the country .The proportion of over-exploited area is highest in Delhi followed by Haryana and Daman and Diu. The number of States/ UTs affected due to salinity is only 6; but among these States/UT, the problem of salinity is somewhat significant in Puducherry and Gujarat.

Table 8 : Classification of Area Units by Usage of Ground Water Resources

% of Units	Safe	Semi-critical	Critical	Over-exploited	Salinity affected
90+	Arunachal Pr., Assam, Bihar, Chhattisgarh, Goa, J&K, Jharkhand, Maharashtra, Manipur, Meghalaya, Mizoram, Nagaland, Orissa, Sikkim, Tripura, A&N Islands, Chandigarh, D&N Haveli				
75 - 90	AP, HP, Kerala, WB			Delhi	
40 -75	Gujarat, Karnataka, MP, UP, Uttarakhand, Lakshadweep, Puducherry	Daman & Diu, Lakshdweep		Haryana, Daman & Diu	
20 - 40	TN	Uttarakhand		Karnataka, TN, Puducherry	Puducherry
5 - 20	Delhi, Haryana	AP, Delhi, Gujarat, Haryana, Karnataka,	Haryana, HP, TN	Gujarat, HP, MP, UP	Gujarat

% of Units	Safe	Semi-critical	Critical	Over-exploited	Salinity affected
5 - 20 contd.		Kerala, MP, Maharashtra, TN, UP, Uttarakhand, WB			
<5		Bihar, Chhattisgarh, Jharkhand	AP, Gujarat, Jharkhand, Karnataka, Kerala, MP, Maharashtra, UP		

Agriculture

Agriculture has been the largest consumer of water in India and is likely to remain so because of the large population , dependence on agriculture as a source of income and therefore it is important to analyse the water resources being used for agriculture. Analysing the country-wise geographical area, arable land and irrigated area in the World, it is seen that among the continents, the largest geographical area lies in Africa which is about 23 per cent of the world geographic area. However, Asia (excluding erstwhile countries of USSR) with only 21 per cent of world geographical area has about 32 per cent of world's arable land followed by North Central America having about 20 per cent of World's arable land. Africa has only 12 per cent of world's arable land. It has been seen that irrigated area in the World is about 18.5 per cent of the arable land in 1994. In 1989, 63 per cent of world's irrigated area was in Asia, whereas in 1994 this percentage has gone upto 64 per cent. Also 37 per cent of arable land of Asia was irrigated in 1994.

Among Asian countries, India has the largest arable land, which is close to 39 per cent of Asia's arable land. Only United States of America has more arable land than India[23]. The state wise irrigated area varies and impacts largely on agriculture being the largest consumer of water resources[24].The FAO database appreciates India's land and water data in great detail conveying that almost 51% of the country's land area is cultivated.(Appendix 4) The total ultimate irrigation potential (UIP) of India stands at about 140 MHa. The share of Minor Irrigation is higher by 22.96 MHa as compared to that of Major and Medium Irrigation. Ground Water contributes more than 79% of the total ultimate potential through minor irrigation.

Figure 26: Ultimate Irrigation Potential: India

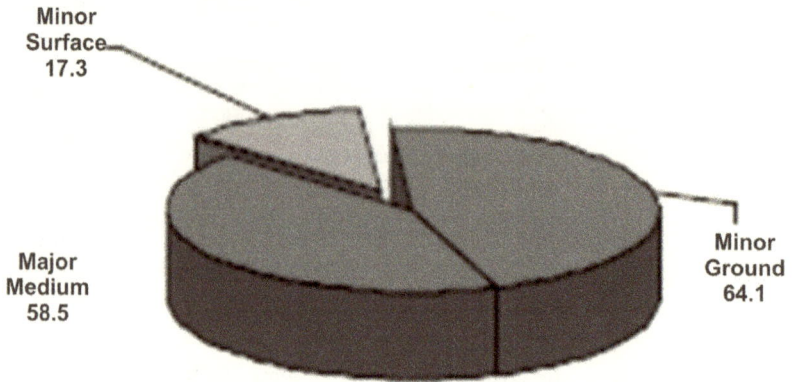

India's own agencies say it must nearly double its annual grain production to more than 450 million tons by 2050 to meet the demands of increasing prosperity and a growing population, or risk becoming a major food importer—a development that will disrupt the already tight international food markets[25].

Rainfed Agriculture

One of the solutions to the problem of pricing or regulating pump water to reduce withdrawals to a sustainable level is too facile. Even if it could be done, practically speaking, what country would be willing to pay the enormous price of this policy in terms of reduced food production and domestic and industrial water supplies? One of the best ways to do this, ironically enough, is to discourage irrigation efficiency, especially by encouraging more paddy irrigation in the wet season. The deep percolation 'losses' of paddy irrigation recharge aquifers and replenish stream flows[26]. A considered decision on this issue must be evaluated in detail and acted upon by India.

Dams Scenario

Central Water Commission maintains the National Register of Large Dams. The State-wise distribution of number of dams is presented in Table below. It reveals that there are 5187 Dams in the country out of which 4839 are completed. The maximum number of dams completed in the country is in Maharashtra (1693) followed by Madhya Pradesh (899), Gujarat (621), Andhra Pradesh (290), Chhattisgarh (243), Karnataka (230) and Rajasthan (201). The number of dams under construction is the highest in Maharashtra (152) followed by Gujarat (45), Andhra Pradesh (44) and Jharkhand (28. The maximum numbers of dams in India were completed during the decades 1971-80 (1294) and 1981-90 (1255).

Table 9 : Number of Dams: Per State

State / UT	Completed	Under Construction	Total	State / UT	Completed	Under Construction	Total
A & N Islands	2	0	2	Maharashtra	1693	152	1845
Andhra Pradesh	290	44	334	Manipur	3	2	5
Arunachal Pr.	1	0	1	Meghalaya	5	1	6
Assam	3	2	5	Mizoram	0	0	0
Bihar	24	4	28	Nagaland	0	0	0
Chhattisgarh	243	14	257	Orissa	198	6	204
Goa	5	0	5	Punjab	14	1	15
Gujarat	621	45	666	Rajasthan	201	10	211
Haryana	1	0	1	Sikkim	2	0	2
Himachal Pr.	13	6	19	Tamil Nadu	116	0	116
J & K	12	2	14	Tripura	1	0	1
Jharkhand	49	28	77	Uttar Pradesh	114	16	130
Karnataka	230	1	231	Uttarakhand	13	6	19
Kerala	58	1	59	West Bengal	28	0	28
Madhya Pradesh	899	7	906				
				Total	4839	348	5187

Source : Central Water Commission, (Dam Safety Monitoring Directorate) National Registrar of Large Dam

Water Resources Projects in India

Water resources projects are broadly categorized into irrigation projects and hydroelectric projects. These projects are planned for various purposes like irrigation, hydro-power generation, water supply for drinking and industrial purpose, flood control navigation etc. Projects which serve more than one purpose are called as multipurpose projects. Generally majority of multipurpose projects are combination of irrigation and hydro-power. There are many irrigation, hydro-power and multipurpose projects which were approved initially as independent projects. Subsequently due to interstate agreements and new projects coming up on downstream and upstream, water planning was done in such a way that operation of these projects are now done in an integrated manner. Such types of projects are now being called as irrigation, hydro power, multipurpose and complex.

Hydro Power Potential and Generation. Data on Hydro Electric Power Potential Development for the country as well as for various States and regions is available. While 32.08 thousand-mega watt (MW) i.e. about 21.6% of country's total hydroelectric potential (148.7 thousand MW identified capacity as per reassessment study) has been developed as on 31.03.2010 and about 14.3 thousand MW (i.e. about 9.6%) has been under development. Contrary to the highest potential assessed in North Eastern Region, the potential actually tapped in this region is not only the lowest but also drastically low as compared to other regions. Next highest in order of potential assessed is the Northern Region where again the progress seems to be rather tardy as evident from only 25.6% of the potential tapped so far, in addition to another 15 % under development[27]. In absolute terms, however, potential developed in the Northern Region is highest at 13.4 thousand MW of developed capacity followed by the Southern region at 9.1 thousand MW. In percentage terms, Western Region promised to the best having tapped 68% of the assessed potential of 8.1 thousand MW followed by Southern region with 57.5% potential development. Among the States Tripura (100%), Punjab (100%), Madhya Pradesh (100%), Haryana (97.5%), Gujarat (89.7%) all the states which have managed to tap a high level of assessed potential. Basin wise Hydro electric Power Potential Development is also available.

Figure 27 : Share Of Hydro-Power Generation : 1947 and 2007-08

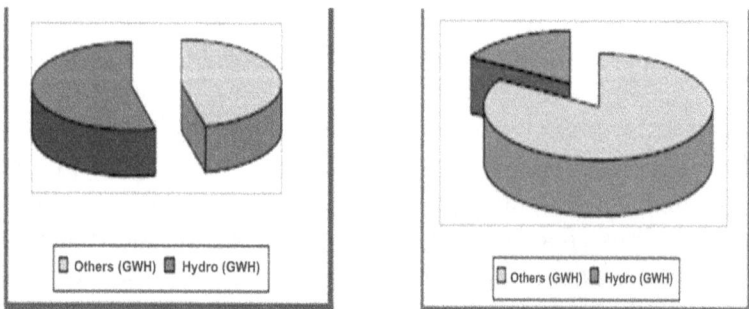

~ 74 ~

National River Linking Project

The 'National River Linking Project' [NRLP] envisages transferring water from the potentially water surplus rivers to water scarce Western and Peninsular river basins. The NRLP proposes to build 30 river links and more than 3000 storages to connect 37 Himalayan and Peninsular rivers[28]. The NRLP water transfers envisage easing the water shortages in Western and Southern India, while mitigating the impacts of recurrent floods in Eastern India. It constitutes two main components - the links, which will connect the Himalayan Rivers, and those which will connect the Peninsular Rivers (Figure)[29]. When completed, the project would transfer 174 billion cubic meters (BCM) of water through a canal network of about 14900 km. It has two distinct components,

- The Himalayan component proposes to transfer 33 BCM of water through 16 river links. It has two sub components : -

  ➢ Ganga and Brahmaputra basins to Mahanadi basin (links 11-14);

  ➢ Eastern Ganga tributaries and Chambal and Sabarmati river basins (links 1-10).

- The Peninsular component proposes to transfer 141 BCM water through 14 river links. It has four sub components: -

  ➢ Mahanadi and Godavari basins to Krishna, Cauvery and Vaigai rivers (links 1-9).

  ➢ West-flowing rivers south of Tapi to the north of Bombay (links 12 and 13)

  ➢ Ken River to Betwa River and Parbati, Kalisindh rivers to Chambal rivers (links 10 and 11).

  ➢ Some West flowing rivers to the East flowing rivers (links 14-16).

Figure 28 : Inter Basin Water Transfer Links Source: WRIS

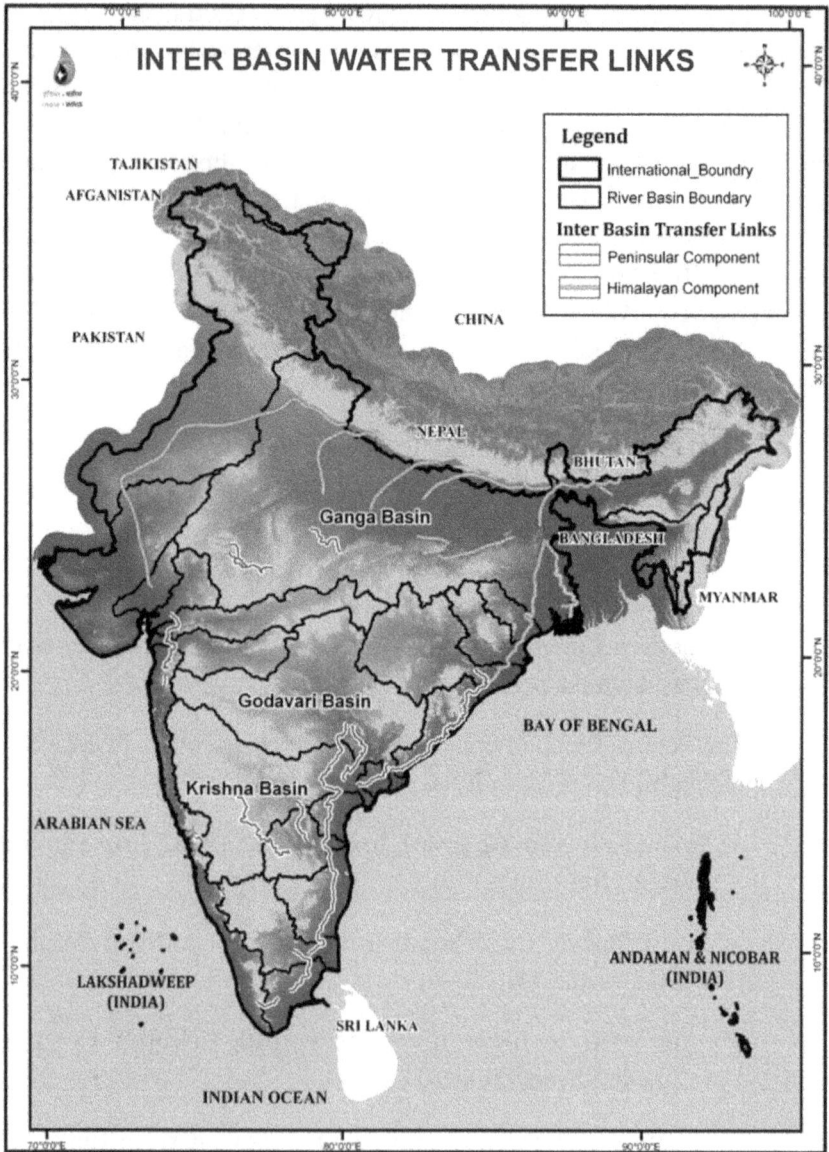

Advantages of the Project. It envisages the following major advantages:-

- Provide additional irrigation to 35 million ha of crop area and water supply to domestic and industrial sectors.

- Add 34 GW of hydro-power potential to the national grid;

- Mitigate floods in Eastern India; and

- Facilitate various other economic activities such as internal navigation, fisheries, groundwater recharge, and environmental flow of water-scarce rivers.

The NRLP, when completed, will increase India's utilisable water resources by 25 percent, and reduce the inequality of water resource endowments in different regions. The increased capacity will address the issue of increasing India's per capita storage. It currently stands at a mere 200 m³/person, as against 5960, 4717 and 2486 m³ /person for the USA, Australia and China, respectively .The NRLP will cost more than USD 120 billion (in 2000 prices), of which the component wise breakdown is :-

- The Himalayan component costs USD 23 billion;

- The Peninsular component costs USD 40 billion; and

- The hydro-power component costs USD 58 billion.

The NRLP water transfers envisage benefiting irrigation the most. It plans to add 34 million ha of new irrigated croplands (24 MHa through surface and 10 MHa through groundwater)[30]. The financial and social benefits, both direct (crop production) and indirect (backward and forward linkages), of irrigation are major components of the benefits. However, achieving this would require committing an outlay of about Rs. one lakh crores (USD 24 billion) annually over the next 50 years. Given the past trends of investments and returns, whether the irrigation benefits that these would generate are worth the cost is indeed a moot point. Indeed, going by the past trends, returns to investments in the major/ medium irrigation show an abysmal picture. Since 1991, India has invested more than Rs. 1.88 lakh crores (USD 53 billion in 2005 prices)[31] in major and medium irrigation alone, yet it has hardly resulted in any addition to net irrigated area by government canals.

The NRLP has three major donor river basins: the Brahmaputra in the Himalayan component, and the Mahanadi and the Godavari in the peninsular component. It proposes to transfer 12.3 km³ from the Mahanadi to the Godavari basin, and 21.5 km³ from the Godavari to the Krishna basin, which includes 6.5 km³ of water transferred from the Mahanadi basin (NWDA 2012). The proposed quantities of water transfer from Brahmaputra to Ganga, Ganga to Subarnarekha, and then from Subarnarekha to Mahanadi, however, are not available yet. However, the issue of surplus surface water in the donor basins is a leading cause of disagreement in the NRLP discourses. An extreme view is that no river basin is water surplus. It is appreciated that a river basin can have surplus water if there is excess river flow after meeting the potential demand of agricultural, domestic and industrial sectors and an adequate allocation for the environment.

The irrigation demand projection by NCIWRD, justifying the NRLP concept, seems an over-estimate. Even under business as usual conditions there is no question that India will need more water supply than the current level of irrigation withdrawals. However, this could be significantly lower than the demand of the high-projection scenario that was used to justify the NRLP. Much of this is due to large over-projections for food grain demand. Unlike in the NCIWRD assumptions, much of the additional water demand in the future could be non-agricultural. They include the rapidly increasing water demand for the industrial and domestic sectors and for ecosystems services.

Some Possible Alternative Options. Some experts have criticised NRLP for inadequate attention given to alternative water management strategies. Three potential areas that are considered suitable alternatives are mentioned here and discussed in brief.

- Increasing water productivity,

- Improving rainfed agriculture in managing the water demand and;

- Artificial groundwater recharge in managing the supply.

Ground Water (Aquifers)

Over the last four decades, while surface irrigation has been gradually declining, groundwater irrigation through small private tube wells has been flourishing. By 2005, groundwater contributed to 61 percent of the gross irrigated area, but this contribution could be even more if it accounts all the conjunctive water use in the canal command areas. Contrary to what most claim, groundwater irrigation has spread everywhere, even outside canal command areas where recharge from surface return-flows could not have reached. The tube well boom has made a significant part of India's agriculture production and rural livelihoods depend on groundwater irrigation, but also made large areas prone to over exploitation. Sustaining groundwater irrigation is essential for a country like India for many reasons:-

- Gives large spatially distributed social benefits to vast rural areas, which surface irrigation has not reached or cannot reach, and benefit a large number of small holders in Indian agriculture.

- Is more efficient, thus allowing better application of agriculture inputs and crop intensification and diversification. This gives higher yields and income per unit land than in canal command areas.

- Is a better mechanism for drought proofing. It can also mitigate impacts due to climate change.

For sustainable groundwater irrigation, India needs to invest more in artificial recharge in many locations and better managements of aquifer storages. India already has in place a National Master Plan for Groundwater Recharge, augmenting the resources annually by another 38 BCM. The program, costing Rs. 24500 crore (USD 6 billion at January 2008 exchange rate)[32], can achieve its potential benefits by addressing the shortcoming of the master plan. In order to meet this increasing demand, there is a need for sustainable management of the ground water resource. One of the solutions to the problem of pricing or regulating pump water to reduce withdrawals to a sustainable level is too facile. A considered decision on this issue must be evaluated in detail and acted upon by India.

It is imperative to demarcate aquifer systems in the country so as to provide critical information to plan for their sustainability. Aquifers, the repositories of ground water, are delineated to assess the ground water resource. In India Central Ground Water Board (CGWB) has collected and integrated information generated on geological, hydrogeological, geophysical, hydrological and chemical aspects of ground water, and collated this into various thematic layers to generate aquifer maps. An Atlas (*"AQUIFER SYSTEMS OF INDIA"*)[33] has been created with an aim to map aquifers on 1:250000 Scale using a GIS platform, to classify the aquifer systems of the country and to depict all the aquifers in an atlas.

This atlas also presents the extent of various aquifer systems in the country along with their hydraulic characteristics.

Population

India's population is set to be the largest in the world by 2030. Based on the predicted figure the Mckinsey Report (2009) suggests that by 2030, water demand in India will grow to almost 1.5 trillion m³, principally driven by population growth and the domestic need for rice, wheat and sugar. According to the Report, the current water supply is approximately 740 billion m³.

Table 10: Water Utilisation by Various Sectors- Present and Projected

| Sector | Present Utilisation (BCM) | Projected Demand (BCM) | | | | | |
| | | Standing Sub-Committee of MoWR | | | NCIWRD | | |
		2010	2025	2050	2010	2025	2050
Irrigation	501	688	910	1072	557	611	807
Domestic	30	56	73	102	43	62	111
Industrial	20	12	23	63	37	67	81
Energy	20	5	15	130	19	33	70
Others	34	52	72	180	54	70	111
Total	605	813	1093	1447	710	843	1180

Source: GoI, Eleventh Five Year Plan: India

The drivers of future water challenge are essentially tied to population increase and it's direct impact on development and economic growth with the agriculture sector as the largest withdrawer of water.

Although India has low per capita water consumption, the efficient use of water across sectors that needs improvement. Population growth, urbanisation and the impact of global warming along with inadequate conservation and huge wastage are putting enormous pressure on water resources. With no proportional increase in water availability and an ever increasing demand, a water security crisis seems imminent.

Water Requirement

The requirement of fresh water both for irrigation and other uses is growing continuously. The requirement of water for various sectors has been assessed by the National Commission on Integrated Water Resources Development (NCIWRD) in the year 2000. This requirement is based on the assumption that irrigation efficiency will increase to 60 % from the current level of 35 -40 %. The Standing Committee of MOWR also assesses it periodically. The total water demand for all the uses is likely to be 1180 BCM by 2050 as per NCIWRD[34]. Though major share of this would be consumed for irrigation purposes, this in no way undermines importance of providing potable drinking water. In fact, it may be presumed that drinking water provision would have to be given an added thrust since the lack of such facility is likely to entail serious social, economic and health impact.

Figure 29: Estimated Sector Wise Demand In India: 2050 (NCIWRD)

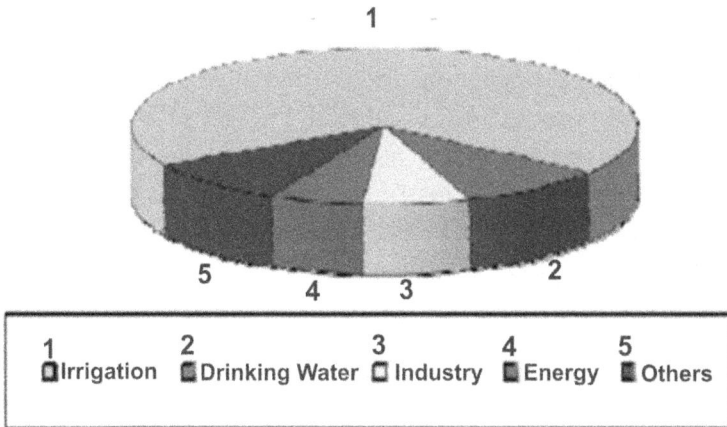

1	2	3	4	5
☐Irrigation	▓Drinking Water	☐ Industry	▓Energy	▓Others

Climate

The presence of the great mountain mass formed by the Himalayas and its spurs on the North and of the ocean on the South are the two major influences operating on the climate of India. The first poses an impenetrable barrier to the influence of cold winds from central Asia, and gives the subcontinent the elements of tropical type of climate. The second, which is the source of cool moisture-laden winds reaching India, gives it the elements of the oceanic type of climate. India has a very great diversity and variety of climate and an even greater variety of weather conditions. The climate ranges from continental to oceanic, from extremes of heat to extremes of cold, from extreme aridity and negligible rainfall to excessive humidity and torrential rainfall. It is, therefore, necessary to avoid any generalisation as to the prevalence of any particular kind of climate, not only over the country as a whole but over major areas in it. The climatic condition influences to a great extent the water resources utilisation of the country.

INDIA'S TRANSBOUNDARY ISSUES

The water issue is gradually becoming the prime focus between the interstate relations. Increasing water shortage has made South Asia a water-stressed region. South Asia has four major rivers basins. They originate from Himalayas and irrigate vast areas of this region; thereby provide edibles and livelihood to the huge population. The four main co-riparian states of the region are India-Pakistan and India–Bangladesh-Nepal are lying in west and east respectively[35]. Water shortage is becoming the bone of contention in this region. With the growing population, industrial, agricultural and domestic uses, glaciers are melting and causing environmental degradation. Conflicts over water issue are growing among the countries and the people of this area.

India's Riparian Status. India, which has multiple riparian identities, is the uppermost riparian on some rivers that originate on its territory, such as the Chenab and the Jhelum, which flow to Pakistan, and the Teesta, which drains a part of Northern Bangladesh. India is the mid-riparian on the Brahmaputra and the main Indus stream. And India is the lowermost riparian on the rivers that begin in Tibet and flow southward via Nepal to empty into the Ganges Basin, such as the Karnali, the Gandak, and the Kosi (Arun). Besides India, few other states in Asia fall in all the three categories—upper, middle, and lower riparian. Indeed, such is India's geographical spread that it has a direct stake in all the important river basins in South Asia. Due to its mottled riparian status, India is potentially affected by water-related actions of states located upstream—China, Nepal, and Bhutan—while its own actions can carry a cross-border impact on Pakistan or Bangladesh. No nation is more vulnerable to China's re-engineering of transboundary flows than India because it alone receives nearly half of all river waters that leave Chinese territory[36]. A total of 718 billion cubic meters of surface water flows out of Chinese territory yearly, of which 48.33% runs directly into India[37] (Some additional Tibetan waters also flow to India via Nepal.). The issues with China in India's context have been discussed in detail in a subsequent chapter. Bangladesh, on the other hand, has one of the world's highest dependency ratios with regard to cross-border inflows, receiving 91.3% of its water from India, although a sizable portion of that water originates in Tibet. India confronts a deepening water crisis, which is more acute than China's. Yet India's per capita capacity to store water for dry-season release (200 cubic meters yearly) is one of the world's lowest; indeed, it is 11 times lower than China's (2,200 cubic meters).[38] The analysis by global think tanks has a dire warning for India: stating that the country is likely to face a 50% deficit between water demand and supply by 2030[39]. The growing water shortages also threaten to slow Indian economic growth and fuel social tensions. With water increasingly at the center of interprovincial feuds in India, the country's Supreme Court has struggled for years to settle water-related lawsuits, with several of the parties returning to litigate on new grounds. Plans for large water projects in India, meanwhile, have run into stiff opposition from influential nongovernment organisations (NGOs), so that it has become increasingly difficult to build a large dam, blighting the promise of hydropower. Yet, seeking to exercise the right of prior appropriation on transnational rivers, the Indian government has since 2012 approved the construction of several dams for electric-power generation in the Himalayan states of Arunachal Pradesh, Sikkim, Uttarakhand, and Jammu and Kashmir. They include the Tawang (800 megawatt), Tato (700 megawatt), Subansiri Upper (1,800 megawatt), and Teesta (520 megawatt) projects[40]. Cost and time overruns are common problems in every dam project in India

Most transboundary water conflicts arise not over natural supplies but over human interventions to manage them[41]. Dams, irrigation diversions, and other infrastructure alter both hydrological relations, affecting the quantity, quality, and timing of down river flows, but also relations between upstream and downstream riparians. The management of transboundary water resources takes place across a range of scales from the local to the global system, but water treaties often lack sufficient specificity or resolution mechanisms to avoid tensions between states. Further, international law in general is vague, often contradictory, and does not demand standards .

South Asian Transboundary Issues

The water issue is gradually becoming the prime focus between the interstate relations. Increasing water shortage has made South Asia a water-stressed region. South Asia has four major rivers basins. The main co-riparian states of the region are India-Pakistan, India–Bangladesh-Nepal and India-China. Water shortage is becoming the bone of contention in this region. India's external dependency ratio is 33.9%, it thus becomes imperative to secure the supply of these waters by way of treaties or agreements. With the growing population, industrial, agricultural and domestic uses, glaciers are melting and causing environmental degradation. In South Asia, three distinct treaties cover the Indus, the Ganges, and the Mahakali rivers. The three agreements adopt very different approaches. The Indus accord physically shares the basin, giving the three Western branches of the river to Pakistan and the three Eastern branches to India. The Ganges Treaty shares the river water between India and Bangladesh.

Table 11 Renewable Water Resources in Asia

Country	Population (1996)	Precipitation (mm)	Internal* million m³	Internal* m³ per inhab (1996)	Country	External** million m³	Total million m³	Total m³ per inhab (1996)	External Dependency Ratio (%)
(Formula)	(1)	(2)	(3)	(4)=3*10⁶/(1)		(5)	(6)=(3)+(5)	(7)=(6)*10⁶/(1)	(5)/(6)
Bangladesh	120,073,000	2,320	105,000	874	Bangladesh	1,105,644	1,210,644	10,083	91.3
Bhutan	1,812,000	4,000	95,000	52,428	Bhutan	0	95,000	52,428	0.0
Brunei	300,000	2,654	8,500	28,333	Brunei	0	8,500	28,333	0.0
Cambodia	10,273,000	1,463	120,570	11,737	Cambodia	355,540	476,110	46,346	74.7
China	1,238,270,000	648	2,812,000	2,271	China	17,169	2,829,569	2,285	0.6
India	944,580,000	1,170	1,260,540	1,334	India	647,220	1,907,760	2,020	33.9
Indonesia	200,453,000	2,700	2,838,00	14,158	Indonesia	0	2,838,000	14,158	0.0
Japan	125,351,000	1,728	430,000	3,430	Japan	0	430,000	3,430	0.0
Korea, DPR	22,466,00	1,054	67,000	2,982	Korea, DPR	10,135	77,135	3,433	13.1
Korea, Rep.	45,314,920	1,274	64,850	1,431	Korea, Rep.	4,850	69,700	1,538	7.0
Lao, DPR	5,035,000	1,600	190,420	37,782	Lao, DPR	146,130	331,550	66,181	42.9
Malaysia	20,581,000	3,000	580,000	28,183	Malaysia	0	580,000	28,183	0.0
Maldives	263,000	1,883	30	114	Maldives	0	30	114	0.0
Mongolia	2,515,000	251	34,800	13,837	Mongolia	0	34,800	13,837	0.0
Myanmar	45,922,000	2,341	880,600	19,176	Myanmar	165,001	1,045,601	22,769	15.8
Nepal	22,021,000	1,500	198,200	9,000	Nepal	12,000	210,200	9,545	5.7
Papua New Guinea	4,400,000	3,500	801,000	182,045	Papua New Guinea	0	801,000	182,045	0.0
Philippines	69,283,000	2,373	479,000	6,914	Philippines	0	479,000	6,914	0.0
Sri Lanka	18,100,000	2,000	50,000	2,762	Sri Lanka	0	50,000	2,762	0.0
Thailand	58,703,000	1,485	210,000	3,577	Thailand	199,944	409,944	6,983	48.8
Vietnam	75,181,000	1,960	366,500	4,875	Vietnam	524,710	891,210	11,854	58.9

* Internal: Originating within a country.
** External: Originating outside a country.

It stipulates how much water each party should receive each ten days during the yearly wet season between 1 January and 31 May. The Mahakali Treaty was supposed to share development of the river, but the intended common project between India and Nepal is in the process of developing to meet both parties requirements. Of the three agreements, only the Ganges accord makes explicit provisions for substantial shortfalls in river flow of the kind that climate change might engender. Experience with the Indus Treaty illuminates how international tensions are shaped and aggravated by domestic ones, and shows how water policy solutions can be generated that link and ameliorate local, regional, and global tensions

South Asia has four major river basins, i.e., the Brahmaputra, Indus, Ganges and the Meghna which provide livelihood to millions of people in this region. The South Asian river basins irrigate millions of hectares of fields and provide livelihood to millions of people in this geographical location. Water distribution, its utilisation, its management and above all the hydro-electric power projects are affecting the upper and lower riparian countries. Water security is gradually becoming an epicenter of interstate relations and water scarcity is increasing the miseries of people of this area.

India's Water Concerns

The dawn of 21(st) century conveys a challenging picture for future generations of India because of increasing water scarcity. Water is a critical shared resource, and its flow is not restricted to any political boundaries. This necessitates peaceful sharing of water resources both within and among countries. India, as a water prosperous country in the past, today is moving towards becoming a water stressed nation due to rapid population upsurges and unequal distribution. Although India has made considerable efforts in resolving some long standing water disputes in South Asian with her neighbours on distribution of water resources particularly rivers. As the resource depletes further these disputes are likely to increase in their intensity. India is geographically in a better position than Pakistan because of her proximity to Tibet, Kashmir, the Himalayas, and the Bay of Bengal[42].

The relations India shares with all its co riparians are varied and yet cooperative. The unique entity of being an upper, middle and lower riparian necessitates Indian policy makers to maintain a fine balance on the decisions taken and strategy for the future. In this chapter the relations with Bangladesh, Nepal and Bhutan are covered in brief with the larger focus on Indo- Pak and Sino- Indian relations covered in greater detail in the following chapters. The geographic proximity of India as also the relative location of the Tibetan Plateau is a very vital issue.

The Northern and North Eastern parts of India receive greater quantities of water in comparison to the peninsular regions. The water issues with the countries is deliberated upon in the subsequent paragraphs.

Figure 30: : The Hindu- Kush Himalayan Range With Basins

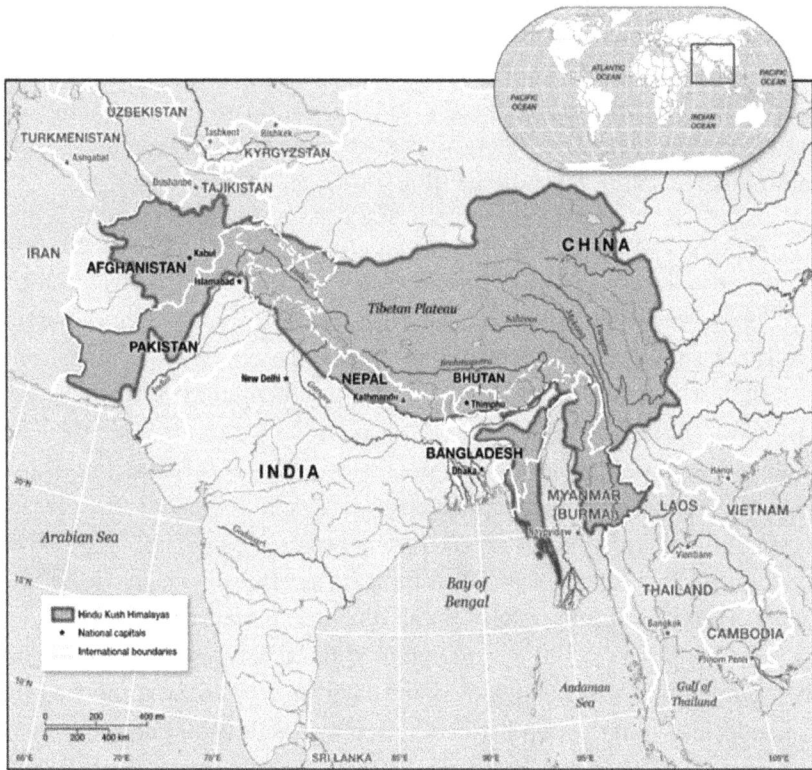

FIGURE S.1 The Hindu-Kush Himalayan region extends over 2,000 km across South Asia and includes all or parts of Afghanistan, Bangladesh, Bhutan, China, India, Nepal, and Pakistan. The region is the source of many of Asia's major rivers, including the Indus, Ganges, and Brahmaputra.

India- Bangladesh

Relations with Bangladesh are interwoven with numerous issues. Water is a very vital link between the two neighbours,there are 54 common rivers shared between the two countries. The river Ganga or Ganges rises in the

Gangotri glacier in in India, at an elevation of about 3139 m above sea level. Many important tributaries including Mahakali, Gandak, Kosi, and Karnali originate in Nepal and China (Tibet). The Ganges river has total length of about 2600 kilometers and the total drainage area is of about 1080000 square kilometers and is shared by China, Nepal, India and Bangladesh[43].

Some issues of disagreement over the Ganges water between Bangladesh and India date back to 1951 when India constructed the Farakka barrage to divert the water from the Ganges to the Hooghly river with a 42-kilometer long feeder canal . The barrage started operation in 1975. Issues of sharing and controlling of the Ganges water have been an issue of discussion and cooperation between these two nations. The two nations signed two treaties in 1977 and 1996 and two Memorandums of Understanding (MOU) in 1983 and 1985 to share Ganges water and to find out long-term solution by augmenting lean season Ganges flow.

A new chapter in the Indo-Bangladesh relations opened up with signing of a Treaty by the Prime Ministers of India and Bangladesh on 12th December 1996 (Appendix 5) on the sharing of Ganga/Ganges waters. The Treaty shall remain in force for a period of thirty years to be renewable by mutual consent. For monitoring the implementation of the Treaty, a Joint Committee has been set up. In a year, the Committee meets three times and observe the Joint measurements on Ganga at Farakka (India) and Ganges at Hardinge Bridge (Bangladesh) during lean season[44]. The Treaty is being implemented to the satisfaction of both the countries. There exists a system of Transmission of flood forecasting data on major rivers like Ganga, Teesta, Brahmputra and Barak during the monsoon season from India to Bangladesh. The transmission of flood forecasting information during the monsoon has enabled the civil and military authorities in Bangladesh to shift the population affected by floods to safer places.

The headwaters of the Ganges and its tributaries lie primarily in Nepal and India, where snow and rainfall are heaviest. During the monsoon period, which occurs from June to October there is abundant water but during non-monsoon months (January-May) the countries become water stressed. The Ganges has an average annual flow (1949-1973) rate of 12105 m3/sec and a flow volume of 382 billion cubic meters (bcm). During June-October the average flow is 24526 m3/sec whereas during January-May it is only 2199 m3/sec. The details of the basin are given in Table below[45].

Table 12 : Ganges Basin Area Distribution And Water Resources

Country	Drainage Area (1,000 km²)	Arable Land (1,000 km²)	Population (2001) (million)	Surface Water Availability (104 m²)	Ground Water Availability (104 m²)
India	861	602	440	525	171
Bangladesh	46	30	37	197	22
Nepal	140	26	23	208	12
China	33	Negligible	1	n/a	n/a
Total	1080	658	501	930	205

The Problem

The problem over the Ganges is typical of conflicting interests of up and down-stream riparians. The dispute over the Ganges revolves around the question of how its water is to be shared during the five dry- season months. During the rest of the year, there is more than sufficient water The problem is in the dry seasons when the average minimum discharges to Farakka falls below 55,000 cusecs. India asks for 40,000 cusecs while Bangladesh needs all it can get for her requirements out of 55,000 cusec availability at that period. This clause also guaranteed Bangladesh a minimum of 80 percent of its share during each period whatever low the flow of the Ganges may be during that period. This is widely known as 80 percent guarantee clause.

(a) **Art. III.** Only minimum water would be withdrawn between Farakka and the Bangladesh border.

(b) **Art. IV-VI.** Provision was made for a Joint Committee to supervise the sharing of water, provide data to the two governments, and submit an annual report.

(c) **Art. VII.** Provisions were made for the process of conflict resolution: The Joint Committee would be responsible for examining any difficulty arising out of the implementation of the arrangements of the Agreement.

(d) Any dispute not resolved by the Committee would be referred to a panel of an equal number of Indian and Bangladeshi experts nominated by the two governments.

(e) If the dispute was not resolved, it would be referred to the two Governments which would, "meet urgently at the appropriate level to resolve it by mutual discussion and failing that, by such other arrangements as they may mutually agree upon.

(f) **Art. VIII.**   The Joint Rivers Commission was again vested with the task of developing a feasibility study for a long-term solution to the problem of the augmentation of the dry season flows of the Ganges.

The Agreement would initially cover a period of five years. It could be extended further by mutual agreement. By the end of the five-year life of the agreement, no solution had been worked out.

Discussions have been continuing with Bangladesh for sharing of waters of Teesta and Feni rivers besides six other common rivers namely; Manu, Muhri, Khowai, Gumti, Jaldhaka and Torsa. Govt. of India is at its endeavour to conclude the agreement of the sharing of waters of Teesta and Feni rivers with Bangladesh, which is acceptable to all parties concerned and which protects the interests of all stakeholders. An Indo-Bangladesh Joint Rivers Commission (JRC) is functioning since 1972. It was established with a view to maintain liaison in order to ensure the most effective joint effort in maximizing the benefits from common river systems. The JRC is headed by Water Resources Ministers of both the countries[46].

Bangladesh: Perspective on Limitations of 1996 Treaty.

(a) Decrease in water allocated to Bangladesh.

(b) No provision of minimum guaranteed flow.

(c) Arrangement and time-frame for dispute settlement not included.

(d) No arrangement For long-term solutions of the dry season water scarcity. Unlike the 1977 Agreement, the 1996 Treaty did not include any arrangement for long-term solution of the dry season water scarcity.

(e) Other Riparian Countries not part of Treaty. Nepal and China are not party to the treaty, have their own development plans that could impact the agreement.

(f) Disadvantageous Arrangement in case of Disagreement on Adjustments of the Water Sharing. The 1996 treaty allowed India to reduce the release to Bangladesh by 10 percent in case of disagreement on adjustments of the water sharing arrangement.

(g) No Authority or Responsibility to the Indo-Bangladesh JRC for Implementing the Treaty.

Positive Aspects of 1996 Treaty

The 1996 treaty incorporated the principle of equitable and reasonable utilisation, obligation not to cause significant harm, principles of cooperation, information exchange, notification, consultation and peaceful settlement of disputes. The inclusion of these principles was the major breakthrough of the Treaty that would in turn reduce conflict and promote cooperation.

Current Issue; Augmentation of The Ganges Lean Season Flow

This is the heart of the problem. So far India and Bangladesh have not been able to arrive at a consensus on the how to deal with this issue. In a series of five Commission meetings during the negotiation years the general approach of the two countries for augmenting Ganges flow was as follows: -

(a) **India's Position**[47]. India had proposed augmentation of Ganges at Farakka by a link canal through diversion of water from the Brahmaputra. The justification given was as under:-

  (i) Additional storage possibilities in India are limited, and not sufficient to meet Indian development needs.

  (ii) The most viable option both to supplement the low flow of the Ganges, and for regional development, is a link canal and storage facilities on the Brahmaputra, to be developed in stages for mutual benefit; India's proposal states that diverting water from the Brahmaputra to the Ganges is the best solution for flow augmentation during the dry season and for reducing flood during monsoon.

(iii) Approaching Nepal or other third countries is beyond the scope. Also, India has rejected any proposals which suggest amending the existing pattern of diversion of water at Farakka into the Bhagirathi-Hooghly.

(iv) Constructing a separate navigation canal is not connected to the question of optimum development of water resources in the region.

(b) **Bangladesh's Position**[48]. Bangladesh had suggested that augmentation of lean flows during the dry season should be done by creating additional storage facilities within the Ganges basin. The justification given was as under:-

(i) There is adequate storage potential of monsoon flow in the Ganges Basin for Indian needs.

(ii) A feeder canal from the Brahmaputra to the Ganges is both unnecessary and would have detrimental effects within Bangladesh , one of which would be requirement of massive population resettlement.

(iii) Indian needs would be better met through amending the pattern of diversion of Ganges water into the Bhagirathi-Hooghly, and constructing a navigation link from Calcutta to the sea via Sunderban.

(iv) The augmentation of the Ganges water should be solved within the   Ganges basin through constructing storage reservoirs in upstream Nepal and that there is enough water. Hence there is a need to approach Nepal for participation.

India's Mega River Linking Project. Due to the problems that Farakka barrage in the Ganges river has caused, Bangladesh was worried that India had a similar plan to siphon off water from the Brahmaputra river as well as the Meghna river through the proposed River Interlinking Project or New Indian Line , by way of aqueducts and pumping stations to transport water from the Ganges River to parts of Southern and Eastern India that are prone to water scarcity.

Apart from the Ganges, the other major rivers that flow between the two countries are the Teesta, Brahmaputra and Barak. The sharing of Teesta waters has assumed priority in the discussion between the two states.

The Teesta Issue

River Teesta, flowing South from Sikkim, flows through the entire length of Sikkim before joining the Brahmaputra as a tributary in Bangladesh. India and Bangladesh have been engaged in dialogue on the sharing of the Teesta since 1974. During dry season, like most rivers, the river faces a water shortage as India has constructed the Gozaldoba Barrage in the upstream and diverts water from the river that enters Bangladesh's greater Rangpur region. The sharing of the existing Teesta flow of 5,000 cusecs forms the core of the negotiations. According to the Bangladesh Water Development Board, the country is dependent on the Teesta for its irrigation projects covering 750,000 hectares of land and has accordingly built a barrage (1st Phase) on the Teesta. Any water shortage in the Teesta very often disrupts irrigation in the vast tracts of land and undermines Bangladesh's need for water.

Tipaimukh Project

India plans to build the Tipaimukh Project on the Barak river in Manipur. The project is designed to generate 1500-MW hydropower and ensure flood control for both Manipur and Mizoram. This involves building a 162.8 metre high dam around 500 metres downstream of the confluence of river Barak with Tuivai. Bangladesh, as a down stream riparian, is very concerned as the share of the Barak will be greatly reduced thus affecting Bangladesh economically and ecologically. The proposed project has also faced protests from within the Indian northeast states on the issues of displacement and doubtful compensation. Not to be seen as an unconcerned upper riparian, India has opened channels of discussion and invited Bangladesh for on-site visits to dispel any concerns over the project.

India – Nepal

India is a lower riparian vis-à-vis Nepal. But given Nepal's water surplus, India, as a friend does not fear being either denied water or being flooded. The potential for harnessing maximum benefits mutually by both the nations is great. Even though many of the joint projects with India relating to flood control, irrigation and hydroelectricity have not lived up to expectations.

Both India and Nepal share many rivers such as Kosi, Gandak, Karnali and Mahakali. Water is a sensitive issue in the relationship between India and Nepal. The two countries have a long history of water cooperation and have signed several water sharing treaties like the Gandak (1957), Kosi (1962), and the Mahakali (1997). The Mahakali Treaty (1997), a comprehensive document on water cooperation, however, remains merely a paper document. Since a very large Indian population lives in the Ganges, Brahmaputra and Meghna region, India needs Nepal not only to meet some of its growing energy needs but equally critical for flood management and navigational uses. Nepal can benefit, by the optimum utilisation of its water resources, by meeting some of India's energy requirements. The shared benefit will give major earnings to Nepal and also help it become self sufficient in energy. Nepal's major rivers Kosi, Gandak, Karnali and Mahakali are snow-fed and flow in the lean season..Some major hydro-power projects for joint development and for electricity exports to India that are under consideration/feasibility stage are as follows:

- 10,800 MW Karnali Chisapani Multipurpose Project

- The Mahakali Pancheswar Project.

- Upper-Karnali Hydroelectric Project, which is being considered for joint development by Nepal Electricity Authority and NHPC of India.

In order to harness the benefits of the Mahakali river between India and Nepal, a multipurpose project was planned. The Mahakali treaty though provides for a construction of a project on the Mahakali river however it has its background to various historical events, which led to the conclusion of these agreements. As regard to the Indo Nepal Water Treaty, the water resource development dates back to 1920 when the British Indian government decided to build the Sarda barrage to irrigate the United Province. As per the treaty, Nepal government agreed to transfer 4093.88 acres of her land on the Eastern banks of Mahakali river to build a barrage. In exchange Nepal received an equal amount of forest land from the British Indian government to the east. In addition the British Indian government also agreed to give 50,000 rupees, a supply of 4.25 cubic meters per sec (cumsecs) out of an annual flow of 650 cumsecs during dry season and 13 cumsecs of water in the wet season which could be further increased to 28.34 cumsecs if water was available. The project was undertaken by the British Indian government for its own benefit and at her own cost in addition to an equitable transfer of land with some benefits as regard to sharing of water is concerned ,being provided by the Nepal Government.

In 1954 India and Nepal signed the Kosi agreement which entailed construction of a dam on the Kosi river for the use of the river water. One of the peculiarities of the river being that it shifts its course frequently and used to flood the plains of Bihar. The Kosi project agreement was signed with the aim of preventing floods in Bihar, diverting the confined water for irrigation and hydropower generation (20,000 KW). The 1.15 km barrage was completed in 1962. The barrage was entirely in Nepal with the Eastern main canal in India. The project was seriously criticised at all levels in Nepal, the complaint being that it was a sell out of national property for India's benefits and that nothing had been obtained for Nepal in return for a huge expenditure of resources. Subsequently on Nepal's insistence, talks were held to revise the agreement in 1966. Later in 1982 the Western main canal was completed of which 35 km stretch of the canal passed through Nepal which was designed to irrigate 3,56,000 hectares of land in India towards the west and 11,000 hectares of land in Nepal. Though the project was completed; however there arose a discontented feeling in Nepal. Nepal's concerns were that the project gave limited benefit to her compared to India. Though India adjusted to the concerns of Nepal, the agreement created a rift in the relations between the two countries and Nepal became cautious for initiation of any new agreement.

In 1959 India and Nepal signed the Gandak Irrigation and Power Project Agreement. Nepal's deep-seated mistrust and grievance towards India on water cooperation are historically rooted in the Kosi and Gandak treaties of the 1950's. In retrospect, both the treaties lacked vision. The projects also suffered from poor design, inefficient implementation and bad maintenance. Though both the treaties were amended Kosi in 1966 and Gandak in 1954 the level of confidence never reached the levels necessary to forge future riparian cooperation. As per the agreement, Nepal government allowed India to construct a barrage at her own cost. The barrage was designed to irrigate 9,20,000 hectares of land in the state of Bihar and 37,000 hectares in Western Nepal from the Eastern main canal and similarly 9,30,000 hectares in Uttar Pradesh and 20,000 hectares in Nepal from the Western main canal. The barrage was constructed on the Indo - Nepal border. The agreement met similar criticism as had the Kosi project. The discontented feelings arising from the Kosi and the Gandak irrigation projects were the reasons which inhibited any progress on the projects to include the Pancheswar and Saptakosi to name a few later on. Furthermore a constitutional amendment made Parliamentary ratification necessary by two third majorities for any treaty or agreement relating to natural resources which affect the country in a pervasively grave manner or on a long term basis.

In the meantime, in 1983, India began constructing the Tanakpur Project. The project was started unilaterally on the land which was transferred to India under the Sarda agreement. Problems started on the Eastern afflux bund that required tying the barrage to the high ground on the left bank in Nepal. India needed about 2.9 hectares of Nepalese land to construct an embankment to prevent back water effects due to the barrage. In lieu Indian agreed to provide 25,000 cusecs of water as well as supply 25 MW of electricity. Nepal however demanded 50 and 59 percent share in water and electricity respectively. Nepal's public stand was that India never brought to notice any prior information on the issue. The project arrived at a political stalemate. In December 1991 during the visit of Nepalese Prime Minister to India, it was concluded that Nepal would allow construction of the 577 meters left afflux bund in its territory so as to prevent a recurrence and to ensure pondage of water at the dam site. In return India agreed to provide 1000 cusecs of water annually with 10 million units of electricity. However the issue led to a political turmoil in Nepal. The opposition in Nepal wanted the project understanding to be treated as a treaty and thus requiring ratification. In October 1992 under a new Memorandum of Understanding (MoU), India agreed to provide 20 million units of electricity units to Nepal. The Supreme Court of Nepal affirmed its verdict on a petition filed on the issue that the MoU between the governments was indeed a treaty but left it to the government of Nepal to decide whether a simple majority or a two-third majority would be required for its ratification. The political turbulence on the issue led to the Prime Minister of Nepal dissolving the Parliament and later a new government under Communist Party of Nepal United Marxist - Leninist (CPN – UML) came in power. Under the new government renegotiations were sought on the Tanakpur project. The Nepalese government demanded increase in quantum of electricity as well as water and construction of a storage high dam at Pancheswar upstream of Tanakpur site on the Mahakali river.

The Mahakali Treaty

The flow of the Mahakali river is through the districts Danchula, Baitadi and Dadeldh in the hills and subsequently the river flows through the Kanchanpur district in the plains. After the river arrives into the plains it turns into a border between both the countries at major stretches. The river joins the Ghagra river in the Indian territory . In 1971, Nepal began her Mahakali Irrigation project. Under the 1920 Sarda agreement, Nepal was permitted to utilise its share of river water. For the project, World Bank provided the assistance.

In 1977 both India and Nepal agreed to jointly investigate the possibilities of harnessing the Mahakali river further between the two countries. It was the fourth major water treaty being considered between the two countries. The treaty concerned the development of Mahakali river for the benefit of both the countries. The treaty was signed between India and Nepal in 1996. The treaty was signed under the back drop of previous treaties which had led to a feeling of mistrust as far as water agreements were concerned and to a great extent shaped the outcome of the Mahakali treaty. The treaty tried to bring within its fold other treaties and tried to arrive with principle of cost benefit sharing. The treaty provides for the construction of and use of a giant, multipurpose project on the Mahakali river called as the Pancheswar project.

In January 1996 the Mahakali treaty was ratified in Nepalese Parliament by more than two third majorities. However prior to ratification, the Nepalese Parliament unanimously passed a 'stricture' on the treaty which redefined the water rights. The main features if the strictures are as follows:-

(a) The electricity generated by Nepal would be sold to India as per the avoided cost principal.

(b) Constitution of Mahakali Commission on agreement with the main opposition party in the Parliament as well as with the recognised national parties.

(c) Equal entitlement in the usage of the waters of the Mahakali river.

(d) The saying that Mahakali is a boundary river on major stretches between the two countries implies that it is basically a border river.

Challenging Issues. The treaty came into existence on 12 February 1996. The articles lacked specificity which led to ambiguity over the interpretation of the treaty. The differences which emerged out after the treaty came into existence are given in succeeding paragraphs.

> The Issue of Border River and Prospect of Equal Sharing . As far as border river is concerned, the river acts as boundary river on major stretches. Nepal interprets it as a border river. As far as equal sharing is concerned, Nepal argues that as the river belongs to both the countries therefore each country owns 50 percent water. The river flows as a boundary river between Pancheswar and Banbassa. As Nepal has interpreted the issue of equal entitlement, it claims half of the share of the river water between the locations. However India's stand is that equal sharing implies that the river per se does not belong to either of the country and can be used by either as per the requirement. Upper riparian country cannot own any water and subsequently sell it to lower riparian country where the lower riparian country as such would receive the water due to natural flow. For India, equal sharing implies that both the countries equally share the incremental benefit and cost that is attached to the Pancheswar Project.

> Existing Consumptive Use. Another major difference that exists is regarding the protection of existing consumptive use. Nepal's concern is that in the treaty, only Nepal's existing consumptive usage has been quantified and not of India. Furthermore as per the treaty (Article 3), the sharing of the capital cost of the Pancheswar project would be proportionate to the relative incremental benefit which have to be considered after protecting existing consumptive use of water of the river. Nepal's concern is that the 2 MHa land irrigated from lower Sarda barrage is outside the scope of the agreement as it is mostly dependent on the water from Ghagra or Karnali river for most part of the year and is dependent on the Mahakali river only from July to October. However India's differs on the issue.

> The Kalapani Issue. Kalapani as experts feel is a disputed area. It is roughly a 35 sq km area at the junction of India, Nepal and China. Indian troops have been stationed there since 1962. There is though no relation between the boundary issue at Kalapani and the Pancheswar project but one of the strictures passed along on Mahakali in Nepalese Parliament states Mahakali as well as the location of its sources as a border river. A Parliamentary committee took up studies to clarify the status of the Mahakali river and the issue of Kalapani emerged. As per the 1816 Segauli Treaty between Nepal and British India, Mahakali river would mark as the border between India and Nepal. The issue of contention is as to which of the stream actually constitutes as the source of the river. Nepal's stand is that the Lipu Gad rivulet should mark as the border which implies that the area of Kalapani which is to further east should be part of Nepalese territory, however Indian experts feel that the Mahakali river beings much downstream where the stream from Kalapani spring and Lipu Gad meet. India however reiterates that the issue should be settled based on old records, documents and survey reports.

> Site for Re-regulating Structure. A site was needed below the main dam to store and subsequently make controlled release of water passing through the Pancheswar dam to meet the irrigation requirements further downstream. There were two locations which rose for discussion for construction of re regulating structure. First was at Rupaligad which Nepal preferred during the negotiation of the treaty. A re regulating structure at Rupaligad could generate about 240 MW of electricity owing to low height, of about 60 m and it would have limited storage capacity. For India, the site does not offer much benefit owing to lower production of energy and offers little of her irrigation demand. Indian experts feel that the site further downstream at Poornagiri would enable construction of a re regulating structure of 180 m height which would produce up to 1000 MW of energy as well as provide adequate storage. Nepal's concern on this issue is that a dam at this site would inundate 2, 50,000 hectares of agricultural land and also displace 56,000 people in Nepal. Nepal looks at the proposal as a project designed by India to irrigate vast tracts of agricultural land in Uttar Pradesh.

➢ The Question of Power Tariff. With the project in place a maximum of 6480 MW of electricity can be derived. As per Article 3 of the treaty, the power stations of equal capacity should be constructed on either side of Mahakali river and the total energy generated would be equally shared between both the countries. The article further points out that a portion of the Nepal's share of energy shall be sold to India on a mutually agreeable cost. Nepalese experts feel that if Nepal decides to sell 3000 MW of energy from Pancheswar project, whatever energy is being sold would be a saving for India. Nepalese infer the article on 'avoided cost principle' which means that India has to pay an amount according to the cost of generation of electricity through other alternative means and argue that India would have produced the equivalent energy which is being sold from coal costing anything up to four to five rupees per kilowatt of power Indian experts however argue that alternative mean need not be thermal power but can be gas based project or HEPs.

Peculiar situation of Nepal

➢ India is the only potential buyer for electricity produced in Nepal and in that Nepal faces tough competition from Bhutan which is providing cheap hydro electricity to India.

➢ Both India and Nepal need perennial irrigation. For India the criticality is for the state of Uttar Pradesh and Bihar and for Nepal, its economy itself is largely dependent on agriculture which is currently dependent of rain fed water system.

➢ In Nepal's internal politics the water relationship between both the countries occupies a centre stage. The survival of many Nepalese governments was linked with policy they made with India.

➢ In terms of energy, for Nepal major source of energy is in the form of hydropower or firewood .No other energy resources have been discovered in any significant quantity. Also only 20 percent of the population has access to electricity. Moreover, though fresh water is in abundance, only about one third of the population has got access to clean drinking water and of the net available land only 42 percent has been irrigated so far.

> ➤ Mahakali is a successive boundary river. Pancheswar project is linked to other projects like the Tanakpur barrage. Mahakali treaty is supporting a right based approach.

In order to resolve and expedite the Pancheswar Multipurpose project a decision was taken by the Prime ministers of Nepal and India during July/ August 2000 to form the Indo-Nepal Joint Committee on Water Resources (JCWR). Since the formulation of the joint committee, five meetings have been held with the most recent one held at Pokhara, Nepal in November 2009. The major developments since the formulation of the committee towards completion of the project is as follows:-

> ➤ Rupaligarh, which is located downstream of Poornagiri, the original site has been chosen to minimise the submergence and displacement of people. The relocation implies less generation of power but faster completion of the project.

> ➤ It has been decided that 5600 MW of power generated would be shared on 50:50 basis.

> ➤ On an issue of the alignment of a 13 km road in Tanakpur – Mahendranagar link, along with the canal as decided by Nepal based on tri party meet, some minor changes in the alignment and positions of the crossing structure were reported while maintaining the original alignment of the main canal. Indian side reiterated that the detailed project report required revision after considering the re alignment and also wanted up gradation of the road to Asian Highway Network Standard. Also, the new alignment requires 7000 sq m of land to be acquired in Nepal which Nepal agreed to after the Link road delineated at the site.

> ➤ An agreement was arrived at to evolve a three tire mechanism at the level of ministers, secretaries and technical experts to oversee the project.

> ➤ It has been decided to set up a Pancheswar Development Authority (PDA) in accordance with the Article 10 for the development, execution and operation of the Pancheswar Multipurpose project[49].

> ➤ On the outcome of joint instructions of the Tanakpur barrage in March 2005, the sill level of the head regulator has been proposed

at EL 245.0 m by Indian side as against the request of EL 241.5 m as this was required to operate the power plant to allow the flow of committed discharge of water from Tanakpur barrage through the existing regulator. In response to Nepal's request to expedite the construction of canal for a capacity of 2000 cusecs to take care when Sarda barrage became defunct, India said that flow of 1000 cusecs had been planned with the already constructed crest level of the head regulator at EL 245.0 m. A new canal of additional 1000 cusecs would be made operational once the Sarda barrage became defunct.

➢ Finally the JCWR finalised the terms of reference for establishment of the PDA to be approved by January 2010.

The establishment of the JCWR to expedite the construction process and resolve various issues bilaterally are definitely a positive step however there are major issues which require a holistic approach so as to mitigate the differences. Nepal has been advocating a right based approach and insisting on the principle of equality to share the river water and the benefits of the project which may not lead to an acceptable solution. Today there is still no agreement on the price of the Nepalese electricity to be sold to India. As far as water sharing is concerned, the treaty mentions that both the countries have an equal entitlement to the utilisation of the water of the Mahakali river. Nepal interprets it as the right to an equal amount of the river water. For that reason, Nepal had been asking for compensation for the unutilised share of the river water. The Kalapani issue still persists

Mitigating The Issues of Concern

After understanding various international principles and law governing international rivers, the areas of conflict, the situation of each of the country on the basis of its geo political and socio economical condition and drawing up conclusions from LHWP treaty which also revolves under similar background, the solution to the conflict lies on the theory of equitable apportionment i.e. sharing of the trans boundary river in terms of sharing of benefit as well as the cost on the basis of social and economic needs of the riparian countries as it is a case of cross asymmetries. The important part is to be aware that equal right does not correspond to equal share of river water but to equal right to use water depending on each riparian states need and find fair ways of compensation. The areas of conflict which still needs to be addressed can be resolved in the manner as suggested in the succeeding paragraphs.

➤ The Kalapani Issue. This issue is of a territorial dispute. The area in question is either of India or it is not and the matter has got no connection as far as the treaty is concerned. The approach should be to resolve this issue with reference to old records, documents, maps and survey reports.

➤ Boundary River. In the context of the Nepal's stand on the issue of the river as a boundary river, no incorrect inference should be drawn. Again the reference of records on boundary should be supplemented to the issue and if there lies no conflict on territorial issue then in that respect the issue should not in anyway impede the development of the project.

➤ The Question of Equal Sharing. The presumption that the river belongs equally to both the countries and each country has half share on the water may not be correct. Equal sharing should be based on the incremental benefits to be created by the project and the relative benefits gained by the two countries should determine the respective share of the capital cost of the project. Any loss in the project due to submergence of agricultural land or displacement of humans, the compensation should also be shared on the relative benefits gained by either of the country.

➤ Protection of Existing Consumptive Use Under the Treaty, the sharing of the capital costs of the Pancheswar project would be in proportion of the relative incremental benefits and the incremental benefits have to be reckoned after protecting existing consumptive uses of the waters of the Mahakali. India has claimed that there is such an existing consumptive use at the lower Sarda, but Nepal questions this on certain grounds. This issue too can be easily resolved by analysing how much are the farmers' dependent on Mahakali river and since when. Also if the farmers on Indian side are deprived of the river benefit, how much would they be affected? Another aspect that India needs to analyse is that is it merely a question of reckoning this against India's share of the benefits arising from the Pancheswar project and thus requiring India to pay more (perhaps a few hundred crores) towards the capital cost of the project? Or is there a danger of an actual denial of Mahakali waters to the farmers in question? In the event of the farmers being denied Mahakali waters, will they have any alternative water source, or will they be subjected to distress? As a result of this examination it may possibly be found that there is no real problem, or that it is marginal, and that solutions are available; but it is necessary to study the matter first.

> Power Tariff. Finally on the issue of power tariff, the cost laid by Nepal should be such that both countries are benefited in selling of surplus power by Nepal. As per the side letter to the treaty the power benefits are to be assessed on the basis of saving in cost as compared with alternatives available. For the alternative, all the means of generating energy should be considered and not just thermal or hydroelectric. The price of power is one that can be negotiated. The cost should be attractive enough for Nepal to warrant the undertaking of a big project and affordable enough for India to warrant purchase from this source. Keeping in the backdrop the geopolitical, the socio economic condition and the large dependency of Nepal on its water as a source of income, India could plan at a price which is favours Nepal's interest more.

Though the importance of politics cannot be discounted in India's water relations with Nepal and Bangladesh, there is however far more scope to overcome and break political deadlocks through sensible water sharing arrangements and resource development. Water here can be regarded as a catalyst for cooperation. The visit by the Prime Minister Modi was an important step in initiating a relationship of trust and mutual benefit between the countries.

India- Bhutan

India's water linkages go back many decades when in 1955, the Ministry of External Affairs (MEA), Govt. of India had sponsored a scheme for the purpose of flood warning measures in India. Accordingly, numerous surveillance and monitoring stations were set up under the control of MEA and subsequently handed over to Royal Government of Bhutan[50]. The hydropower cooperation between Bhutan and India started with the signing of the Jaldhaka agreement in 1961. The Jaldhaka hydropower plant is located on the Indian side of the Indo-Bhutan border in the state of West Bengal. In July 1979, it was decided that a separate scheme may be drawn for setting up flood forecasting system on rivers common to India and Bhutan run by Ministry of Water Resources in Bhutan for the development of mutual cooperation between the two countries in the field of Hydro-meteorological data collection and flood forecasting activities on rivers common to India and Bhutan. Accordingly, the network was expanded to include more stations on common rivers under the funds provided by Ministry of Water Resources, Govt. of India.

India's water relations are stress-free and unproblematic with Bhutan. The relationship is essentially one of hydro-electricity generation. India aids and assists the construction of hydro projects in Bhutan and then buys the power. The monetary gain by Bhutan has helped it and established a confidence in the fairness of the agreements. With Bhutan, unlike Nepal, the success of one project has cascaded to another, based on confidence, economic viability and shared benefits. The growing confidence has led to a recent agreement between the two countries to develop 10 hydropower projects with a total capacity of 11,576 MW by 2020 in Bhutan[51].

The major rivers transit through the country from north to south and finally join the Brahmaputra. The estimated hydropower potential being 30,000 MW. The Master Plan, developed with World Bank assistance, estimates that the four major rivers the Ammochu (Torsa), Wangchu (Raidak), Punatsangchu (Sankosh) and Manas alone have the potential to economically generate around 20,000 MW of hydroelectricity[52].

Bhutan exports most of its electricity India needs it and they have mechanisms in place to achieve this. Therefore the hydro-power projects are beneficial for both India and Bhutan. The major relations and progress was made with the Chukha Hydel Project, which was the commencement of a mutually beneficial relationship between the two countries. It generated substantive revenues for economic development for Bhutan, and also fulfilled the energy requirements of the two countries[53]. The Chukha was built under a 99-year agreement between India and Bhutan, whereby India provided a financial package that was 40 per cent loan and 60 per cent grant. Later a guaranteed power buy-back provision was also included in the agreement this arrangement has been mutually beneficial to both .

The other projects jointly shared by the two countries are :-

➢ The Kurichu Dam (60-MW) project on the river Kurichu, esatabilished in 1994. The project is a 55-metre high concrete dam with a surface powerhouse on the base of the dam . It has four generating units with an installed capacity of 15 MW. Ninety per cent of the power generated by the dam is exported to India.. The project was envisaged to stimulate growth of industries and create job opportunities for the local people of Eastern Bhutan.[54]

➢ The Tala Agreement, signed in 1996. The Tala HE Project is located immediately downstream to the existing Chukha HE Project. The Project based on the river Wangchu has a 91-metre high dam and stores 3.20 Mcum , it can produce 1040 MW of power annually. It was commissioned in 2006-07. Although the project is funded by India through with a grant (60 per cent) and loan (40 per cent), the power surplus is being sold to India. As per the agreement the project is solely owned by Bhutan.

Endnotes

1   Minister for Water Resources, River Development and Ganga Rejuvenation, Government of India. http://wrmin.nic.in/forms/list.aspx?lid=297

2   FAO, Aquastat, Water resources and MDG Water Indicators, March 2013

3   Hegde Narayan G. , Water Scarcity And Security In India

4   India's Water Wealth. Water Resource Information system of India , http://india-wris.nrsc.gov.in/wrpinfo/index.php?title=India%27s_Water_Wealth

5   India's National Water Policy, 2012; Government of India, Ministry of Water Resources India, Pages 3 and 5 http://wrmin.nic.in/writereaddata/NationalWaterPolicy/NWP2012Eng6495132651.pdf

6   ibid http://wrmin.nic.in/writereaddata/NationalWaterPolicy/NWP2012 Eng 6495132651.pdf

7   'Water stress', according to the Falkenmark index, which this report uses, indicates water availability between 1000 to 1700 cubic meters per person per year. 'Water scarcity', indicates water availability between 500 to 1000 cubic meters per person per year.

8   Ibid,4,   http://india-wris.nrsc.gov.in/wrpinfo/index.php?title=India%27s_ Water_ Wealth

9   Water And Related Statistics, Water Resources Information System Directorate Information System Organisation, Water Planning and Projects Wing Central Water Commission, DECEMBER 2013. http://www.cwc.nic.in/main/downloads/Water%20and%20Related%20Statistics-2013.pdf

10 ibid,9

11 Ibid,9

12 ibid,1

13 ibid,2; http://www.fao.org/nr/water/aquastat/countries_regions/IND/index.stm

14 Upali A. Amarasinghe, Tushaar Shah, Hugh Turral and B. K. Anand, Research Report 123 India's Water Future to 2025–2050: Business-as-Usual Scenario and Deviations http://www.iwmi.cgiar.org/Publications/IWMI_Research_Reports/PDF/PUB123/RR123.pdf

15 ibid,9

16 ibid,2 http://www.fao.org/nr/water/aquastat/countries_regions/IND/index.stm

17 World Bank (2010), *Deep Wells and Prudence: Towards Pragmatic Action for Addressing Groundwater Overexploitation in India*, World Bank..

18 Ibid

19 Rodell, M., Velicogna, I. and J. Famiglietti (2009), 'Satellite-based estimates of groundwater depletion in India', *Nature*, Vol. 460, pp. 999-1002.

20 Government of India (2010), *Groundwater Scenario of India 2009–10*, Central Ground Water Board, Ministry of Water Resources: http://www.cgwb.gov.in/documents/Ground Water Year Book%2 02009-10.pdf

21 Shah, T. (2011), 'Innovations in Groundwater Management: Examples from India', International Water Management Institute:http://rosenberg.ucanr.org/documents/argentina/Tushar Shah Final.pdf.

22 World Bank (2010), *Deep Wells and Prudence: Towards Pragmatic Action for Addressing Groundwater Overexploitation in India*, World Bank.

23 ibid,1

24 ibid,1   http://wrmin.nic.in/writereaddata/WatertheResource/statewiseirrigated 2079753822.pdf

25 Commission for Integrated Water Resource Development, *Integrated Water Resource Development: A Plan for Action*, vol. 1 (New Delhi: Commission for Integrated Water Resource Development, Ministry of Water Resources, 1999); National Water Development Agency, Indian Ministry of Water Resources, "The Need," <http://goo.gl/bIuvm

26 Hayato Kobayashi, Exploring Alternative Futures Of The World Water System. Building A Second Generation Of World Water Scenarios. Driving Force: Agriculture, , 2010; United Nations World Water Assessment Programme.

27 ibid,9

28 Upali Amarasinghe, The National River Linking Project of India: Some Contentious Issues, Water Policy Research,www.iwmi.org/iwmi-tata/apm2012

29 ibid,28

30 ibid,28

31 ibid,28

32 ibid,28

33   Singh Dhruv Vijay, erstwhile Secretary, Minister for Water Resources, River

Development and Ganga Rejuvenation, Government of India.

34   ibid, 9

35   Iram Khalid, Trans-Boundary Water Sharing Issues: A Case of South Asia , Journal of Political Studies, Vol. 1, Issue 2, 79-96; pu.edu.pk/images/journal/pols/Currentissue-pdf/Iram5.pdf

36   CHELLANEY BRAHMA , Water, Power, and Competition in Asia, Posted on August 18, 2014 Asian Survey, Vol. 54, Number 4, pp. 621–650. ISSN0004-4687, electronic ISSN1533-838X. (Copyright 2014 by the Regents of the University of California.)

37   ibid, 2. http://www.fao.org/nr/water/aquastat/data/query/results.html

38   Chellaney B, *Water, Peace, and War*, p. 287.

39   2030 Water Resources Group (Barilla Group, Coca-Cola Company, International Finance Corporation, McKinsey and Company, Nestlé S.A., New Holland Agriculture, SABMiller PLC, Standard Chartered Bank, and Syngenta AG), *Charting Our Water Future* (New York: 2030 Water Resources Group, 2009), p. 10.

40   Ibid, 37

41   Fresh Water Futures: Imagining Responses to Demand Growth, Climate Change, and the Politics of Water Resource Management by 2040, Prepared by-The Stimson Center, www.stimson.org/images/uploads/.../StimsonCenterConfWaterReport.pdf

42   Ismail Serageldin, Roshni Chakraborty,Sharing of River Waters among India and its Neighbors in the 21st century: War or Peace?

43   Rahaman, M.M.: "The Ganges Water Conflict", p.196. http//www.lib.tkk.fi

44   ibid,1

45   Ibid, 44

46   ibid,1

47   Ibid, 44

48   Ibid, 44

49   ibid,1

50   ibid,1 http://wrmin.nic.in/forms/list.aspx?lid=350&Id=4

51 "Indo-Bhutan hydropower initiative increase installation capacity", Economic Times, March 26, 2009, at: http://economictimes.indiatimes. com/News/News-By-Industry/Indo-Bhutan-hydropower-initiative-increase-installation-capacity/articleshow/4320446.cms.

52 Nepali Times, 30 August - 5 September 2000, http://himalaya.socanth.cam. ac.uk/collections/journals/nepali times/ pdf/Nepali_Times_007.pdf

53 Agreement between The Government Of India And The Royal Government Of Bhutan Regarding The Chukha Hydro-Electric Project, 23 March 1974, New Delhi, http://www.bhutanpeoplesparty.org/ lawtreaty/chukhahydro.htm

54 Cooperation with Neighbouring Countries, July 2008, http ://www. cea.nic. in/ hydro/ Cooperation%20with%20Neighbouring%20Countries.pdf

CHAPTER - 3 : INDO PAK WATER IMBROGLIO

"Water Is A Friendly Element For Those Who Are Familiar With It And Know How Best To Treat It".

—Goethe

The Common Dilemma

South Asia's earliest civilizations arose on the banks of the Indus, encompassing sites in both modern day Pakistan and India. Recent archaeological evidence suggests that climatic shifts dried the rivers that once watered the irrigated agriculture on which those Bronze Age cities depended, precipitating the ultimate collapse of Harappan civilization[1] .

Water is a vital but finite renewable resource. Rainfall, snow and ice melt, seepage between surface waters and groundwater, and return flows from irrigation and other uses ultimately drain to the Indus River and recharge aquifers to varying degrees. For any given source, however, renewals vary over time and place. Natural processes may only recharge underground aquifers over tens, hundreds, or even thousands of years, and the glaciers that nourish many watercourses have accumulated over millennia[2]. Every watershed is only replenished by a certain amount of renewable water every year. The waters of the Indus basin begin in the Himalayan mountains of Indian held Kashmir. They flow from the hills through the arid states of Punjab and Sind, converging in Pakistan and emptying into the Arabian Sea south of Karachi. Where once there was only a narrow strip of irrigated land along these rivers, developments over the last century have created a large network of canals and storage facilities that provide water for more than 26 million acres - the largest irrigated area of any one river system in the world.

Today , India and Pakistan again face significant water resource challenges. The Indus River is one of the most important water systems in Asia. With looming water wars in South Asia, India cannot afford to be casual about harnessing and utilising its water resource, particularly when China is behaving like a hydraulic empire[3] . The Indus originates in China on the Tibetan Plateau and runs for 3,200 km across Northern India and the length of Pakistan before emptying into the Arabian Sea near the port city of Karachi. While the Indus system counts 27 major tributaries, the six most significant branches — the Chenab, Ravi, Sutlej, Jhelum, Beas and the Indus itself— flow west through India before crossing into Pakistan. A seventh major tributary, the Kabul River, rises in Afghanistan and flows east into Pakistan. Many of the Himalayan rivers are intimately tied up with the issue of territory, as the rivers enter areas where there is contestation over the demarcation of borders.

For example, the Indus flows through parts of Kashmir that is labeled as "disputed" territory. For Pakistan, laying claim on Kashmir in effect means claiming the waters of the Indus river system. Almost 65 percent of the total area of Pakistan, 14 percent of the Indian land mass, 11 percent of Afghanistan, and one percent of China's land area lie within the Indus Basin[4].

Figure 31: The Indus River Basin

Indus river basin

The boundaries and names shown and the designations used on this map do not imply official endorsement or acceptance by the United Nations.

Dotted line represents approximately the Line of Control in Jammu and Kashmir agreed upon by India and Pakistan. The final status of Jammu and Kashmir has not yet been agreed upon by the parties.

0 75 150 300 450 km

Albers Equal Area Projection, WGS 1984

Today, the Indus supplies the needs of some 300 million people living throughout the basin. Together, India and Pakistan represent almost all of the demand on the river's resources, with Pakistan drawing 63 percent of water used in the basin and India drawing 36 percent[5]. Pakistan depends critically on the Indus, as the country's other rivers run only seasonally and their total flows equal less than two percent of the mean annual inflow entering Pakistan through the Indus system. For India, meanwhile, the Indus furnishes about seven percent of the annual utilisable surface water available nationwide. In addition to sharing the Indus' surface waters, India and Pakistan also share important — though inadequately mapped and characterized — transboundary aquifers in the basin[6]. Groundwater constitutes an essential additional source of freshwater for the region. Groundwater and surface water resources in the Indus Basin are closely linked both hydrologically and socio-economically. The renewable water resources are at critical levels for both.

Figure 32: Renewable Water Resources and Withdrawal: Indus River Basin

Country	India	Pakistan	Total
Average long-term available renewable water supplies in the IRB	97 km³/year	190 km³/year	287 km³/year
Estimated renewable surface water supplies in the IRB	73 km³/year	160-175 km³/year	239-258 km³/year
Estimated renewable groundwater supplies in the IRB	27 km³/year	63 km³/year	90 km³/year
Estimated total water withdrawals in the IRB	98 km³/year	180-184 km³/year	257-299 km³/year
Estimated total surface water withdrawals in the IRB	39 km³/year	128 km³/year	
Estimated total groundwater withdrawals in the IRB	55 km³/year	52-62 km³/year	

Note: Figures for surface and groundwater supplies may not sum evenly to figures for total renewable water resources because a large fraction of groundwater and surface water resources overlap, so that separate supplies cannot be absolutely distinguished.

Source: Derived from FAO, *Irrigation in Southern and Eastern Asia in Figures: AQUASTAT Survey 2011*, Karen Frenken ed. (Rome: FAO, 2012); A.N. Laghari et al., "The Indus basin in the framework of current and future resources management," *Hydrology and Earth Systems Sciences* 16, no.4 (2012); Bharat R. Sharma et al., "Indo-Gangetic River Basins: Summary Situation Analysis," International Water Management Institute, New Delhi Office, July 2008.

Ground Water Woes. India and Pakistan are likewise rapidly depleting the basin's groundwater resources. Indeed, abstractions from the Indus aquifers reflect both the most intensive and the most unsustainable levels of groundwater exploitation on Earth[7]. Studies in Pakistan reveal water tables plummeting by two to three meters a year, with groundwater levels falling to inaccessible depths in many wells. Because groundwater salinity in these aquifers typically increases with depth, dropping water tables lead farmers to irrigate with ever more saline water, salinizing the soils and degrading their production potential. Salt-affected soils now afflict 4.5 million hectares, amounting to over 22 percent of Pakistan's irrigated lands.[8] Similarly, a review by India's Central Ground Water Board determined that overdrafts exceeded rates of recharge in the states fed by The rivers of the Indus Basin. As a result, the Indus Basin is literally losing water.

Figure 33: Ground Water Stress: Indus River Basin

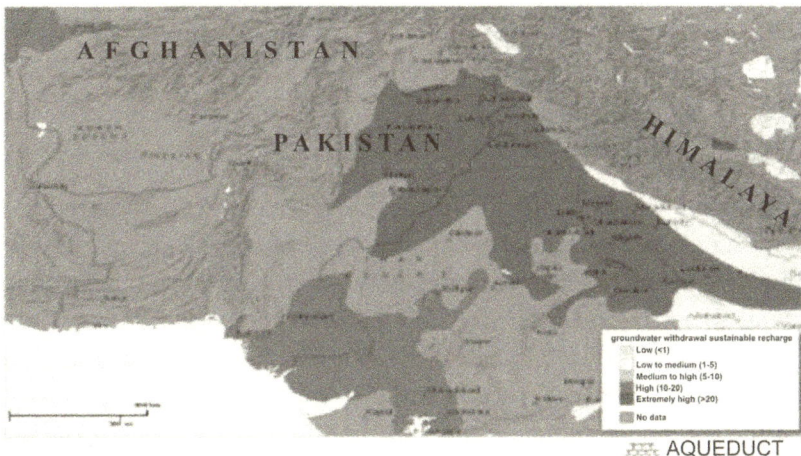

The UN expects that India's population will increase by almost a quarter in the next 20 years, topping 1.5 billion in 2030 and approaching 1.7 billion by 2050. Pakistan will witness even more spectacular growth. From 174 million inhabitants in 2010, its population will surge to 234 million in 2030 and near 275 million in 2050[9]. Within the confines of the Indus, one assessment projects that 383 million people will be living in the basin — including populations in Afghanistan and China — by 2050. Annual renewable water availability across the basin would then be under

750 m3 per capita. Another model evaluation by the International Water Management Institute calculates that total annual availability of renewable water on the Indian portion of the Indus Basin will slip from 2,109 m3 per capita (in 2000) to 1,732 m3 in 2050. On the Pakistani portion of the basin, yearly per capita water availability is expected to slide from 1,332 m3 to 545 m3[10].

According to the McKinsey & Company and the International Finance Corporation, international assessment — assuming that present policy regimes continue and existing levels of efficiency and productivity persist — renewable water supplies will fall 52 percent short of annual demands on the Indian side of the Indus Basin in 2030. The consortium's findings echoed an earlier Indian prognosis concluding that total utilisable freshwater resources in the Indian reaches of the Indus will meet less than half of the basin's requirements in 2050[11]. The situation is equally alarming on the other side of the frontier. There, the World Bank figures that Pakistan has already breached the limit of its available resources. Yet by 2025 the country will require 30 percent more water than today to meet its rising agricultural, domestic, and industrial needs[12].

Climate Change

According to recent studies the Himalayan glaciers will continue to retreat over the next 50 years and beyond as a result of climate change. This will cause a shrinking of glaciers, erratic snow patterns, erratic rainfall patterns, natural disasters and influence flow patterns in the Himalayan Rivers, particularly the Indus. Indus River flows are heavily dependent on glacial and snow melt (jointly termed melt water) and hence all the riparians will face the impact of climate change in the future[13]. On several occasions Indian dams in J&K have been blamed instead of climatic factors for low flow periods as well as flash floods in Pakistan, however, these allegations benefit neither side. Eventually, cooperation and not accusations will help reduce the impact of climate change in the two countries. Pakistan will benefit greatly because it receives more than 80% of its water supply from the Indus River, India's cooperation will ensure a greater trust relationship with Pakistan and joint studies on climate change will offer a more comprehensive understanding about the water situation in the region, including not just man-made issues but environmental factors as well. Meltwater constitutes the main flow of the Indus River; 1.5 times that of rain. According to the International Centre for Integrated Mountain Development in Kathmandu (ICIMOD) meltwater contributes 44.8% of the river flow, out of which, 40% is derived from glacial ice and from seasonal snows. As weather patterns become erratic and the Himalayan glaciers begin to melt, the flow patterns in the Indus River will increase in the short term but decrease dramatically in the long-term. Climate change is a reality that still needs to be factored in when discussing Transboundary Rivers in this region. In the next few years, as the flow of the Indus becomes more erratic and flash floods become more frequent, it will be essential for Pakistan to accept that Indian dam building has very little to do with this. Only then can progress on cross-border water issues be made in an effective manner. Both India and Pakistan are victims of climate change. In August 2010, Ladakh in India witnessed one of the most devastating flash floods in its history. As the Himalayan glaciers retreat, the most important short-term impact will be the Glacial Lake Outburst Floods (GLOFs).[14] A GLOF occurs when a glacier that contains a lake collapses, causing a sudden outburst of water. The Indus basin has a total of 2,420 glacial lakes 52 of which are potentially dangerous, in the ten sub basins of Indus River system namely Swat, Chitral, Gilgit, Hunza, Shigar, Shyok, Upper Indus, Shingo, Astor and Jhelum[15]. These sub-basins cover the Hindu Kush-Himalayan region in Pakistan.

Glaciers of the Hindu Kush Himalayan (HKH) region affect the hydrological regimes of 10 of the largest river systems in Asia. These glaciers help regulate water flows, control the regional and global climate systems on several time and spatial scales, and help sustain the livelihood of more than 1.3 billion people. The Indus Basin is uniquely dependent on these glaciers — snowpack- and glacial melt account for more than 50 percent of the Indus' annual average flow volume, and melt waters constitute roughly the same portion of flow volume for the river's primary tributaries. The arrival of snowpack- and glacial melt waters is particularly vital to downstream water users during the spring and fall shoulder months that come before or after the westerly monsoons, when these waters account for a significant portion of the base flow volume of the Indus and its tributaries[16].

Figure 34: Glaciers: Indus River Basin

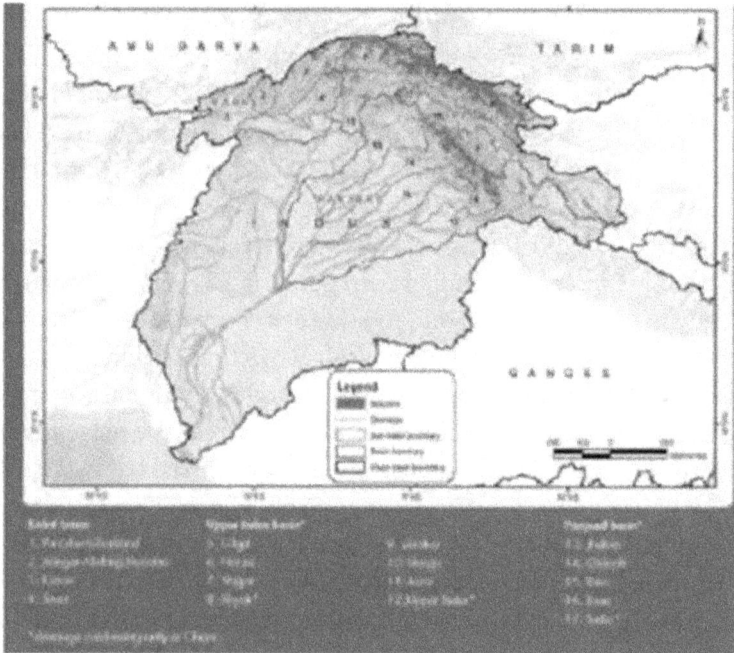

Source: Bajracharya, SR (2012) Status of glaciers in the Indus Basin. Kathmandu: ICIMOD

The rivers in the Indus Basin send to the Arabian Sea approximately 238,000 million cubic metres (mcm) of water each year, in comparison to the Nile's historic contribution to the Mediterranean Sea of 84,000 mcm[17]. The River Ravi, even during the dry winter months, has on average more water than the River Jordan; 1,500 mcm compared to 1,200 mcm respectively [Nijim, 1969: 38]. The above figures denote the average annual water supply, but hide a crucial factor - variability, both seasonal and between years. Large year-to-year variations in annual precipitation induce corresponding variability in the Indus' annual flow. Despite all the water, the Indus Basin is largely an arid or semi-arid area because of an uneven distribution of water. Most of the basin's rain falls within two months during the summer, and is transported out of the basin to the Arabian Sea. For the remaining ten months, very little rain falls in the basin. Even so, all the basin catchments show substantial seasonal fluctuations, with river flows peaking during June-September when the monsoon brings intense rainfall to the Lower Basin and higher temperatures increase snow and glacier melt in the Upper Basin[18].

Figure 35: Seasonal Variability : Indus River Basin

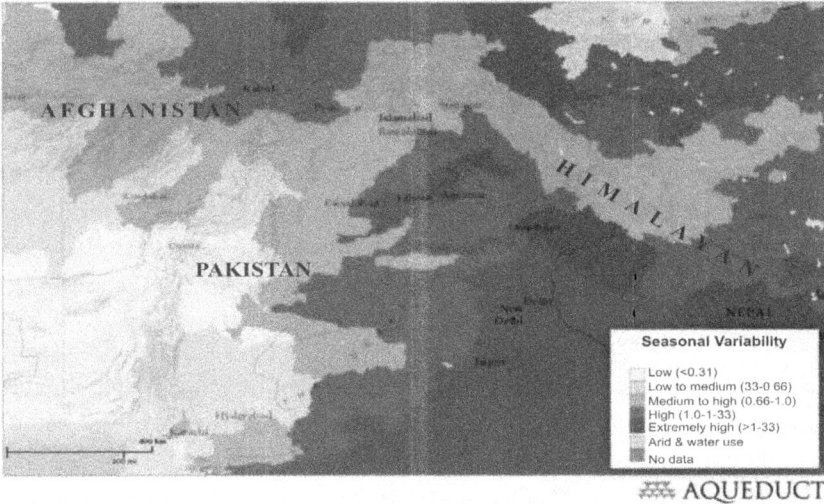

AQUEDUCT

To fully appreciate the long lasting issue it is imperative to have a detailed understanding of the historical perspective and the present compulsions of both countries .

Historical Perspective

The partition of the Indian subcontinent created a conflict over the plentiful waters of the Indus basin. The newly formed states were at odds over how to share and manage what was essentially a cohesive and unitary network of irrigation. These irrigation projects had been developed over the years under one political authority, that of British India, and any water conflict could be resolved by executive order. The Government of India Act of 1935, however, put water under provincial jurisdiction, and some disputes did begin to crop up at the sites of the more-extensive works, notably between the provinces of Punjab and Sind.[19.]

The British, in the mid 18th century developed a complex Irrigation System based on the Indus River System. Irrigation in the Indus River basin dates back centuries, by the late 1940s the irrigation works along the river were the most extensive in the world. The irrigation in the unified Punjab of the pre-independence era was dependent on the Indus and its tributaries. The water available in the individual rivers was not sufficient for the area to be irrigated. Some of the main tributaries namely Jhelum, Chenab and Ravi were also linked to one another through link canals in order to transfer water to the requisite areas[20].

Furthermore, the geography of partition was such that the source rivers of the Indus basin were in India. Pakistan felt its livelihood threatened by the prospect of Indian control over the tributaries that fed water into the Pakistani portion of the basin. Where India certainly had its own ambitions for the profitable development of the basin, Pakistan felt acutely threatened by a conflict over the main source of water for its cultivable land.

Before a decision could be reached, however, the Indian Independence Act of August 15, 1947 internationalized the dispute between the new states of India and Pakistan[21]. Partition was to be carried out in 73 days, and the full implications of dividing the Indus basin seemed not to have been fully considered, although Sir Cyril Radcliffe, who was responsible for the boundary delineation, did express his hope that, "some joint control and management of the irrigation system may be found" (Mehta 1986, p. 4). Heightened political tensions, population displacements, and unresolved territorial issues, all served to exacerbate hostilities over the water dispute. As the monsoon flows receded in the fall of 1947, the chief engineers of Pakistan and India met and agreed to a "Standstill Agreement," which froze water allocations at two points on the river until March 31, 1948, allowing discharge from headworks in India to continue to flow into Pakistan. During the first years of partition the waters of the Indus were apportioned by the Inter-Dominion Accord of May 4, 1948. This accord required India to release sufficient waters to the Pakistani regions of the basin in return for annual payments from the government of Pakistan[22]. The accord was meant to meet immediate requirements and was followed by negotiations for a more permanent solution. Neither side, however, was willing to compromise their respective positions and negotiations reached a stalemate. Pakistan wanted to take the matter to the International Court of Justice but India refused, arguing that the conflict required a bilateral resolution. On April 1, 1948, the day that the

"Standstill Agreement" expired, in the absence of a new agreement, India discontinued the delivery of water to the Dipalpur Canal and the main branches of the Upper Bari Doab Canal. The dispute commonly known as the 'canal water dispute' was in a larger sense about the rights of the lower and upper riparian and about equitable distribution.

Even before the partition of India and Pakistan, the Indus posed problems between the states of British India. The problem became international only after partition, and the incessant hostility only compounded the issue. Pakistani territory, which had relied on Indus water for centuries, now found the water sources originating in another country, one with whom geopolitical relations were increasing in hostility[23].

The resumption of water delivery to Pakistan from the Indian headworks was worked out at an Inter-Dominican conference held in Delhi on 3-4 May 4 1948. India agreed to the resumption of flow, but maintained that Pakistan could not claim any share of those waters as a matter of right (Caponera, 1987, p. 511). This position was reinforced by the Indian claim that, since Pakistan had agreed to pay for water under the Standstill Agreement of 1947, Pakistan had recognized India's water rights. Pakistan countered that they had the rights of prior appropriation, and that payments to India were only to cover operation and maintenance costs (Biswas, 1992, p. 204). An agreement was signed, later referred to as the Delhi Agreement, in which India assured Pakistan that India would not withdraw water delivery without allowing time for Pakistan to develop alternate sources despite both maintaining their own perspectives. By 1951, the two sides were no longer meeting and the situation seemed intractable. Despite the unwillingness to compromise, both nations were anxious to find a solution, fully aware that the Indus conflict could lead to overt hostilities if unresolved.

After visiting India and Pakistan on Nehru's invitation David Lilienthal, former chairman of the Tennessee Valley Authority (TVA) apprised his friend, David Black, president of the World Bank, with recommendations on helping to resolve the dispute. As a result, Black contacted the prime ministers of Pakistan and India, inviting both countries to accept the Bank's good offices. In a subsequent letter, Black outlined "essential principles" that might be followed for conflict resolution. These principles included the following: that water resources of the Indus basin should be managed cooperatively; and that problems of the basin should be solved on a functional and not on a political plane, without relation to past negotiations and past claims. After three weeks of discussions, an outline was agreed to, whose points included :-

➢ Determination of total water supplies, divided by catchment and use

➢ Determination of the water requirements of cultivable irrigable areas in each country.

➢ Calculation of data and surveys necessary, as requested by either side.

➢ Preparation of cost estimates and a construction schedule of new engineering works which might be included in a comprehensive plan.

In a creative avoidance of a potential and common conflict, the parties agreed that any data requested by either side would be collected and verified when possible, but that the acceptance of the data, or the inclusion of any topic for study, would not commit either side to its "relevance or materiality." When the two sides were unable to agree on a common development plan for the basin in subsequent 5 meetings in Karachi, November 1952, and Delhi, January 1953, the Bank suggested that each side submit its own plan. Both sides did submit plans on October 6, 1953, each of which mostly agreed on the supplies available for irrigation, but varied extremely on how these supplies should be allocated (Table 2).The Indian proposal allocated 29 million acre-feet (MAF) per year to India and 90 MAF to Pakistan, totaling 119 MAF (MAF = 1233.48 million cubic meters; since all negotiations were in English units). The Pakistani proposal, in contrast, allocated India 15.5 MAF and Pakistan 102.5 MAF, for a total of 118 MAF[24]. The basis of justification was because Pakistan insisted on the "Historical use rights" of waters from Indus and its tributaries whereas India argued that the historical distribution should not dictate the future of water sharing. India suggested that the waters of Western tributaries go to Pakistan and those of the Eastern tributaries to India.

Indus Water Treaty (IWT) 1960

The IWT, a trilateral agreement between Pakistan, India and the World Bank, basically agrees to the splitting of the Indus Rivers, awarding rights over the Eastern Rivers (Ravi, Sutlej, Beas) to India and the majority of the flow in the Western Rivers alone. Chenab, Jhelum) to Pakistan[25]. India however, is accorded customary usage of water in the Western Rivers for agricultural purposes and run-of-the-river electricity-generation projects. Before the partition in 1947, Pakistan had an extensive network of canals, supplied by the waters from the Sutlej, the Ravi and the Beas. The division of Punjab by the Radcliffe Award resulted in the headworks of Madhopur and Ferozepur in East Punjab while the canals were in West Punjab. With the division, the sharing of the waters of the Sutlej, the Ravi and the Beas became an issue that urgently needed to be resolved[40]. The treaty has proved to be robust, surviving the 1965 and 1971 wars, the Kargil conflict, the worsening of relations in the wake of the parliament attack in 2001 and the Mumbai terror strikes in 2008. As such, it is lauded as an example of successful negotiation on a contentious issue like water sharing between two hostile states.

For Pakistan the importance of the quietly flowing rivers of the Indus Basin are vital for the survival of Pakistan and parts of Northern India. For centuries, the Indus River Basin constituted a unified geography in today's Tibet, India, Pakistan and Afghanistan. In 1960, it was divided under the Indus Waters Treaty. Accordingly, the three Western rivers Indus, Jhelum and Chenab were awarded to Pakistan and the three Eastern rivers Ravi, Beas and Sutlej to India. This division provided Pakistan with 56 per cent of the catchment area and India with 31 per cent.[26] The authors of the Treaty then hoped that the division of the Indus Water Basin would eventually lead to the unity of people in Pakistan and India. Fifty years later, they seem to be proved wrong. In fact, the concern over the distribution of the Indus catchment area raises a basic question: whether short term divisive solutions can be sustained in the long run, or whether they can actually worsen the situation. Perhaps water would not have been a central issue had it been utilised efficiently over the last half century. Unfortunately, that has not been the case .In fact, only four of the transnational river basins in Asia are subject to treaties covering water sharing or other institutionalized cooperation[27]. These are the Mekong (where the non-participation of China, the dominant upper riparian nation, has stunted development of a genuine basin community), the Ganges (between Bangladesh and India), the Indus (between India and Pakistan, with the greatest guaranteed cross-border flows of any treaty regime in the world) and the Jordan (a four-nation basin whose resources are the subject of a treaty arrangement restricted to Israel and Jordan).

The Structure of the Indus Water Treaty 1960

The Indus Water Treaty (IWT) is a technical treaty which partitions the rivers of the Indus basin. It consists of a preamble, twelve articles delineating the rights and obligations of both countries, including mechanisms to deal with disputes and eight technical annexures (A to H) which lay down in great detail the responsibilities and obligations for both parties[28]. It seeks to fix and delimit 'rights and obligations of each in relation to the other concerning the use of these waters'. These are summarised below:-

(a)	Article I.	Definitions.
(b)	Article II.	Provisions Regarding Eastern Rivers.
(c)	Article III.	Provisions Regarding Western Rivers.
(d)	Article IV.	Provisions Regarding Eastern Rivers and Western Rivers.
(e)	Article V.	Financial Provisions.
(f)	Article VI.	Exchange of Data.
(g)	Article VII.	Future Cooperation.
(h)	Article VIII.	Permanent Indus Commission.
(j)	Article IX.	Settlement of Differences and Disputes.
(k)	Article X.	Emergency Provisions.
(l)	Article XI.	General Provisions.
(m)	Article XII.	Final Provisions.
(n)	Annexure A.	Exchange of Notes between Governments of India and Pakistan.
(o)	Annexure B.	Agricultural Use by Pakistan from Certain Tributaries of the Ravi.
(p)	Annexure C.	Agricultural Use by India from the Western Rivers.
(q)	Annexure D.	Generation of Hydroelectric Power by India on the Western Rivers.
(r)	Annexure E.	Storage of Waters by India on the Western Rivers.

(s)   Annexure F.   Neutral Expert.

(t)   Annexure G.   Court of Arbitration.

(u)   Annexure H.   Transitional Arrangements. (Annexure H is no longer valid as the Transition Period, during which Pakistan was required to make alternate arrangements for the loss of waters of the Eastern rivers, has long expired)

Main Provisions of The Indus Water Treaty 1960

> The IWT allocated the three Eastern rivers, Ravi, Beas and Sutlej to India and the three Western rivers Indus , Jhelum and Chenab largely to Pakistan . The Treaty permits India to draw water from the Western rivers for irrigation of 642,000 acres that existed on the date of the treaty and in addition, an entitlement to irrigate an Irrigated Cropped Area (means the total area under irrigated crops in a year, the same area being counted twice if it bears different crops of *kharif* and *rabi*.) of **701,000 acres**[29]. (Figure)

Agricultural Use Permitted to India from Western Rivers

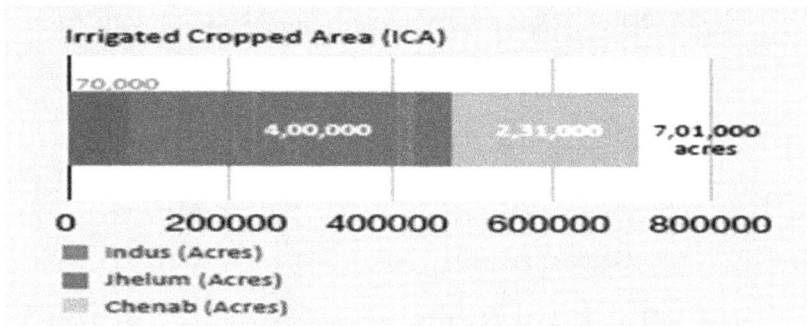

Irrigated Cropped Area (ICA)

70,000			
4,00,000	2,31,000	7,01,000 acres	

| 0 | 200000 | 400000 | 600000 | 800000 |

- Indus (Acres)
- Jhelum (Acres)
- Chenab (Acres)

Figure 36: Agricultural Use Permitted to India: Western Rivers

➢ The waters of the three Eastern rivers - the Ravi, the Beas and the Sutlej - would be available for unrestricted use by India, after a transition period.

➢ Pakistan may withdraw from the Basantar Tributary of the Ravi, as maybe available and necessary for irrigation of not more than 100 acres of land annually[30]

➢ All the waters of any tributary and in its natural course, while flowing in Pakistan, that joins the Satluj Main or the Ravi Main after these rivers have finally crossed into Pakistan shall be available for unrestricted use by Pakistan. India shall not construct this provision as giving Pakistan any claim or right to any releases in any such territory.

➢ Pakistan shall receive for unrestricted use of all the waters from the Western rivers which India is under obligation to let flow. India shall not permit any interference with these waters except for the following:-

(a) Domestic use.

(b) Non consumptive use.

(c) India may make following maximum withdrawals from the Chenab Main for agricultural use :-

(i) Ranbir Canal. 100 cusecs from 15 April to 14 October and 350 cusecs from 15 October to 14 April.

(ii) Pratap Canal. 400 cusecs from 15 April to 14 October and 100 cusecs from 15 October to 14 April.

(d) India could continue to irrigate from the Western rivers from areas that were irrigated as on 01 April 1960.

(e) India could also make further withdrawals from the basins of Indus, Jhelum, Chenab and Deg rivers for a Maximum Cropped Area of 70,000 acres, 400,000 acres 225,000 acres and 6000 acres respectively.

(f) Generation from hydro-electric power run-of-river-plants which were in operation or under construction as on 01 April 1960.

(g) India can also develop new runoff river plants or store water subject to criteria outlined in Annexure D and E of the Treaty.

➢ Storage. It permits India to build storage facilities to the tune of 3.6 MAF on the Western rivers within specified parameters.[31] This is in addition to the storage that already existed on these rivers before the coming into force of the treaty.

Figure 37: Storage Permitted To India: Western Rivers

River Systems	General Storage Capacity (MAF)	Power Storage Capacity (MAF)	Flood Storage Capacity (MAF)
Indus	0.25	0.15	Nil
Jhelum	0.50	0.25	0.75
Jhelum Main	Nil	Nil	As provided in para 9, Annexure E of the IWT
Chenab	0.50	0.60	Nil
Chenab Main	Nil	0.60	Nil
Total	1.25	1.6	0.75+Annx E of IWT

Source: Indus Water Commission

➢ Each Party agreed that any non-consumptive use made by it shall be such as not to materially change the flow in any channel to the prejudice of the uses of that channel by the other party under the provisions of the Treaty.

➢ Both sides are required to exchange information related to river flows observed by them, not later than three months of their observation and to exchange specified information on Agricultural Use every year.

➢ Each Party declared its intentions to prevent as much as possible the pollution of the river waters which adversely affect the uses similar in nature to those to which the waters were put on 01 April 1960. Both countries agreed to take all reasonable measures to ensure that any sewage or industrial waste would be treated before being discharged into the rivers.

➤ During the transition period of ten years, India would continue to give Pakistan some supplies from the Eastern rivers, in accordance with detailed regulation set out in the Treaty. The period may be extended at Pakistan's request up to a maximum of another three years. If so extended, India would deduct from its contribution Rs. 4.16 crores for one year's extension and Rs. 8.54 crores for two years' extension and Rs. 13.13 crores if the extension is sought for three years.

➤ Pakistan would build works in the transition period to replace, from the Western rivers and other sources, waters she used to get in her canals from the Eastern rivers.

➤ Agreement to create a permanent post of Commissioner for Indus Waters to serve as the channel of communication for the implementation of the Treaty and form the Permanent Indus Commission (PIC). The PIC was supposed to meet at least once a year alternately in India and Pakistan and submit an annual report to their respective Governments before June, 30th every year.

➤ Nothing contained in the Treaty, and nothing arising out of the execution thereof shall be construed as constituting a recognition or waiver whether tacit, by implication or otherwise of any rights or claims whatsoever of either of the parties.

➤ The IWT also enunciated a mechanism for regular exchange of flow-data of rivers, canals and streams.

➤ Pakistan may also withdraw from the following tributaries of Ravi as maybe available and necessary for the irrigation for the limits specified below39:-

	Tributary	Maximum Annual Cultivation (Acres)
(a)	Basantar	14000.
(b)	Bein	26600.

(c)   Tarnah   1800.

(d)   Ijh   3000.

> Dispute Settlement Mechanism. The IWT lays down the procedure for settlement of differences and disputes both bilaterally and through International arbitration. A condensed version of the dispute settlement process is given below:-

(a) Any question that might be a breach of IWT shall be first examined by the PIC.

(b) A difference is deemed to have arisen if the PIC could not reach an agreement.

(c) The difference shall be dealt with by a neutral expert who may opine if it is a dispute or not. If not, he shall resolve it. Such a neutral expert shall be a highly qualified engineer and appointed by the two Governments in consultation, or failing which, by the World Bank. Such a neutral expert can deal with any of the questions mentioned in Part-I of Annexure-F. The expert's decision is final and binding.

(d) In case of a dispute, the Commissioners report to their respective Governments which shall then strive to resolve the dispute.

(e) A Court of Arbitration shall be setup to resolve the dispute, if no decision is reached by the above process.

Such a Court will consist of seven members, two from each party and three including a Chairman from a panel to be chosen by the two Governments. If no consensus on names can be arrived at, the IWT has given a list of persons from whom to choose such as the Secretary General of the U.N. or International Bank for Reconstruction and Development (IBRD) for the Chairmanship and President of M.I.T., Cambridge, the Rector of Imperial College, London, the Chief Justice of the USA, or the Lord Chief Justice of England for panel membership.

Figure 38: Process of Arbitration: IWT

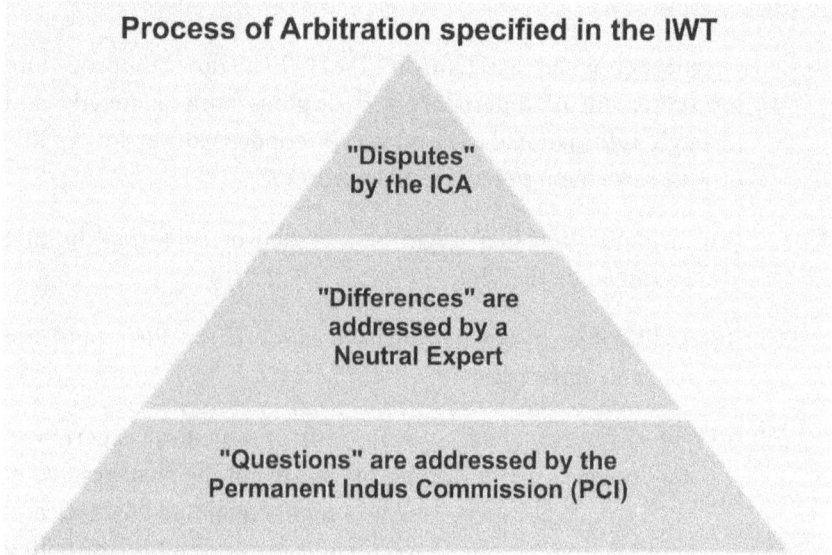

Process of Arbitration specified in the IWT

"Disputes"
by the ICA

"Differences" are
addressed by a
Neutral Expert

"Questions" are addressed by the
Permanent Indus Commission (PCI)

Advantages of the IWT Pakistan

The principal benefits for Pakistan were[32]:-

➤ Gaining part independence from India for ensuring its supplies by binding the latter to a formal international treaty .

➤ The treaty helped regulate the flows of the Indus and its tributaries.

➤ It helped to overcome shortcomings and revolutionise agriculture in Pakistan .

Drawbacks

➤ About 80 per cent of the total water is produced during the monsoon period July to September. However, this loss was compensated by the construction of storage reservoirs, canals and diversions which ensured water availability during winters and enhanced canal diversions.

➤ The other drawback was the rise in inter-provincial discord, especially in recent years, due to reduced flows in the Indus.

Sindh's stance towards Punjab is comparable to that of Pakistan towards India.

Situation For India

The partition gave India very little of the already-developed areas of the canal and irrigation system. India was free to undertake development works on the Eastern rivers, thus helping in irrigating even arid areas like Rajasthan. However, having previously enjoyed complete rights over the waters of these rivers, the treaty was a compromise. The major benefits that accrued from the treaty are:-

- ➤ Fully harness the Eastern rivers to its benefit. It helped in diverting waters to arid areas like Rajasthan and develop irrigation facilities.

- ➤ Could build run-of-river hydroelectric plants on the Western rivers and flood control storage facilities.

The disadvantages accruing to India were as follows :-

- ➤ Ceding Western rivers to Pakistan hampered growth of Jammu & Kashmir, as water resources in the state could not be harnessed (this part is discussed later)

- ➤ Increased differences amongst basin states as they began contending higher allocation of water.

- ➤ The treaty does not augur well as it has no exit clause, though Article XII of the treaty provides for a modification of the treaty.

Shortcomings in the Indus Water Treaty

In 1960, the IWT offered a simple bifurcation of rivers as a solution to the water problems between India and Pakistan. Analysts have stated this one point as both the main benefit as well as the main disadvantage of the Indus Water Treaty – on the one hand, it allows both countries to pursue their individual interests, without much need for cooperation in the field of water. On the other hand, it restricts cooperation on integrated water basin management, information sharing and disaster management measures. A major achievement of the treaty was to end the decade-long bitter controversy since partition. So far water disputes between India and

Pakistan have arisen because of the different interpretations of the IWT on both sides rather than the lack of provisions in the treaty. It opened the way for large development works in the basin in both countries. The post-treaty period led to an agricultural boom in both the countries, leading to higher levels of production, acreage, yield and rapid growth. According to an analysis, while building dams on the Western Rivers, Pakistani engineers interpret the technical annexures of the IWT very literally while Indian engineers tend to emphasize the clause in the treaty that emphasizes the need for a techno economically sound project design. In some cases techno-economical soundness of the project has been given priority over certain annexures in the IWT and this was the case with the Baglihar Dam project wherein the neutral expert conceded to the fundamental design issues that India was facing, given certain restrictions in the IWT. Experts elaborate that - "given the high seasonal flow variability... (and)... some of the highest silt loads in the world, projects often simply cannot be technically or economically viable without a liberal interpretation of the limitations on regulating structures...". Most analysts believe that the IWT has been largely successful in its endeavour to prevent a 'water war' between India and Pakistan. There have been disagreements over water over the years but there hasn't been any indication of outright conflict over water. It has faithfully served both the countries as a means of forestalling water-related disputes. And despite being the upper riparian state, India has never used it as a 'black mailing' tool in spite of two major wars and constant skirmishes However - because the treaty was designed in 1960 and since water availability, demand and supply mechanism have changed considerably since then question is less about the IWT's durability and more about its adaptability. Some experts believe that India and Pakistan, despite their longstanding hostility, are **'water-rational'** states interested in securing long-term supplies of fresh water[33] . For much of the IWT's history, the sharing of the Indus basin system[34] calmly worked through the mechanisms, and disputes were mutually resolved by the Permanent Indus Water Commission (PIC).[35] In recent years, however, water has gained political ascendancy and doubts have arisen about the durability of the water-sharing arrangement. Over the years, the following major shortcomings have been observed in the Treaty:-

(a) The depletion in the Indus waters due to climate change was not perceived and hence was not factored into the treaty.

(b) The treaty divided the rivers without taking the volume of water into account .

(c) It made no provisions for joint management.

(d) The treaty does not augur well as it has no exit clause, though Article XII of the treaty provides for a modification of the treaty , through a mutual agreement.

(e) India, though an upper riparian, has certain responsibilities with regard to the use of the waters as explained in articles II, III and IV.[46]

(f) Despite the major sources of Indus waters in Jammu and Kashmir, provision of providing share of its benefits to the people of the State were not built into the Treaty.

(g) Although India is the upper riparian state in the Treaty, it gets only 31 percent of the share while Pakistan enjoys 56 percent share. Some estimates place the ratio at 20 percent and 80 percent respectively.

Pakistan's Water Woes: The Cauldron Within

Pakistan's water woes are often blamed on the upper riparian nation India with accusations that India is responsible for blocking Pakistan's water supply. However, the reality is that the water shortage problems in Pakistan are not a case of obstruction by external forces but rather a case of wastage and unequal distribution and utilisation by internal forces.

Pakistan's per capita availability of water has declined from 5600 cubic metres in 1947 to approximately 1100 cubic metres in 2010 fast approaching the threshold level of less than 1000 cubic metres by 2025. The decline in water availability has particularly meant disaster for irrigation. In Pakistan, over 80 per cent of the cropland is irrigated. The country has the world's largest contiguous irrigation network. The rivers of the Indus Basin provide 60 per cent of the water utilised for irrigation, while groundwater accounts for the rest. The inflow of water for irrigation has declined from 140 MAF in the 1980s to an average of 100 MAF in 2005.[36] In Pakistan, total annual water withdrawals have risen from 153.4 km3 in 1975 to 183.5 km3 in 2008, while total annual renewable water resources per capita have plunged from 3,385 cubic meters (m3) in 1977 to 1,396 m₃ in 2011.[37] For the Indus Basin as a whole, the United Nations Environment Programme (UNEP) calculates that per capita annual renewable water availability stands at 1,329 m₃. Another analysis by the International Centre for Integrated Mountain Development (ICIMOD) estimated yearly water supplies in the basin at 978 m₃ per person. Both figures indicate that the basin's inhabitants face severe water stress[38]. It is feared that it will decline further as the flows in the three rivers are reducing at the rate of 6.6 per cent per year.

Figure 39: Per capita Water Availability: Pakistan

Per Capita Water Availability in Pakistan

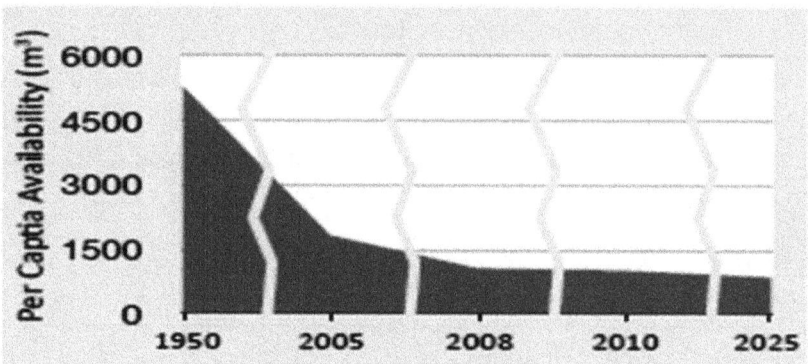

Sources: Final Settlement (SFG), Agricultural Water Demand Management in Pakistan (Kochi University Japan), Dr. Zakir Hussain VC University

Ground Water. PG 36 of Module 2 Most urban and rural water is supplied from groundwater sources. Salt-water intrusion is a problem in Pakistan with about 36% of the groundwater classified as highly saline. The ground water resources are also fast depleting. As compared to 3.34 MAF in 1959, ground water pumping is reached 55 MAF by 2009. Groundwater is pumped with the help of tubewells. Average Annual Freshwater Availability, which accounts mainly for the Indus River Basin flow is pegged at 130MAF (million acre feet) but can reach as low as 116MAF per year.[39] In 2008, total water withdrawal was estimated at 148.68MAF (183.4 km³) creating a deficit of roughly 18MAF. Surface water withdrawal accounted for 98.74MAF (121.8 km³) and groundwater withdrawal accounted for 49.94MAF (61.6 km³). The withdrawal refers mainly to the Indus Basin Irrigation System (IBIS) as withdrawals outside of this are negligible. If the network of canals and tubewells continue to provide gradually reducing quantities of fresh water. Already the country faces a shortfall in foodgrain availability of more than 4 million tonnes per year. By some assessments, 45 percent of Pakistan's renewable groundwater supply originates in leakage from the canal system, 26 percent comes from irrigation return flows, and six percent derives from river recharge. In India, an estimated one-fifth of the surface water withdrawn from the Indus for irrigation subsequently drains into groundwater aquifers as return flow.[40] Socio-economically, many water users in the basin rely on groundwater to supplement or supplant surface water supplies where these prove inadequate, intermittent, or unavailable.

Siltation in Dams. Increasing silt levels in dams result in poor dam storage capacity. According to former Chairman of the Indus River System Authority (IRSA), very little attention is paid to the effects of silting on dam storage capacity in Pakistan. According to him, the Tarbela, Mangla and Chashma reservoirs together have silted up to 6.6 MAF in the last 36 years.[41] He says that the rapid silting has adversely affected the storage capacity created under the IWT and has harnessed inter-provincial disputes between Sindh and Punjab. Watershed management measures like check dams, built along the catchment area, can reduce the speed of rainwater run-off and check soil erosion, thereby, increasing the lifespan and capacity of these dams. But as of 2012, no watershed management measures have been carried out in the catchment area of any of these dams. Pakistan's solution to silting so far has been to raise the level of the dam, which leads to the displacement of people and environmental damage. Silting in dams in Pakistan could reduce the original storage capacity by more than 45% in the future.

Figure 40: Storage Losses In Dams Due To Silting: Pakistan

Storage Loss due to Silting, measured in MAF			
Reservoir	Storage Loss by 2001	Storage Loss by 2010	Est. Storage Loss by 2020
Tarbela		2.92	
Mangla (after raising)		3.16	
Chasma		0.44	
Total	3.46	6.52	8.3745
Storage Capacity after Storage Loss due to Silting, measured in MAF			
Tarbela	9.69	6.77	
Mangla (after raising)	8.22	5.06	
Chasma	0.70	0.26	
Total	18.61	12.09	10.23

Source: Final Settlement and ibrat newspaper, Sindh (15 Apr 2011)

Annual precipitation in Pakistan is roughly 500mm although this varies with less than 100mm in certain parts of Baluchistan and Sindh and 1,500mm in the foothills and mountains of Punjab and NWFP. There is also an extreme variability in rainfall between the seasons. There are 2 main rainfall seasons in Pakistan – Rabi season (October-March) and Kharif Season (April-September). 60% of the annual rainfall is received during the peak of the Kharif season from July-September. Similar to the rainfall periods, 85% of the flow of the Indus is received during the Kharif Season (April to September) and the remaining 15% is received during the Rabi season (October to March). In addition, 80% of the water in the Kharif season is received from melt water.[42]

Figure 41: Total Average Renewable Freshwater Availability 2008

River Basins	MAF	Km³
Indus River Basin (Western Rivers)	124-138	170.27
Makran and Karan Basins	Less than 4	Less than 5
Afghan Use of Kabul River	-8	-
Final Total	120-134	

Source : FAO, Aquastat, 2010 version & Eng. Abdul Majidh Kazi

Overall Supply and Demand. Historically, more attention has been given to water supply in Pakistan and measures that would help to enhance this supply such as dams and irrigation systems. However, little attention has been given to the demand side of Pakistan's water nexus with negligible efforts to improve utilisation and mitigate water losses. There is an urgent need to introduce demand-based management into the country, especially in Pakistan's agricultural sector. In addition, marginal water, i.e. desalination and wastewater, is not pursued actively in the country, however, it could contribute substantially to enhancing water supplies. According to Rao Irshad Ali Khan, Chairman of the Indus River System Authority (IRSA) Pakistan's demand for water has already outstripped total supply by 11-12MAF. This gap between water demand and water supply is projected to reach around 31MAF by 2025[43]. It is pertinent to mention that the gap between demand and supply widens in the summer (Kharif) season and towards the end of the watercourses.

Figure 42: Supply and Demand Gap : Pakistan

Pakistan's Supply and Demand Gap

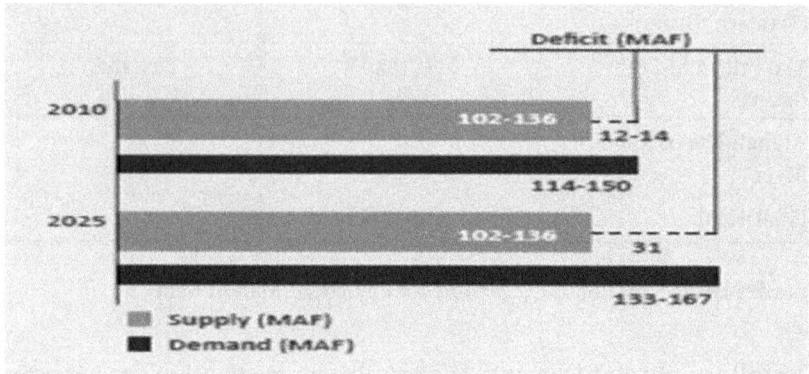

Deficit (MAF)

2010
102-136
12-14
114-150

2025
102-136
31
133-167

■ Supply (MAF)
■ Demand (MAF)

* Supply here refers mainly to surface water availability and
largely represents the Indus Basin.
Sources: The following figures were derived from
statements made by IRSA Chairman Rao Irshad Ali Khan
and a paper by Shaheen Akhtar of the Institute of Regional
Studies, Islamabad.

The main factors driving water demand in Pakistan are agriculture, hydro-electricity and storage capacity. Consumption of water is heavily skewed towards agriculture – as of 2008 the agricultural sector constituted 94% of total water withdrawal (172.4 km³), municipal use was estimated at 5.2% (9.7 km³) and industrial use constituted 0.76% (1.4 km³)[33]. This pattern is unlikely to change as agricultural output constitutes roughly 21% of the GDP, 50% of employment and provides 60-70% of Pakistan's exports[44]. Pakistan has also developed agriculture in parts of the country that are not actually conducive to the practice. The Northern Territories in Pakistan have a substantial amount of rainfall. Most of the crops here are grown through rain-fed agricultural practices and are less dependent on irrigation. Sindh and Punjab on the other hand depend substantially on groundwater tubewells and surface water irrigation during crop production. Yet only 20% of PoK's irrigable land is currently developed whereas 80% of the land in the rest of Pakistan is used for irrigation. This 80% is considered arid and semi-arid and is therefore highly dependent on the Indus Basin irrigation network and not rainfall to support its agricultural practices.

Figure 43: Sector Wise Water Demand: Pakistan

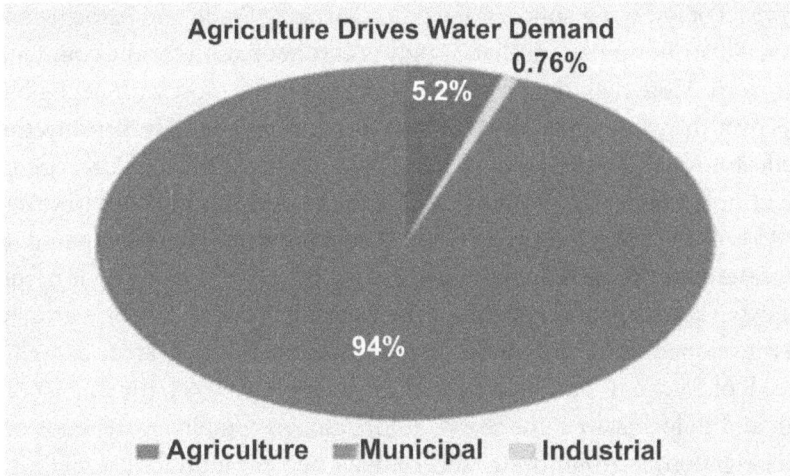

Irrigation Inefficiency. While Pakistan's irrigation network is vast, it is managed in an extremely inefficient manner. Seepage from irrigation canals has resulted in water logging in low-lying areas, disturbing the composition of salts in the soil. It has reduced the delivery efficiency of the canal system to hardly 40 per cent. The Indus River System carries about 43,500 hectare metres of silt every year. About 40 per cent of the silt load settles before reaching the Indus mouth and erodes the storage capacity of the three main dams Tarbela, Mangla and Chashma. In particular, the Tarbela dam is losing storage capacity of 100,000 cusecs each year. Pakistan's irrigation sector has some of the lowest conveyance efficiencies in the world. Conveyance losses result in water wastage within Pakistan. According to a 'Special Report on the Water Crisis in Pakistan' by Pakistan (Pakistan's largest agri web portal), 25% of the water diverted to the country's canal system is misplaced in 'line losses' or pipe leakages.[45]

The overall irrigation efficiency in the Indus Basin Irrigation System is low at around 40%. Pakistan has one of the world's largest contiguous irrigation systems. Consequently water losses through the system can be substantial and can be quite costly for Pakistan's agri-economy. Pakistan has one of the world's largest contiguous irrigation systems. Consequently water losses through the system can be substantial and can be quite costly for Pakistan's agri-economy.

Uneven Water Distribution Amongst The Provinces. Pakistan's Punjab province receives the lion's share of the water resources in the country, while the impact of low water supply is felt much harder in Sindh and Balochistan. Unequal distribution rather than supply is another reason for the country's water woes. More than the provinces, PoK suffers the most with negligible rights over the water resources that flow from its territory. Historically, the benefits for water development projects have not benefited the PoK region. Agriculture provides livelihood to 84% of the households in PoK. However, only 13% of the cultivable area in PoK is actually irrigated as compared to 80% of the cultivable area in the rest of Pakistan[46]. Despite having one of the most extensive irrigation systems in the world, irrigation in PoK is grossly underdeveloped. Inter provincial discords are rife in other areas as well, while all of Pakistan is affected by declining supply of water, the impact on Sindh and Balochistan is the worst. Sindh, almost completely depends on canal irrigation, as groundwater sources have become unfit for use. Salinity and waterlogging has affected 88.8 per cent of Sindh's agricultural land[47]. Sindh has had to bear the maximum brunt of the large and inefficient irrigation network. The diversion of water upstream has resulted in the decline of water downstream to Sindh. As a result, discharge of freshwater into the sea has come down, thus causing intrusion of sea waters into the mainland. Sea intrusion has already destroyed 1.5 million acres of farmland in the two coastal districts of Badin and Thatta.[48] Sindh often claims that upper riparian state Punjab siphons excess water from the Indus River System through excessive groundwater pumping and canal diversions when this water rightfully belongs to Sindh. The 1991 Accord has been the most recent document that specifies the distribution of water between Pakistan's provinces Sindh and Punjab (figure). Although it is controversial, the agreement has largely been established as the basis for water-sharing.

Figure 44: Water Distribution Accord, 1991 : Pakistan

Water Distribution According to the 1991 Accord (In MAF)

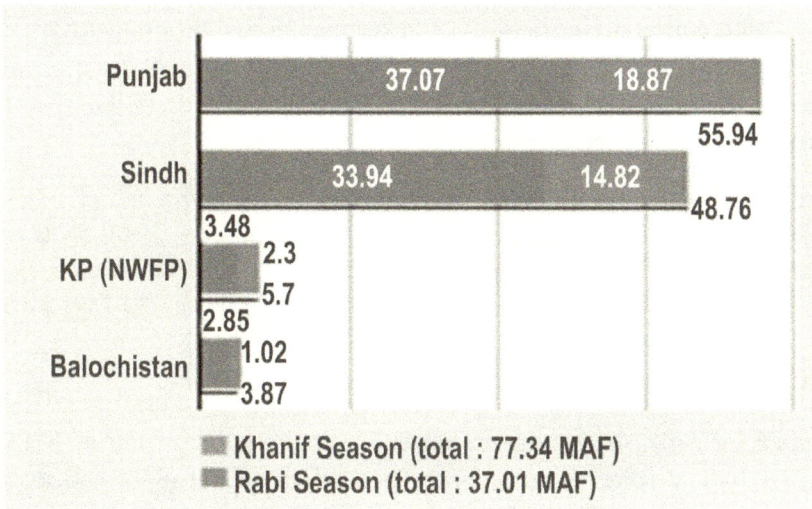

■ Khanif Season (total : 77.34 MAF)
■ Rabi Season (total : 37.01 MAF)

Source: Final Settlement, SFG, 2005
"Please not that PoK does not feature in this allocation.

To add to the woes, a scheme to divert the Chenab to join it with the Ravi and Sutlej is on the anvil[49]. Punjab has commenced on a five-year project worth ₹20 billion to revamp the irrigation system in the province to overcome system losses.. Punjab and Sindh always have been and currently are, at loggerheads over deciding a formula to distribute shortages in water flows. Sindh demands the implementation of the Water Accord of 1991, whereas Punjab insists on a formula worked out in 1994. With Punjab's exclusive rights on the Mangla, it is able to draw sufficient waters. Sindh is left dry and to the mercy of the rain gods.

Neglected Water Sector Development. Low Expenditure on water sector development has decreased measures to enhance the water supply and control the rising water demand. Pakistan has never spent much on water sector development, utilizing only 0.25% of its GDP. To put this in perspective, military spending in Pakistan is 47 times this amount. An ADB report released in 2007 advised Pakistan to increase its water sector spending to a minimum of 1% of GDP[50], stating that the water use in Pakistan amounted to a zero in terms of efficiency. The federal government is often unable to provide financial assistance to Sindh and PoK for their water development projects. Most of the schemes in these provinces are managed and funded by the provincial government through foreign loans.

With a brief understanding of Pakistans internal turmoil with water resources management it is important to analyse the issues of discord with India over this critical shared resource. Pakistans attitude to the crisis is exemplified in this statement

"Insisting on our water rights with regard to India must be one of the cornerstones of our foreign policy. The disputes of the future will be about water."

–Ayaz Amir, The News, Pakistan, 01 May 2009.

Ongoing Contentious Issues With India

The IWT clearly conveys the responsibilities of both the signatories to the treaty . India despite being an upper riparian with nearly all the control in their hands have maintained a very creditable record of maintaining their part in the treaty. Notwithstanding the overt and covert hostile actions by Pakistan , it has respected the treaty and continues to do so. Pakistan on the other hand raises a hue and cry blaming India for its water crisis as a perpetual source of all its woes. India has diligently followed the conditions by sharing the relevant data on all the projects undertaken on the Western rivers. This has given Pakistan a certain sense of authoritarian control over the usage of the waters of the Western rivers by India. National interests of all countries are dear to them and ensuring that they are upheld at all costs, is how hydrodiplomacy will be seen in the Indus Basin as well. The ongoing contentious issues could broadly be summarised as follows in succeeding paragraphs.

In the late seventies Pakistan raised serious objections on the design of the Salal dam on Chenab. This delayed the project and also compelled India to make certain design changes which over time has resulted in silting of its reservoir and reducing its intended performance.

Baghliar Project. Pakistan raised six main objections to the design of the Baglihar project and they are mentioned in the table below. Consequently, India gave responses to each of these 6 objections and ultimately, the Neutral Expert, Raymond Lafitte, gave his ruling on all of these six points.

Figure 45: Decision Made By Neutral Experts: Baghliar

Decision Made by the NE on the 6 points of Contention		
Indian Perspective	Pakistani Perspective	Neutral Expert's Decision
Pondage of 37.5MCM.	Excessive. Pondage of 6.22MCM would be adequate.	Reduce Pondage to 32.58MCM.
Freeboard Height of 4.5 metres.	Freeboard of 1.5 metres would be adequate.	Reduce Pondage to 3 metres.
Gated spillway required.	Gated spillway not required.	Pakistani objections rejected. Gated spillway required.
Gated spillway at right height.	Gated spillway not at highest possible level.	Pakistani objections rejected. Gated spillway required for efficient maintenance. Recommended lowering of the spillway by another 8 metres.
Probable Maximum Flood (PMF) of 16,500 cumecs.	Too large. PMF of 14,900 cumecs would be adequate.	Pakistani objections rejected.
Water intake at 818 metres.	Water intake at Dead Storage Level 835 metres.	Raise water intake to 821 metres.

Lafitte's ruling on the Baglihar Dam elucidates the fact that Pakistani objections to Indian run-of-the-river projects on the Western Rivers of the Indus are more a reflection of Pakistani 'lower riparian' anxieties than an actual Indian violation of the IWT. With regards to run-of-the-river projects on the Western Rivers of the Indus, disagreements between India and Pakistan arise over the interpretation of the IWT. As per experts of United States Institute for Peace (USIP), Pakistani engineers interpret the technical annexures of the IWT very literally while Indian engineers tend to emphasize the clause in the treaty that emphasizes the need for a techno-economically sound project design. The Indus River Basin carries some of the highest silt loads in the world – an estimated 400 million tonnes while the Ganga carries 159 million tonnes and the Nile River 150 million tonnes. In the case of Baglihar and now in the case of Kishanganga (where a similar argument is being made) reservoir flushing is absolutely necessary. If this maintenance is not conducted then the reservoir will silt up rapidly and will subsequently become inoperable. Perhaps this is what Pakistan wants as it would ensure that the run-of-the-river projects have an extremely short lifespan. There have been no incidents concerning this run-of the-river project since 2008 and Pakistan has agreed that it will not pursue the Baglihar filling issue any longer. As a side note it is also important to note that there are other inflows to the Chenab River apart from the flow that runs through the Baglihar Dam and all of these should be taken into account in the case of reduced water flow to Pakistan.

Tulbul Navigation Project (Wullar Barrage). The main argument on the Tulbul Navigation Project[51] is the effect that this structure could have on the flow of the Jhelum River. Pakistan believes that the structure is in violation of the IWT design specifications and it will hamper the flow of the Jhelum River during the low flow periods. India has provided reassurance that it will modify the design to suit the specifications in the IWT and it has said that the aim of the barrage is to enhance the level of flow in the Tulbul Navigation Project which could regulate the flow of the Jhelum and benefit both sides of the border in terms of agriculture; dam maintenance and flood control. However, Pakistan's objections are driven more by lower riparian anxiety than technical specifications. If Pakistan insists on considering every development project on the Kashmir Rivers as a geo-strategic threat rather than development works then the treaty will not survive for much longer. Pakistan cannot abuse the IWT simply to use its rights and hamper development in lean months and not the other way around.

Figure 46: Tulbul Navigation Project (Wullar Barrage)

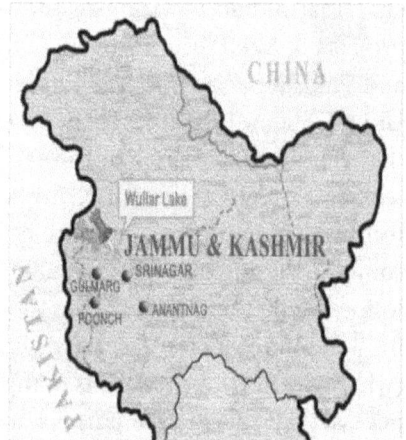

1984	India starts work on the Tulbul Navigation Project.
1986	Pakistan refers its objections (questions) to the Permanent Indus Water Commission.
1987	After deliberation between the two sides the Indus Water Commission records a failure to resolve the matter.
1989	Pakistan agrees to the barrage, but only after Pakistani inspection. India rejects the offer.
1991 1992	India offers to forgo initial storage capacity. Pakistan makes its agreement conditional on the cessation of work on the Kishanganga Projects. India rejects the offer.

Source: The Times of India (http://timesofindia.indiatimes.com/photo.cms?msid=794766)

Pakistan's first point of contention is that by controlling the flow of the Jhelum River through the Tulbul or Wullar Barrage, India is turning the Wullar Lake, a natural structure, into a manmade storage device and this is strictly prohibited under Article III (4) of the IWT. Even if India argues that Article III (4) does in fact allow for a limited amount of 'incidental' storage like flood control purposes on the Jhelum and the Chenab Rivers, Pakistan contends that the storage specified under this clause is 0.01MAF and the storage capacity specified in the original design of the Wullar Barrage is 0.3 MAF. It is therefore 32 times larger than the amount permitted under the IWT. India has already accepted this objection by Pakistan in the past and it modified the design in a draft that it prepared in 1991. The draft agreed to forgo the storage capacity of 0.3 MAF in the barrage (if Pakistan allowed the water level to reach its full operational height of 5,177.90ft)[52]. The main reason for a suspension in an agreement over the Tulbul Navigation Project is Pakistan's insistence on linking the Barrage issue to the Kishanganga hydro-power project. This is the stance that Pakistan took in 1992 to stall the issue, once storage capacity was no longer a problem, and this is the stance that it is likely to take on the Tulbul Navigation Project in the future as well. By linking objections on the Kishanganga project to the Wullar Barrage, Pakistan is hoping to derail both the projects at once. In response to Pakistani fears of water obstruction, India has maintained on several occasions that the overall volume of water flowing to Pakistan will remain intact. The barrage is a navigational structure and the aim of this structure is not to store or impound water but to control the flow for navigation. The problem with navigation in the Jhelum arises in the lean season from October to February. During this period the flow of the water in the river is 2,000 cubic feet per second and its depth is about 2.5 feet which cannot support navigation. The aim of the structure is to maintain the flow, depth and a minimum draught of 1.37m in the river during the winter season in order to make trade along the river possible.

Kishanganga Dam and Neelam-Jhelum Dam

- On May 17, 2010, the Islamic Republic of Pakistan instituted arbitral proceedings against the Republic of India under Paragraph 2(b) of Annexure G to the Indus Waters Treaty 1960.[61]

- A Court of Arbitration composed of seven members has been constituted pursuant to Annexure G. The Permanent Court of

Arbitration acts as Secretariat to the Court of Arbitration pursuant to Paragraph 15(a) of Annexure G.

- On December 20, 2013, the Court of Arbitration rendered its Final Award.

- On December 20, 2013, the Court of Arbitration issued a *Decision on India's Request for Clarification or Interpretation dated 20 May, 2013.*

- On February 18, 2013, the Court of Arbitration rendered a Partial Award.

- On August 31, 2012, the Court of Arbitration concluded a two-week hearing on the merits.

- On August 20, 2012, the Court of Arbitration commenced the hearing on the merits.

- The Court of Arbitration conducted a visit of the Neelum River Valley.

- On September 23, 2011, the Court of Arbitration issued an *Order on Interim Measures.*

- The Court of Arbitration conducted a visit of the Neelum-Jhelum and Kishenganga Hydroelectric Projects and surrounding areas in June 2011.

The Indian project plans to divert the flow of the Kishanganga, a tributary of the Jhelum (called the Neelam in Pakistan), to another tributary known as the Bunar-Madmati Nallah through a 22km long tunnel. After generating hydro-electricity at a power house in Bunkot, the river will join the main Jhelum River, via the Wullar Lake, near the town of Bandipur (Baramullah District) in J&K. This will change the course of the river by roughly 100km; instead of the Neelam and Jhelum meeting in Pakistan, at Domail near Muzaffarabad, the tributary will meet the Jhelum in J&K. Thus the river will be returned to Pakistan after use for power generation however it will be via another route. It should be noted that 30% of the Jhelum River arises in India, of which the Kishanganga is one part, while the river accrues the remaining 70% of its flow after it crosses the LoC.[53]

The main argument raised by Pakistan on the Kishanganga project does not pertain to technical objections; it pertains to India's legal interpretation of the IWT itself. This is why Pakistan has skipped referring the case to the Neutral Expert and has referred it directly to the Court of Arbitration, the highest IWT mechanism for resolving water disputes between India and Pakistan. Pakistan's arguments on Indian projects in the past have lacked technical accuracy, so perhaps it has decided to take a different approach this time around. In addition, India had made major design changes to the Kishanganga project in 2004 and this apparently took 'the sting' out of the more mechanical problems that Pakistan had raised with the dam initially. Only one 'technical' or 'design oriented' objection remains and it pertains directly to the Baglihar proceedings – It is the issue of spillway gates, their necessity in Indian dams and the height at which they should be placed. Despite the legal and binding decision by the Neutral Expert Lafitte, this issue seems to be a recurring theme in Pakistan's stance on Indian dams and it should be addressed once and for all. Perhaps Pakistan is hoping that it can reduce the silting process downstream if it takes measures to ensure that Indian structures store some of the silt discharged in the upper reaches of the river. In any case, referring the Kishanganga project to the Court of Arbitration will amount to an astronomical cost and a large amount of spent resources. The cost of arbitration aside, both Pakistan and India risk suspension of their individual dam projects and the timeline for the completion of these projects is directly correlated to the final cost. The cost of the Kishanganga project is now Rs.3,700 crores or 68% more than its original estimation 20 years ago[54].

As of Dec 2013 after the issuance of the clarifications sought by India, The international court of arbitration has allowed India to go ahead with construction of the Kishanganga dam in Jammu & Kashmir, over which Pakistan has raised objections.

The court delivered its "final award" after India requested clarification of an order issued by it in February. In its "partial award" in February 2014, the court upheld India's main contention that it has the right to divert waters of Western rivers, in a non-consumptive manner, for optimal generation of power. The Western rivers are allocated to Pakistan under the Indus Waters Treaty of 1960. The "final award" specifies that 9 cumecs of natural flow of water must be maintained in Kishenganga river at all times to maintain the environment downstream[55].

Bursar Dam. The Bursar Dam, constructed on the Marusudar River (Chenab tributary) in the Doda District, is the biggest project among a host of others built by India on two major rivers – Jhelum and Chenab, with a generation capacity of 1,020MW and a height of 252ft. According to Pakistan these specifications will be in gross violation of the IWT and will block 2.2MAF of water to Pakistan, however the Indian government has not confirmed the design and has stated that it will give Pakistan notice 6 months before it starts construction or work as is stipulated in the IWT[56]. The Pakistani media has already released information about the potential ecological damage that the dam can cause and the potential humanitarian consequences. It is claiming that 4,900 acres of thick forest would be submerged under water and the entire population of the Hanzal village will have to be displaced.

Pakistan's latest complaint is over the cumulative storage capacity of all the current as well as planned run-of-the-river projects on the Western Rivers of the Indus, particularly those on the Chenab and the Jhelum Rivers. Pakistan claims that individually, the storage capacity in Indian projects on Western Rivers might adhere to the specifications of the IWT; however, their combined capacity will allow India to affect the flow of Western Rivers to Pakistan, especially during the dry season when the flow is extremely low. According to Late Mr B.G. Verghese, a water expert associated with the Centre for Policy Research, "there is no drying up because run-of-the-river projects deplete water only at filling time of new dams. Whether there are 50 or 100 it doesn't matter. You can't store running water." [57] So far India has built 3 major run-of-the-river hydel dams on the Chenab – Salal I & II, Baglihar and Dul Hasti - and they have a combined live capacity or pondage of 264,000 acre feet or 0.264MAF. India's entitled pondage capacity for power storage on the Chenab River, as per the IWT stipulations, is 1.2MAF[58]. According to official figures on the flow of the Chenab the lowest flow, received in the months of January and December, is 0.5BCM or 0.4MAF. The current dam capacity in these three projects is half the quantity of Pakistan's lowest flow period in the Chenab and well below the stipulated capacity of the IWT1.

Pakistan : Delusions of Persecution

To the outside world, it is projected that Pakistan is supporting a struggle for self-determination for the people of Kashmir. However, the mindset of

Pakistan politico –Military leaders can be clearly comprehended with an understanding of Gen Pervez Musharraf's dissertation in 1990 at the Royal College of Defence Studies in London with the title - 'The Arms Race in the Indo-Pakistan Subcontinent, Conflicts with the Pressing Requirements of Socio-economic Development. What are its Causes and Implications? Is there a Remedy?' The paper provided a new analytical framework to define the security paradigm in South Asia. In essence it stated that the basic problem in the region was the divide between the Hindu and Muslim mindset. Since it was a psychological problem, nothing much could be done about it. He reasoned that there were two other core problems and since they wereof practical nature it should be possible to resolve them. One of them was the issue of Jammu & Kashmir, which was known to the international community. The other was about the distribution of the Indus Rivers between India and Pakistan[59]. After General Pervez Musharraf's elevation as Army Chief, he conveyed that the only solution acceptable to Pakistan, to settle its conflicts with India, was *the Chenab Formula*. It was decided that the Chenab Formula should be the basis of discussion with India to resolve the Kashmir conflict. In subsequent deliberations it was conveyed that finding a permanent solution to the India-Pakistan conflict would depend on ensuring Pakistan's water security beyond the Indus Waters Treaty of 1960. Pakistan has directly or indirectly emphasised the Chenab Formula as the most preferred option. It is based on the 'Dixon Plan', proposed in 1950 by Sir Owen Dixon, who came as a United Nation's representative for India and Pakistan. The proposal, though accepted by Pakistan, was rejected by India fifty years ago. As per this formula, the city of Jammu and some districts of Jammu province would go to India, while the city of Srinagar and most parts of the Kashmir valley as well as parts of Jammu region would be transferred to Pakistan. This division would be based on the flow of the Chenab, but it would to some extent coincide with religious demography. An interesting aspect of Pakistan's claim over these districts is that the catchment areas of all the rivers important to Pakistan Indus, Jhelum and Chenab would come under Pakistan's jurisdiction, evidently, the issues of Kashmir and Indus are complex and interconnected.

Criticalities Facing India.

Apart from the common issues already discussed above India is faced with some critical issues of it's own which have sparked the debate seeking abrogation of the IWT or atleast seek a fair review. Pressure on national water resources is said to be high when water withdrawal exceeds 25% of total renewable water resources. This ratio is 34% for India. The fastest increase in water demand in Asia, however, is coming not from agriculture but from the industrial sector and urban households[60]. The United Nations projects that industrial water withdrawals in the world will double between 2000 and 2025, with much of the increase likely to occur in the Asia-Pacific region, 'given its rapidly rising status as a global industrial production centre and the fast growth in subsectors with high water consumption, such as the production of transportation equipment, beverages and textiles'.[61] The fastest rise is projected for India, whose economy is currently led by the services sector but where industrial water use is expected to almost quadruple by 2050 as manufacturing rapidly expands.

Water Availability: Northern India. India's overall per capita water availability has declined from over 5000 cubic metres in 1950 to 1800 cubic metres in 2005. India may reach the threshold level of 1000 cubic metres per capita in 2025[62]. However, some parts of the country are already facing water scarcity conditions below the threshold level. The Northern states of Punjab and Haryana, which form part of the Indus River Basin along with Jammu & Kashmir and Himachal Pradesh, are fearful of a substantial decline in water availability in the next 5-10 years. The underground water levels have been falling at the rate of 5 per cent per year in Punjab and Haryana.

Under Development in J&K. People in J&K have voiced their concerns about this matter several times, stating that the IWT restricts them from using their own waters for agriculture and power generation. The state of Jammu & Kashmir is landlocked and has no significant renewable natural resources other than water. The development potential of this water, however, is highly restricted under the Indus Waters Treaty. The total hydel potential in the state has been assessed at about 20,000MW, mostly on the basis of 'run of the river' schemes with some small storage capacity in the upper reaches of the three Western Rivers, but due to restrictions and pressure from Pakistan J&K's current hydro-electric production stands at 181MW in the State Sector and 690MW in the Central Sector. As per the Jammu and Kashmir planning department the estimated hydro power potential of the Jammu and Kashmir is 20,000 Megawatts (MW), of which about 16480 MW have been identified. Out of the identified potential, only 2457.96 MW 15 % (of identified potential) has been exploited so far, consisting of 760.46 MW in State Sector from 21 power projects, 1680 MW from four power projects under Central Sector i.e. {690 MW Salal Hydel Electric Project, 480 MW Uri-I Hydel Electric Project, Dulhasti 390 MW and 120 MW Sewa-II} and 17.5 MW from two private sector projects. The installed capacity of 760.46 MW from state sector projects includes the 450 MW of Baghlihar Phase–I constructed at a cost of ` 5827 crores by the J&K State Power Development Corporation which was commissioned on 9-10-2008. This State of the Art project is located on Chenab basin at Chanderkote in district Ramban. Energy loss incurred on hydel projects in the entire state, as a result of the IWT restrictions, is around 30-50%. There is practically no effective storage on the main Chenab up to Kishtwar, there is no live storage at Salal and only weekly storage at Baglihar (0.03MAF), Dulhasti (0.007MAF) and a proposed 1.1 MAF on the Bursar project. As a result the potential energy loss in projects like Uri and Salal are 44% and 55% respectively[63]. If J&K was allowed adequate storage capacity during the summer months it could store the surplus water and use it to generate electricity in the winter months. Instead, the state has to pay exorbitant rates for gas based power generation and even has to import power from the central government power stations. In this regard it is important to bear in mind that the J&K State Hydroelectric Projects Development Policy 2011, unveiled in July of that year, clearly spells out plans for setting up several power plants of varying capacities under the state, central, and private sector, which, when completed, will result in the production of 5,756.5 MW of electricity. It is estimated that the state's power demand is likely to be 2,600 MW in 2012–13 and 5,500 MW by 2025–26. It has also been stated that the state will enjoy a power surplus by 2018. Given these figures, one can safely conclude that the state's requirements can easily be fulfilled, provided adequate capacities are built quickly.[64] Jammu and Kashmir is currently undergoing severe shortage of electricity and could gain immensely from tapping into its hydropower potential.

Crystal Ball Gazing

Pakistan's awareness of its vulnerability to its upstream neighbour for economic viability grew during the period of formulating the treaty. Furthermore, its justification for acquiring the Kashmir valley also found credence with the signing of the treaty. The then President Ayub Khan in his broadcast to the nation on September 4, 1960 had stated: "The very fact that we will have to be content with the waters of three Western rivers will underline the importance for us of having physical control on the upper reaches of these rivers to secure their maximum utilisation for the ever growing needs of West Pakistan." The treaty has thus far safeguarded Pakistan's water requirements. It now argues that by submitting to man-made reservoir water, which has inherent complications, Pakistan has accepted an unjust principle of replacing perennial stream water. But it has to be borne in mind that had it not been for the treaty, Pakistan would have remained in eternal conflict with its neighbour. Post-treaty, after more than 50 years, Pakistan has not done enough to manage the ever reducing availability of water . Pakistan still has a solution in hand by improving management of water resources and developing new projects, though it involves huge capital outlay. India, on its part, has never used the treaty as a bargaining lever to restrain Pakistan from providing support to anti national activities in Kashmir. There is an perpetual sense of insecurity in Pakistan's mind given that any call on India's part to change or abrogate the treaty can jeopardise Pakistan's water supply situation. Physically, India is the geographical and political owner of the three rivers ceded to Pakistan by the treaty. If the treaty is revoked, Pakistan stands to lose its lifeline. Assessing the present water situation, it is evident that India has had much to lose while Pakistan has been exposed far less to the water-related adversities. For India, abrogating the treaty is an extreme step, which may be taken only under coercive circumstances as it would violate the treaty. On the other hand, given the bounty that the treaty has bestowed on Pakistan, the country might not entertain even the proposition of renegotiating the treaty. Yet it is Pakistan who continues to misinform it's own citizens and is not taking sufficient measures to manage this ever depleting resource till faced by a crisis.

The Indus Water Treaty is likely to subsist till such time that: -

> India demands an irrevocable renegotiation of the treaty, for reasons including, inter alia, water shortage.

> The political status of Kashmir changes drastically.

> India decides to abrogate the treaty as an extreme step in retaliation to cross-border terrorism.

Endnotes

1   Liviu Giosan et al., "Fluvial landscapes of the Harappan civilization," *Proceedings of the National Academy of Sciences*, Early Edition on-line, forthcoming 2013, http://www.pnas.org/content/early/2012/05/24/1112743109.full.pdf.

2   Connecting The Drops . *An Indus Basin Roadmap for Cross-Border Water Research, Data Sharing, and Policy Coordination*. Indus Basin Working Group http://www.stimson.org/images/uploads/research-   pdfs/connecting_the_drops_stimson.pdf

3   Uttam Kumar Sinha, INDIA'S WATER WOES Sunday, 16 March 2014 | | in Agenda   http://www.dailypioneer.com/sunday-edition/agenda/cover-story/indias-water-woes.html)

4   FAO, "Indus river basin," in *Irrigation in Southern and Eastern Asia in Figures: AQUASTAT Survey 2011*, Karen Frenken ed. (Rome: FAO, 2012), http://www.fao.org/docrep/016/i2809e/i2809e.pdf. Note that some other studies cited in this report furnish slightly different figures for the total basin area and its distribution between the riparian states.

5   Ibid, 2

6   S. Puri and A. Aureli eds., *Atlas of Transboundary Aquifers* (Paris: UNESCO, 2009), http://www.isarm.org/publications/324.

7   Yoshihide Wada et al., "Nonsustainable groundwater sustaining irrigation: A global assessment," *Water Resources Research* 48, W00L06 (2012), p.11, http://onlinelibrary.wiley.com/doi/10.1029/2011WR010562/pdf.

8   Asad Sarwar Quereshi et al., "Challenges and Prospects of Sustainable Groundwater Management in the Indus Basin, Pakistan," *Water Resources Management* 24, no.8 (2010); FAO, "Pakistan country profile," p.384.

9   Jianchu Xu et al., "The Melting Himalayas: Cascading Effects of Climate Change on Water, Biodiversity, and Livelihoods," *Conservation Biology* 23, no.3   (2009),   http://academic.regis.edu/ckleier/conservation%20biology/melting_himalaya.pdf; ICIMOD, *The Status of Glaciers in the Hindu Kush-Himalayan Region* (Kathmandu: ICIMOD, November 2011), http://books.icimod.org/uploads/tmp/icimod-the_status_of_glaciers_in_the_hindu_kush-himalayan_region.pdf; ICIMOD, *Status of Glaciers in the Indus Basin* (Kathmandu: ICIMOD, March 2012), http://geoportal.icimod.org/MENRISFactSheets/Sheets/2icimod-snow_cover_status_and_trends_in_

the_indus_basin.pdf.

10 Laghari et al. p.1069; Sharma et al., "Indo-Gangetic River Basins," p.4.

11 Garg and Hassan; 2030 Water Resources Group, *Charting Our Water Future: Economic Frameworks to Inform Decision-Making* (McKinsey & Company, 2009), http://www.mckinsey.com/App_Media/Reports/Water/Charting_Our_Water_Future_Full_Report_001.pdf.

12 World Bank, *Pakistan's Water Economy: Running Dry* (Washington, DC: World Bank, 2005).

13 ICIMOD, *Climate Change in the Hindu Kush-Himalayas: The State of Knowledge* (Kathmandu: ICIMOD, 2011), National Research Council, *Himalayan Glaciers: Climate Change, Water Resources, and Water Security* (Washington, DC: National Academies Press, 2012).http://lib.icimod.org/record/9417/files/icimod-climate_change_in_the_hindu_kush-himalayas.pdf

14 Ibid, 13

15 Ibid,13

16 ICIMOD, *Climate Change Impacts on the Water Resources of the Indus Basin* (Kathmandu: ICIMOD, March 2010), http://books.icimod.org/uploads/tmp/icimod-climate_change_impacts_on_the_water_resources_of_the_indus_basin:_.pdf.

17 With the advent of the Aswan High Dam, and increased withdrawals within Egypt for agriculture, the amount of fresh water flowing from the River Nile into the Mediterranean Sea is now estimated to be approximately 30,000 mcm or 30 billion cubic metres (bcm) [Gleick, 1993b: 158].

18 FAO, "Indus river basin"; J. Eastham et al., "Water-use accounts in CPWF basins: Simple water-use accounting of the Indus basin," CPWF Working Paper BFP07 (Colombo, Sri Lanka: CGIAR Challenge Program on Water and Food, 2010), http://cgspace.cgiar.org/handle/10568/4696.

19 *AaronT.WolflandJoshua.T.Newton.* ,Case Study of Transboundary Dispute Resolution: the Indus Water Treaty. http://www.transboundarywaters.orst.edu/research/case_studies/Documents/indus.pdf

20 Mark Giordano, Alena Drieschova, James A. Duncan, Yoshiko Sayama, Lucia De Stefano & Aaron T. Wolf , A review of the evolution and state of

transboundary freshwater treaties, 2013 ,. http://www.transboundarywaters. orst.edu/publications/publications/Giordano%20et%20al.%20Treaty%20 Update%204-13.pdf

21 *Ibid,19*

22 The Indus Waters Treaty: A History, Research Pages, Stimson Centre- **http:// www.stimson.org/research-pages/the-indus-waters-treaty-a-history/**

23 *Ibid,19*

24 Maj Rajiv Ahlawat , Dissertation Water Resource Management And Study Of It's Potential As A Source Of Future Conflict In South Asia. Need For A Comprehensive Strategy To Avert Such Regional Crisis, DSSC, 2010

25 The Indus Equation, Strategic Foresight Group. Strategic Foresight Group, 2011 http://www.strategicforesight.com/publication_pdf/10345110617.pdf

26 "Final Settlement: Restructuring India-Pakistan Relations' Strategic Foresight Group, 2005. , Chapter7   http://www.strategicforesight.com/finalsettlement/ lifeline.pdf

27 Brahma Chellaney, Asia's Worsening Water Crisis- Posted on March 17, 2012..:. *Survival* | vol. 54 no. 2 | April–May 2012 | pp. 143–156, DOI: 10.1080/00396338.2012.672806   http://chellaney.net/2012/03/17/asias-worsening-water-crisis/

28 Uttam Kumar Sinha , Arvind Gupta & Ashok Behuria: Will the Indus Water Treaty Survive?, Strategic Analysis, 36:5, 735-752, (2012) http://dx.doi.org/10 .1080/09700161.2012.712376

29 Subrahmanyam Sridhar, The Indus Water Treaty, Security Research Review, Volume 13, www.bharat-rakshak.com.

30 Dr Parajuli U et al; Water Sharing Conflicts Between Countries, and Approaches to Resolving Them , Water and Security in South Asia (WASSA) Projects, Volume III, p42 http://www.gee-21.org/publications/Water-Sharing-Conflicts-Between-Countries-and-Approaches-to-Resolving-Them.pdf

31 Article III, 'Provisions Regarding Western Rivers' of the Indus Water Treaty with details in Annexure C, D and E. Under agricultural use, the total area permitted to be irrigated by India is 1.34 million acres. Out of the 3.6 MAF, 1.25 is general storage, 1.6 is for generation of hydroelectricity and 0.75 for flood control. In terms of rivers, 0.4 MAF is permitted on the Indus, 1.5 on

helum and 1.7 on Chenab.

32 Ibid, 30 http://www.gee-21.org/publications/Water-Sharing-Conflicts-Between-Countries-and-Approaches-to-Resolving-Them.pdf

33 Undala Z. Alam, *Water Rationality: Mediating the Indus Water Treaty*, September 1998, (unpublished PhD thesis from University of Durham, UK, 1998) (Accessed 22 March 2014). According to the water rationality thesis, countries would prefer cooperation to conflict to promote long-term security of their water supplies (p. 24).

34 The Indus basin is an important geophysical part of the Indian subcontinent. The Indus, together with the Chenab, Ravi, Sutlej, Jhelum, Beas and the extinct Sarasvati, constitutes the basin. TheIndus basin has a total area of 11,65,500 km2 with annual available waters of 207 Billion Cubic Meters (BCM). The basin countries are Pakistan (632,954 km2), India (374,887 km2), China (86,432 km2) and Afghanistan (76,542 km2). Downloaded by [117.222.208.6] at 07:08 03 March 2014 .*Strategic Analysis* 749

35 Ibid, 33

36 Ibid,26

37 Abdul Rauf Iqbal, ISSRA PAPERS VOL-V, ISSUE-I, 2013Institute for Strategic Studies, Research and Analysis (ISSRA) National Defence University, Islamabad http://www.ndu.edu.pk/issra/issra_pub/issra_paper/ISSRA-PAPERS-VOL-V,ISSUE-I,-2013.pdf

38 Mukand S. Babel and Shahriar M. Wahid, *Freshwater Under Threat: South Asia* (Bangkok/Nairobi: Asian Institute of Technology/UNEP, 2008), p.14, http://www.unep.org/pdf/southasia_report.pdf; Mats Eriksson et al., *The Changing Himalayas: Impact of Climate Change on Water Resources and Livelihoods in the Greater Himalayas* (Kathmandu: ICIMOD, 2009), p.2, http://books.icimod.org/index.php/search/publication/593.

39 Ibid, 25

40 Ibid, 2

41 Ibid, 2

42 Ibid, 25

43 Ibid, 25

44 'Water not Stolen in India but Wasted in Pakistan: Qureshi' Outlook India, April 2010. http://news.outlookindia.com/item.aspx?678581

45 Ibid, 25

46 Ibid, 25

47 Bharat Verma , Indian Defence Review:, Lancer Publishers Oct-Dec 2010,

48 'ibid,26

49 Ibid,26

50 Ibid, 25

51 The Tulbul project is a "navigation lock-cum-control structure" at the mouth of the Wullar Lake. It envisages regulated water release from the natural storage in the lake to maintain a minimum draught of 4.5 feet in the river up to Baramulla during the lean winter months. This is to ensure round-the year navigation from Anantnag to Srinagar to Baramulla, a distance of over 20 km. India views it as permissible under the IWT, while Pakistan maintains that the project is in violation. India says suspension of work is harming the interests of people of Jammu and Kashmir and also depriving the people of Pakistan of irrigation and power benefits that may accrue from regulated water releases.

52 "Draft: Indus Water Treaty and Managing Shared Water Resources for the Benefit of Basin States – policy issues and Options" IUCN, 2010. http://cmsdata.iucn.org/downloads/pk_ulr_d1_2.pdf.

53 Indus Waters Kishenganga Arbitration (Pakistan v. India) http://www.pca-cpa.org/formulier_members.asp?pag_id=1161

54 Iyer, Ramaswamy. "Arbitration & Kishanganga Project" The Hindu, 25 June 2010. http://www.thehindu.com/opinion/ lead/article485555.ece

55 India allowed to go ahead with J&K's Kishanganga project. The Times of India, 21 Dec 13 http://timesofindia.indiatimes.com/india/India-allowed-to-go-ahead-with-JKs-Kishanganga-project/articleshow/27738180.cms

56 Hasan, Munawar "India Gives Go Ahead to another Dam on Chenab IHK" International The News, 14 March 2010. http://thenews.jang.com.pk/TodaysPrintDetail.aspx?ID=27783&Cat=13&dt=3/14/2010

57 Verghese, B.G. "An inconvenient truth: Responding to Pakistan's Water Concerns and Challenges" Writings and Commentaries – BG Verghese, 8

June, 2010. http://www.bgverghese.com/PakistanWater.html .

58 Avoiding Water Wars: Water Scarcity and Central Asia's Growing Importance for Stability in Afghanistan and Pakistan . Prepared for the Committee on Foreign Relations United States Senate, 22 February 2011

59 Ibid,26

60 Asia's Worsening Water Crisis- Posted on March 17, 2012. Brahma Chellaney.: http://chellaney.net/2012/03/17/asias-worsening-water-crisis/. *Survival* | vol. 54 no. 2 | April–May 2012 | pp. 143–156, DOI: 10.1080/00396338.2012.672806

61 UN Economic and Social Commission for Asia and the Pacific, *State of theEnvironment in Asia and the Pacific*, p. 63.

62 Ibid,26

63 Akhtar, Shaheen. "Emerging Challenges to Indus Waters Treaty". Institute of Regional Studies, Islamabad. http://www.irs.org.pk/PublFocus.htm#_ftn1

64 Arpita Anant, Beyond the Indus Water Treaty: A Perspective on Kashmir's "Power" Woes http://www.idsa.in/idsacomments/BeyondtheIndusWaterTreaty_aanant_020212 . - IDSA COMMENT February 2, 2012

CHAPTER – 4 : SINO – INDIAN ISSUES

*"If mediation is successful, the parties take the credit: if it fails,
the mediator gets the blame"*

– [Bailey, 1985: 222].

Background

Geographically, China's water resources are unevenly distributed, with Northern China's water availability per person only a fraction of that in the rainy South. China's huge population of more than 1.3 billion, a third of which is concentrated in the relatively dry Huang-Huai-Hai river basins of North China, is a major factor in China's low per capita water availability[1]. A detailed look at the related statistics of water, land us, water use, arable land etc gives a lucid picture of China's dilemma of water despite having a considerably high per capita availability of water. Climate change is disrupting weather patterns and accelerating the evaporation of glaciers, further diminishing surface water supplies. In addition, increasingly widespread pollution from industrial and domestic wastewater discharges of China's surface water resources and 90 percent of China's rivers near urban areas has not only taken a toll on human health[2], but also has contributed to shortages that have led to a rising dependence on groundwater. A consequence has been that critical rivers, lakes and wetlands are drying up. Water table levels also are falling, causing land subsidence in some areas.[3]

The scramble for control of natural resources to support economic and population growth, combined with the uncertain effects of climate change on the Tibetan Plateau, is raising tensions in Asia over Himalayan water resources. Ten of the region's largest and longest rivers (the Amu Darya, Brahmaputra, Ganges, Indus, Irrawaddy, Mekong, Salween, Tarim, Yangtze, and Yellow) originate in the Himalayas (Figure 47)[4].

China's Water Issues

There is ample evidence and literature to prove that China is water insecure and its insecurity primarily relates to the disproportionate availability or uneven distribution of waters within its territory. In the later half of the 20th century, China realized that it was in the midst of an acute water crisis[5]. The water resources are primarily in the South (Tibet) with the North and West excessively water stressed. The region South of the Yangtze river, which accounts for roughly 36 per cent of Chinese territory, has 81 per cent of water resources. The territories North of the Yangtze, where much water is required, make up 64 per cent but have a meagre 19 per cent of water capacity[6].

Figure 47- Rivers of Tibetan Plateau

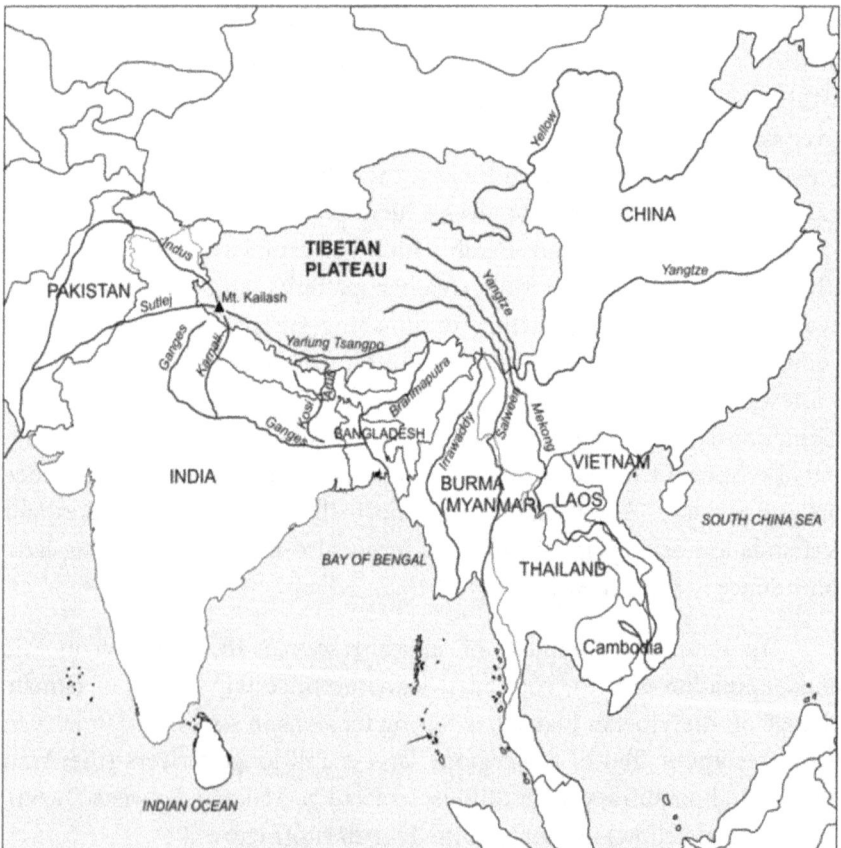

The land of the dragon is quickly turning into the land of the thirsty dragon [7]. The spreading water crisis, which already affects more than half of country's 660 cities, is largely sourced in its strikingly uneven distribution of water resources. The worst affected area in China is the North East region particularly the Huabei region. The Huabei region includes four provinces (Hebei, Shanxi, Shandong and Henan), two cities (Beijing and Tianjing) and one municipality of Inner Mongolia. This region is the Chinese centre of politics, economy and culture besides being an important source of food supplies. The arid North and Northwest, home to 35% of the population, has only 7% of the country's water resources.[8] While China's water reserves, estimated at around 280,000 bcms, accord it the sixth rank in the world in terms of fresh water reserves, due to its huge population, it ranks as low as 121st in terms of per capita availability[9]. Compared to the world average of 10,900 m3 per capita per annum (1997 figures), China's per capita availability, estimated at 2,220 m^3, is less than 1/5th of the world's average. [10]

Figure 48: Water Availability: China

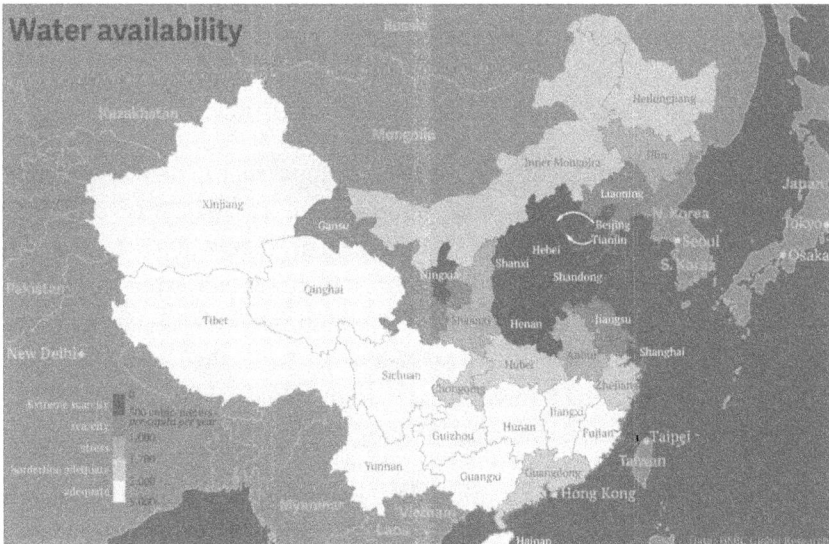

According to the water resources ministry, the total water resources in China in 2007 amounted to 2469.6 billion cubic metres, of which the surface water resources were 2376.4 billion cubic metres.[11] The figures become very interesting when we observe that the amount of water that flowed *into* Chinese territory from outside was only 15.7 billion cubic metres. In comparison, the water that flowed *out* of the territory was 569.9 billion cubic metres. China has much in the total volume of water resources but less in per capita volume. The available water resources per capita were 1869 cubic metres on average. What is to be noted is that the total amount of water resources is decreasing. The amount of total water supply in 2007 was 578.9 billion cubic metres, of which surface water was 470.4 billion (81.2 per cent) and groundwater 105.8 billion (18.3 per cent).[12]

China is expected to face a 25 per cent supply gap in the projected water demand by 2030, with two-thirds of its cities already facing difficulty in accessing water. Having put in place the structures as part of its strategic objective, China in December 2010 decided to accelerate the reform and development of water resources, as per the No. 1 Document in 2011. The document focuses on three 'red lines': over-exploitation, usage efficiency, and pollution[13].

These facts suggest that China is water insecure and its insecurity primarily relates to the disproportionate availability or uneven distribution of waters within its territory, the majority of which are in the South (Tibet) with the North and West excessively water stressed.

Precipitation, Usage and Consumption in China

China has lower levels of precipitation compared to many developed countries. As per the Data and figures from the Ministry of Water Resources, People's Republic of China, Annual Report 2007–2008 , the mean annual precipitation was 606.3 mm, which was converted into a total amount of annual precipitation of 5,741 billion m^3, 0.7% less than that of the year before or 5.7 % less than average year. While the national average rainfall is registered at 2.9 m3/100 acres, in the Huabei region, it is 1/5th or 1/6th that of the national average.

Much of China's water is utilized for irrigation. Apart from inefficient use of water for agricultural purposes, rampant urbanisation and industrialisation have also contributed to the water scarcity. In large cities, the problem has become more critical due to water pollution. Extensive mining has also taken a toll on water, areas which had substantial ground water reserve are now suffering from shortfall. Desertification in the North Western region of China has been taking place for centuries. China's capital

Figure 49 : Population Breakout Per Basin: China

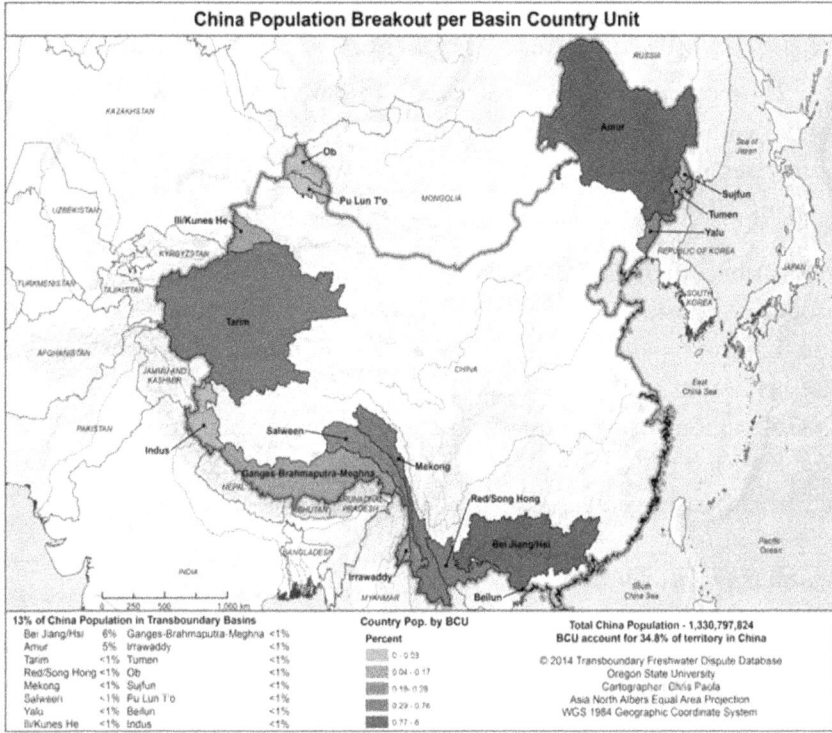

Beijing, Tianjin (the fourth largest city) and the historic city of Xian suffer from an acute water shortage.

While China has 7 % of the world's arable land and only 8% of the world's fresh water, it has to support 21% of the world's population. With the Chinese government laying emphasis on maintaining a 'basic' (i.e at least 95%) grain self-sufficiency, the water utilisation for agricultural purpose would remain high. Since grains, particularly rice, are an important part of Chinese diet, paddy cultivation, which is water intensive, will continue to utilise the bulk of available water. As it is, flood irrigation has led to a major problem of salinity / alkalisation of arable land in China. A clear linkage has been identified by observers between depletion of water resources in the North China plain to the increase in rice cultivation in the area.[14]

China's demand in 2030 is expected to reach 818 billion m3, of which just over 50 percent is from agriculture (of which almost half is for rice),

32 percent is industrial demand driven by thermal power generation, and the remaining is domestic. Current supply amounts to just over 618 billion m³ [15]. Significant industrial and domestic wastewater pollution makes the "qualityadjusted" supply-demand gap even larger than the quantity-only gap: 21 percent of available surface water resources nationally are unfit even for agriculture. Thermal power generation is by far the largest industrial water user, despite the high penetration of water-efficient technology, and is facing increasing limitations in the rapidly urbanizing basins [16].

Water scarcity is already doing measurable harm to China's economic productivity, with reduced river flows affecting hydropower generation and limiting expansion of water-dependent industries—from coal mining and petroleum refining to steel production to higher-tech industries, such as semi-conductors—all are increasingly constrained by the lack of water. Notably, most of China's coal resources are in the arid North whereas some of China's largest coal reserves remain untapped due to water shortages.

Managing The Deficit

Finding ways to augment China's water supply is therefore an increasingly pressing concern of China's policy leaders. Historically, water shortages in China have been redressed principally by engineering physical transfers of water to augment supply [17]. Water conservancy infrastructure has long been an important measure for stabilising the state, developing production and extending territory in China. [18] Dating back to the Han Dynasty, chain pumps were used to move water from lower to higher elevations to irrigate fields or to provide water to urban dwellers. The senior leaders have followed the philosophy of treating this as a very serious issue and sought solutions with aggressive intervention and technology. The past two and half decades have been an era of long-distance water transfer projects—all to dry Northern cities. These have included projects involving transfers from the Biluhe River to Dalian, the Huanhe to Qingdao, the Lanhe to Tianjin, and the Luanhe to Tangshan, among others [19] Much of the one trillion Yuan allocated for public investment in the water sector in China's 11th Five-Year Plan (2006-2010) was for diverting water supplies to cities experiencing water shortfalls [20].

The Water Diversion Projects

South-North Water Transfer Project (SNWTP). The most ambitious and best known of the diversion projects as first mooted by Mao Zedong in the 1952, involves diverting water from the South to the North along three routes.[21] China has completed its ambitious $80 billion 'South-to-North Water Diversion Project' with world's longest canal and pipelines spanning 1400 kms, transferring water to its arid Northern regions including the capital, amid concerns over its adverse environmental impact. The project was approved by the State Council in December 2002, after nearly half-a-century of debate.

The project took eight-years to be completed and involves two 4,000-meter-long tunnels under the riverbed of the Yellow River, China's second largest river[22]. The project will transfer water from the Yangtze river, China's largest river, to the arid Northern regions. In 2003, its project cost was estimated to be around $59 billion which spiralled to $80 billion by the end of its completion. It is the second biggest water project undertaken by China after the Three Gorges dam regarded as the world's biggest hydro-power dam. The first-stage of the project, the Eastern route, went into operation in 2013, sending water to Shandong province. By 2050, as many as 440 million people could benefit from the diversion of 44.8 billion cubic meters of water each year.

The project's transfer of vast volumes of water from the Yangtze River Basin clearly reflects the prioritization of North China's water needs over those of the donor basin region in South-central China. Supplying the NCP with water — while certainly a pressing concern requiring immediate attention for social and economic as well as political reasons , is ultimately more important to the Chinese government at present than maintaining a healthy water supply for other major cities like over the long term. In addition to a 80 billion USD price tag, constructing the world's largest water transfer project to date has required the relocation of more than 330,000 people[23], many of whom are dissatisfied with the compensation packages they have received. Environmental impacts, including a dramatic decline in the volume of the Yangtze River (of which the Han is a major tributary), estuary salinization, and the breakdown of biogeographic barriers[24],[25] are expected as a result of the project. The pattern emerging in the wake of the SNWTP is the reinforcement and potential exacerbation of existing rural-urban and regional inequalities. Rural-urban and regional inequality are a major feature of post-reform China[26]. The case of China's SNWTP reminds us of the fundamentally political nature of water management in the twenty-first century. The SNWTP reflect existing spatially articulated power discrepancies, as it reinforces and potentially exacerbates those inequalities by prioritizing Beijing's present and future water needs above those of its neighbours and locking them in place for the future. The SNWTP, as conceived by the Chinese Government does not envisage diversion of the waters of the Yarlung Tsangpo (tributary of the Brahmaputra). The details of the SNWTP are given in succeeding paragraphs.[27]:-

Figure 50 : Map of the South-North Water Transfer Project China

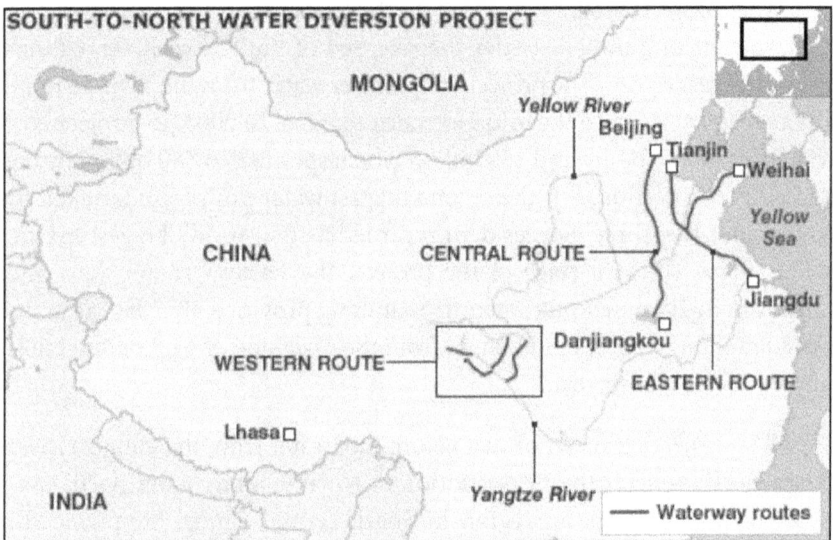

Source: Global Water Forum

Eastern Route. It commenced in December 2002, the waters pumped from the lower reaches of the Chang Jiang will be transferred to North China. Diverted from a major branch of Yangtze River, the water travels along existing river channels to the Weishan mountains of Shandong, before crossing the Yellow River via a tunnel and flowing to Tianjin. It aims to supply Shandong province and the Northern part of Jiangsu, linking Shandong with the Yangtze River and bringing water North to the Huang-Huai-Hai Plain via the Beijing-Hangzhou Grand Canal. The trunk of the water diversion is approximately 1,155 km and involved the construction of 23 pumping stations.

Central or Middle Route. The middle route begins at Danjiangkou reservoir, in Hubei province, and runs for 1,200 km[28]. It will supply 9.5 billion cubic meters of water per year to 100 million people in the Northern regions, including the cities of Beijing and Tianjin. It marks the completion of the middle route's first stage, construction of which began exactly 12 years ago. It took eight years for engineers and workers to complete two 4,000-metre-long tunnels under the riverbed of the Yellow River, China's second largest . The project's Middle Route, completed on December 25, 2013, will transfer 3.5 trillion gallons of water annually from the Danjiangkou Reservoir, fed by the Han River basin in central China, Northward to the North China Plain (NCP)[29] . The route has been designed so that water will flow from its source to its end point by gravity alone. A major engineering challenge has been the need to increase the storage capacity and therefore the height of the Danjiangkou Dam has been increased from its original 157m to 170m. In a striking display of Chinese engineering muscle, both the Eastern and Central routes will run under the Yellow River[30].

Western Route. Construction on the Western route, which involves working on the Qinghai-Tibet Plateau, between 3,000 to 5,000 m above sea level has commenced in 2010 and will involve overcoming some major engineering and climatic challenges. When completed in 2050, the project will bring 4 bcm in the first stage from three tributaries of the Yangtze River (the Tongtian, Yalong and Dadu – in some literature there is a reference to Jinsha) to nearly 500 km across the Bayankala mountains and then on to Northwest China. Construction will involve 300 km relay of tunnels and channels. The project will be completed in three stages. After the three stages are completed, 17 bcm of water is expected to be diverted through this project.

The Eastern and the Middle Route will not have any impact on India. Even the Western Route, as presently approved, will only draw upon the waters of the Yangtze River. However, according to experts, by 2030 the entire Yangtze River Basin will suffer from water shortages[31]. Thus, there will be no surplus water in Yangtze river to redirect Northwards. A severe drought along the Yangtze river region has brought water levels to near record low.

However, according to observers, the SNWTP as it is presently approved, is only Phase I of the project. Phase II of the SNWTP will incorporate the Guo Kai (or He Zuoxiu) proposal of diverting waters from the Yarlung Tsangpo, the Nujiang (Salween) and the Lancang (Mekong) which will sustain the project of bringing waters to the North. Thus, it is the Great Western River Diversion Project (GWRDP) which is presently still in the consideration stage which will, effectively, impact India and Bangladesh.

Guo Kai's Proposal or the Shuotian Canal

Veteran hydrologist Guo Kai[32] advocated the idea of diverting waters from the rivers of Tibet to Northern China , in the 1980s,. The Great Western Route Project of Guo Kai envisaged diversion of, 200.6 bcm waters annually, from Tibetan rivers i.e the Yarlung Tsangpo, Lancang and the Nujiang. The project was to be completed in 10 years as against the Chinese national plan of the SNWTP which would take 50 years to complete and, at approx 200 billion yuan (around US $ 25 billion) would cost roughly only a third of the SNWTP's costs (estimated to cost US$ 62 billion)[33].

After several years of discussions and political support for and against the project surveys were carried out. The proposal remained lo key until November 2005, when the publication of Li Ling's book, "Save China Through Water From Tibet", once again revived the debate.

Figure 51 : The Shuotian Canal

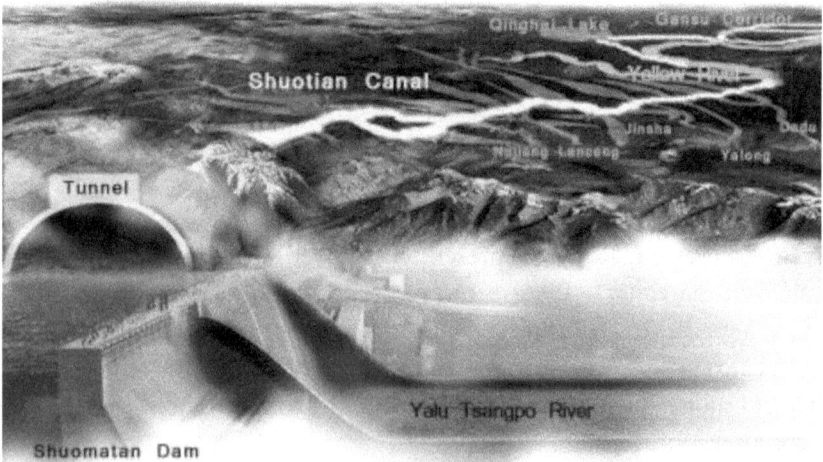

Source: www.water-technology.net

The Shuotian Canal (as the canal connecting Shuomatan (or Chomathang, the mouth of the Yarlung Tsangpo) in Tibet to Tianjin canal in China's east coast). The Shuotian Canal project involves the following :-

(a) Construction of a dam at Shuomatan across the Yarlung Tsangpo in Tibet, thereby raising the water level to a height of 3588 m and drawing water up to Bomi and Song Zong passing through the watershed, at an altitude of 3500 meters into the Nujiang (River Salween).

(b) Construction of a dam on the Dujiang at Xia li Shuo Wa Ba, raising the water level to a height of 3500 m and letting the backwaters, after crossing Jia Yu Qiao enter the Lancangjiang (River Mekong) through a tunnel at Mali.

(c) Construction of a dam at Chamdo to block water, and then drawing into the Jinsha river through tunnels and across the watershed.

(d) Blocking the Jinsha river waters, with a dam to raise water level to a height of 3469 m, allowing the water to enter Zengqu in the Baiyu county of Sichuan province and then diverting the water into the Yalong river through tunnels and across the watershed at Ganze.

(e) Building a dam across the Yalong river to turn the water eastward across the watershed and to enable the water level to reach a height of 3454 m and then through tunnels to take it to the Sequ-Duke rivers in the upper reaches of the Dadu river.

(f) Building a reservoir at the mouth of the Sequ and Duke rivers and then drawing the waters into Maerke river and thereafter up to Abachalisi and across the watershed to enter the Yellow River at an altitude of 3399 m marking the completion of the of the first stage.

(g) After entering the Yellow River, the water will flow into the Yellow River La Jia Gorge Reservoir and then flow in the La Qing Grand Canal for 216 kms to enter the shallow waters of the Erhaiyan Lake, thus becoming a water source for Xinjiang, Gansu, Inner Mongolia, Ningxia, Hebei, Beijing and Tianjin. Part of the water will run down the lower reaches of the Yellow River catering to the needs of Shaanxi, on Henan and Shandong.

The actual length of the project would be 1239 kms. It would involve six tunnels with a length of 240 kms, the longest being 60 kms. Since the route of the project would be over terrain which is sparsely populated and also which allows free flow movement, there would be minimal inundation approximately 25,000 people are estimated to be affected by the project.

Dams : A Solution In China

According to international projections, the total number of dams in developed countries in the next ten years is likely to remain about the same, while much of the dam building in the developing world, in terms of aggregate storage-capacity buildup, is expected to be concentrated in Asia, especially China.[34] which has more than half of the approximately 50,000 *large* dams on the planet [35] . Indeed, about four-fifths of all dams currently under construction in Asia are in China alone[36].

The numerous new dam projects in China and elsewhere show that the damming of rivers remains an important priority for Asian policymakers. Dam building on transnational rivers, however, is already stoking inter-riparian tensions in Asia. China has adopted the doctrine of prior appropriation, which legitimizes the principle "First in time, first in right." Under this doctrine of customary international water law, the first user of river waters (whether an upstream or downstream state) acquires a priority right to the continued utilisation of river waters, as long as those resources are diverted for "beneficial" applications, including irrigation, industrial or mining purposes, electric power generation, and municipal supply. One trend in Asia, best epitomized by China, is toward giant dam projects. China has graduated from building large dams to constructing mega-dams. The world's largest dam, the Three Gorges Dam on the Yangtze in China, has an installed power-generating capacity of 18.3 gigawatts (GW) . Other examples of mega-dams in China include its latest addition on the international Mekong River — the 4,200 megawatt (MW) Xiaowan, which dwarfs Paris's Eiffel Tower in height — and a proposed 38 GW dam on River Brahmaputra at Metog ("Motuo" in Chinese), close to the disputed, heavily militarized border with India. The Metog Dam will be twice as large as the Three Gorges Dam, according to HydroChina Corporation, a leading state-owned dam builder. The 5,850 MW Nuozhadu Dam, nearing completion on the Mekong, is bigger than even Xiaowan.

Most of the new dams and other water diversions in Tajikistan, Kyrgyzstan, Pakistan, Tibet, Nepal India, Bhutan, Burma, and Laos are concentrated in the Great Himalayan Watershed. In fact, two thirds of China's hydropower potential is located on the Tibetan Plateau, including the so-called Tibet Autonomous Region (TAR) and the Tibetan areas in Yunnan and Sichuan provinces. The Great Himalayan Watershed, with the world's third largest ice mass after the Arctic and Antarctic regions, is probably the "most critical region" in terms of the likely impact of the global-warming-induced ,accelerated glacial thaw on water supplies.[37] In the broader Himalayan region, "tensions between countries over the proper management and equitable allocation of water resources mean that the potential for international conflict is high. China's multiple dam projects in the Great Himalayan Watershed, including the Brahmaputra and Arun river basins, have, for example, prompted India to initiate its own dam-building program in the Himalayas. China and India are not only competing to build dams along their disputed high altitude frontier, but also are aiding other states' plans to tap river resources in the Great Himalayan watershed. While Chinese firms are involved in dam building in Pakistan-controlled Kashmir, Nepal, and Myanmar, India is aiding some Bhutanese and Nepalese dam projects.

China, whose major dam building activities have increasingly moved to the Tibetan Plateau, has a hydrological and strategic advantage over other countries in the Great Himalayan Watershed because almost all the major Asian rivers originate on its side of the highlands. The rivers include the Yangtze, the Yellow, the Mekong, the Salween, the Irrawaddy, the Arun, the Brahmaputra, the Karnali, and the Indus. Two key Central Asian rivers — the Amu Darya and the Tarim — rise in the Western rim of this watershed. The Ganges is the only great Asian river that rises on the Indian side of the Himalayan rim. But whereas the Ganges' primary source — the Gangotri Glacier — and point of origin are on the Indian side of the Himalayas, this mighty river's main tributaries flow in from the Chinese controlled Himalayan areas. These tributaries include the Karnali, the Gandak, and the Kosi (whose uppermost part is called the Arun). These actually are Nepal's principal river systems, and they drain into the Ganges in India. These highlands help shape climatic and rainfall patterns in multiple ways. In the summer, the Tibet Plateau's rocky and lofty terrain heats up quickly to form a low- pressure system that helps attract monsoonal currents from the east, Southeast, and Southwest — that is, from the East and South

China Seas, the Bay of Bengal, the Indian Ocean, and the Arabian Sea. By acting as a high-elevation heat pump, this region helps make rain. Chinese experts have estimated that there are about 15,000 large glaciers just in the Himalayan region of China; if the smaller glaciers are also counted, that figure jumps to 36,793 [38]. The Himalayan portion in Tibet has at least three times more glacier area than the part in India. Indeed, other than some glaciers in Xinjiang, China's glaciers are all concentrated on the Tibetan Plateau, including the areas that have been taken out of Tibet and either merged with Sichuan, Gansu, and Yunnan or turned into the separate province of Qinghai. China actually has renamed the Tibetan Plateau the "Qinghai-Tibetan Plateau."

By ramping up the size of its dams, China now not only boasts the world's largest number of mega-dams, but it has also emerged as the biggest global producer of hydropower, with an installed generating capacity of nearly 230 gigawatts [39]. The serious environmental and social problems spawned by the Three Gorges Dam—which officially uprooted 1.7 million Chinese—have failed to dampen China's hyperactive dam building. In its 2013 actions, China's State Council, seeking to boost the country's hydropower capacity by another 120 gigawatts, identified 54 new dams—in addition to the ones currently under construction—as "key construction projects" in a revised energy-sector plan up to 2015. Most of the new dams are planned in the biodiversity-rich Southwest, where natural ecosystems and indigenous cultures are increasingly threatened. Among the slew of newly approved dam projects are five on the Salween and three each on the Brahmaputra and the Mekong. China has already built six mega-dams on the Mekong, the lifeblood for continental Southeast Asia.

The greater the dependence of a river system on glacial meltwaters for sustaining its flows, the greater is its vulnerability to the effects of climate and environmental change. The Yellow and the Yangtze basins, for instance, contain limited glaciated area, but the opposite is true of the Brahmaputra and the Indus, both of which flow extensively through high-altitude terrain along the Himalayas. The late-spring and summer discharges of the Brahmaputra and the Indus are likely to reduce "considerably" between 2046 and 2065, according to one study, "after a period of increased flows due to accelerated glacier melt [40]". Such flow reduction will pose a serious threat to economic security and social stability in their downstream basins. The Brahmaputra is the single largest source of freshwater for Bangladesh, which heavily depends on cross-border inflows. Bangladesh indeed is likely to bear the brunt of climate change because of its low-lying position and lack of money and technology to protect itself. More than half of Bangladesh's transboundary water supplies, totaling 1,106 billion m3 per year, are delivered by the Brahmaputra alone[41].

Chinese Plans for Trans-Border Rivers[42]

The Indus river flows for a very short distance in Indian territory (Ladakh region of Jammu & Kashmir) before entering the Northern Areas occupied by Pakistan. Given the difficult terrain in India, very little survey work has been done on the river; it is exploited only for subsistence irrigation. On the other hand, the Sutlej is one of the largest tributaries of the Indus system and the mainstay of Punjab, Haryana and Rajasthan. Besides irrigation, the Sutlej has several major hydroelectric projects on its waters as already elaborated in the previous chapter. Reportedly, NRSA data indicate the existence of 13 small to medium dam like structures on the Sutlej[43]. A 2006 report also mentioned that a barrage had been built across the Zada gorge on the Sutlej waters in Western Tibet to supply electricity to Zada town [44]. On the Brahmaputra river system, Chinese plans for the Yarlung Tsangpo have three aspects; construction of six dams in the upper reaches[45] to the Yellow River and production of 40,000 MW of hydropower at the Great Bend[46].

Figure 52 : Transboundary River Basins in China

Figure 52 : Transboundary River Basins in China

% of Transboundary Basins in China					
Bei Jiang/Hsi	97%	389,510 (km²)	Yalu	51%	31,724 (km²)
Tarim	96%	1,048,443 (km²)	Amur	43%	889,168 (km²)
Beilun	85%	712 (km²)	Mekong	21%	164,737 (km²)
Pu Lun T'o	80%	38,786 (km²)	Ganges-Brahmaputra-Meghna	19%	317,673 (km²)
Tumen	68%	22,719 (km²)	Ili/Kunes He	14%	57,006 (km²)
Sujfun	60%	10,024 (km²)	Indus	10%	82,276 (km²)
Red/Song Hong	54%	75,049 (km²)	Irrawaddy	6%	21,443 (km²)
Salween	52%	136,762 (km²)	Ob	2%	50,044 (km²)

China BCU total area- 3,336,076 (km²)
China total area- 9,353,837 (km²)
BCU accounts for 35.6% of territory in China
© 2014 Transboundary Freshwater Dispute Database
Oregon State University
Cartographer: Chris Paola
Asia North Albers Equal Area Projection
WGS 1984 Geographic Coordinate System

While reports on possible diversion of the Brahmaputra waters by China cannot be ignored, they are certainly exaggerated. In the year 2000, the Chinese Academy of Engineering (CAE) published its "Strategic Study on Sustainable Development of China's Water Resources in the 21st Century", wherein the technical feasibility and financially viability of the project was analysed[47].

Figure 53 : Transboundary River Basins Withdrawals in China

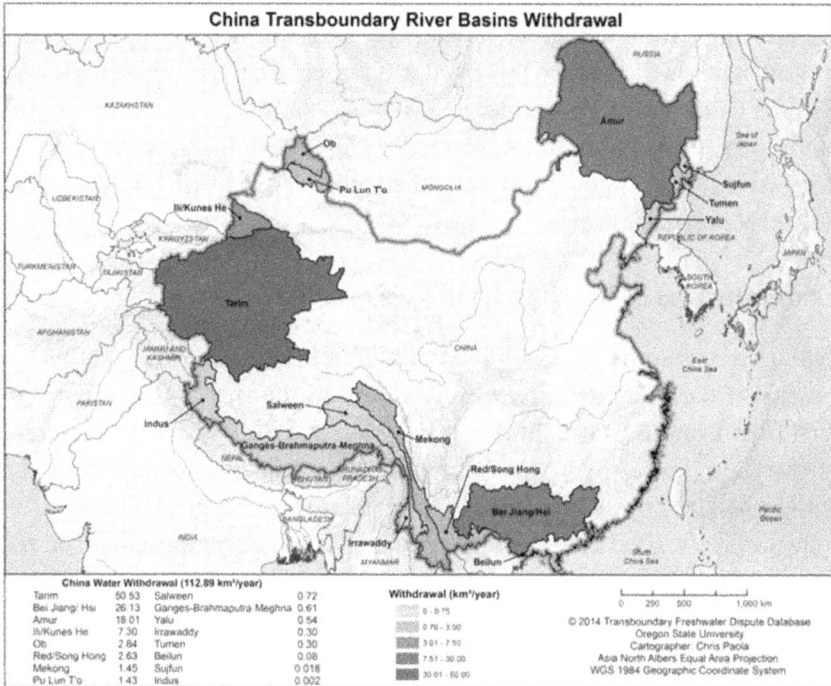

China's Stand and Her Capabilities

Officially, China denies its intention to divert the waters of the Brahmaputra. In November 2006, the state-run "China Daily" published Minister Wang Shucheng's comments on the Guo Kai plan which he termed as "unnecessary, unfeasible and unscientific". The spokesperson of the Chinese Foreign Ministry also stated clearly that the "Chinese government has no plans to build a dam on the Yarlung Tsangpo River to divert water to the Yellow River"[48] Since these statements coincided with the visit of the then President Hu Jintao to India they were obviously made to address Indian concerns over the project. The proposal has its share of critics within China and that the Chinese will carefully examine all parameters before taking such a decision, it does not rule out the project taking shape sometime in the future. It is felt that China's technological capabilities and national determination are stupendous. The completion of the Gormo-Lhasa railway project is proof of their stupendous capabilities. Those who believe that China is likely to go in for such an option point out that the current leadership is optimally placed to take such a decision. The erstwhile President Hu Jintao was a post-graduate in "water conservancy engineering" from Qinghua University, had worked for hydroelectric projects and in the Ministry of Water Conservancy and Power. He was also the Communist Party chief in Tibet, was familiar with the geography of the area and supported the proposal[49]. The present hierarchy is similarly aggressive and technologically qualified and is likely to support major technical projects for national interests.

Consequences of Possible Chinese Projects[50]

While there is some conjecture regarding the Indus river system, there is paucity of hard data on Chinese activities, on the waters within Tibetan territory. Even the yields of the Indus main and Sutlej rivers at the point of entry into India are not available. One view is that any diversion on the Sutlej will have downstream effect and may lead to the type of serious inter-state problems as existing between Punjab, Haryana and Rajasthan, on the issue of Ravi-Beas waters. Also major hydroelectric projects are located on the Sutlej. The breach of a landslide dam on the waters of the Parechu river, a minor tributary of the Sutlej in Tibet, had tragic consequences in Himachal Pradesh in the year 2000; a larger diversion could do far greater damage.

Regarding the Yarlung Tsangpo, there is a large volume of literature available, although most of it is clearly alarmist. Guo Kai had projected the Shuotian Canal project to be beneficial to India and Bangladesh since China could increase water supply to them when they suffer from drought conditions and prevent waters from flowing down when there is flood during the monsoon[51]. If the average annual yield of Brahmaputra at Pandu (Assam) is 493.3 bcm (including the 160 bcm yield available at the boundary) and the Guo Kai proposal involves diversion of 40 bcm (22 bcm during monsoon and 18 bcm in low season) this would amount to less than 10 % of the total yield of the Brahmaputra. If one looks at the yield at the boundary alone, this would amount to diversion of 25% of the Yarlung Tsangpo's waters. However, during lean season, flow at the border is only 85% thus this proposal would lead to 1/7th of the total waters[52] in non-monsoon period being diverted. Interestingly, discourse in China has projected the Shuotian Canal project as being beneficial to India and Bangladesh since China could decrease water supply to these countries when they suffer from floods and increase when they suffer from drought.[53]

How would this affect the North East region of India which primarily depends upon the Brahmaputra ? Considering the medium projection of India's population in 2050 to be at 1.64 billion, the population of North East India by 2050 is estimated to increase to about 80 million from its present 38 million. A gross demand of 62.4 billion cubic meters and a net demand of 27.6 billion cubic meters has been projected by 2050 for meeting domestic, industrial, livestock and agricultural requirements of the region. The dependable flow of the Brahmaputra (and Barak river) in the lean flow period is estimated to be in the order of 3,000 cubic meters per second and 45 cubic meters per second respectively at their exit points. The total groundwater potential of the two sub-basins, at about 31 billion cubic meters per year, can support, for 240 days per year, a draft of about 1,500 cubic meters per second.

According to experts, about 3,000 cubic meters per second of water is available from both surface as well as ground water sources. The net withdrawal from the system, including groundwater, would be in the order of 239 cubic meters per second in February, which is lower than the lean flow of 304 cubic meters per second.[54] Now, if the diversion by China (in worst case scenario) of 25 % of the Yarlung Tsangpo takes place (or 40 bcms), this would amount to less than 10% of the total yield of the Brahmaputra at Pandu; in other words, approximately around 270 cubic meters per second would be available which is far more than the projected demand of 239 cubic meters per second.

Thus, a diversion of waters to the Yellow River by China will not materially affect overall development of the North East region. However, individual projects such as the proposed Upper Siang project (11,000 MW) which were to be constructed close to the boundary and which depend upon the waters of the Siang/Yarlung Tsangpo may have to be scaled down. Reports already suggest that the Chinese have asked for the shifting of the Upper Siang project to an alternative site 49 kms downstream since the original location may lead to flooding across the border.

The effects of climate change with melting and receding glaciers causing floods and thereafter drying up of the rivers may have the same effect as physical diversion of waters by China. Thus, there is a serious case for cooperation between India and China.

Asia's water resources are largely transnational, making inter-country cooperation and collaboration essential. Yet the vast majority of the 57 transnational river basins in continental Asia have no water-sharing arrangement or any other cooperative mechanism. This troubling reality has to be seen in the context of the strained political relations in several Asian subregions. The river basins in the Asian continent that have a treaty-based sharing arrangement currently in place are the Al-Asi/Orontes (Lebanon-Syria), Araks-Atrek (Iran-Russia), El-Kaber (Lebanon-Syria), Euphrates (Iraq-Syria), Gandhak (India-Nepal), Ganges (Bangladesh-India), Indus (India-Pakistan), Jordan (Israel-Jordan), and Mahakali (India-Nepal). Arrangements in some of these basins, such as the Gandhak, Jordan, and Mahakali, do not incorporate a formula dividing the shared waters between the parties but rather center on specific water withdrawals, transfers, or rights of utilisation.

An important arrangement in the Mekong Basin—limited to the lower riparian nations—is centered on the sustainable management of water resources but without any water sharing. China is the source of rivers for a dozen countries. No other country in the world serves as the riverhead for so many countries. This makes China the central driver of inter-riparian relations in Asia. Yet China also stands out for not having a single water-sharing arrangement or cooperation treaty with any co-riparian state. Its refusal to accede to the Mekong Agreement of 1995, for example, has stunted the development of a genuine basin community. By building mega-dams and reservoirs in its borderlands, China is working to unilaterally re-engineer the flows of major rivers that are the lifeblood for the lower riparian states. The plain fact is that China rejects the very concept of water sharing. It also asserts a general principle that standing and flowing waters are subject to the full sovereignty of the state where they are located. It thus claims "indisputable sovereignty" over the waters on its side of the international boundary, including the right to divert as much shared water as it wishes for its legitimate needs[55].

China's new dam projects on the Brahmaputra, the main river running through North Eastern India and Eastern Bangladesh, have meanwhile prompted the Indian government to advise China to "ensure that the interests of downstream states are not harmed" by the upstream works. Water has emerged as a new divide in Sino-Indian relations. Then-

Indian Prime Minister Manmohan Singh personally proposed to Chinese President Xi Jinping and Premier Li Keqiang in separate meetings in the spring of 2013 that the two countries enter into a water treaty or establish an intergovernmental institution to define mutual rights and responsibilities on shared rivers. Both Xi and Li, however, spurned the proposal[56]. The Indian assumption that booming bilateral trade would make Beijing more amenable to solving the border and water disputes with India has clearly been belied. Indeed, China is damming not just the Brahmaputra, on which it has already completed several dams, but also other rivers in Tibet that flow into India. It has built a dam each on the Indus and the Sutlej and unveiled plans to erect a cascade of dams on the Arun River, which helps augment downstream Ganges flows and is thus critical for India to meet its water-sharing treaty obligations vis-à-vis Bangladesh. The flash floods that ravaged India's Himachal Pradesh and Arunachal Pradesh states between 2000 and 2005 were linked to the unannounced releases from rain-swollen Chinese dams and barrages. The Brahmaputra is a huge attraction for China's dam program because this river's cross-border annual discharge of 165.4 billion cubic meters into India is greater than the combined transboundary flows of the three key rivers running from the Tibetan plateau to Southeast Asia—the Mekong, the Salween, and the Irrawaddy. More fundamentally, China's new focus on building dams in its Southwest carries transnational safety concerns because this is an earthquake-prone region. Indeed, some Chinese scientists blamed the massive 2008 earthquake that struck the Tibetan Plateau's Eastern rim, killing 87,000 people, mainly in Sichuan Province, on the newly constructed Zipingpu Dam, located beside a seismic fault[57].

Common Trans-Border Rivers Between India And China And Their Status

The Brahmaputra and Indus are the two trans-border river systems between India and China. Between the two river systems, there are six trans-border rivers which are known by different names in the two countries.[58]

Figure 54 : Origin of the Indus in Tibet, China

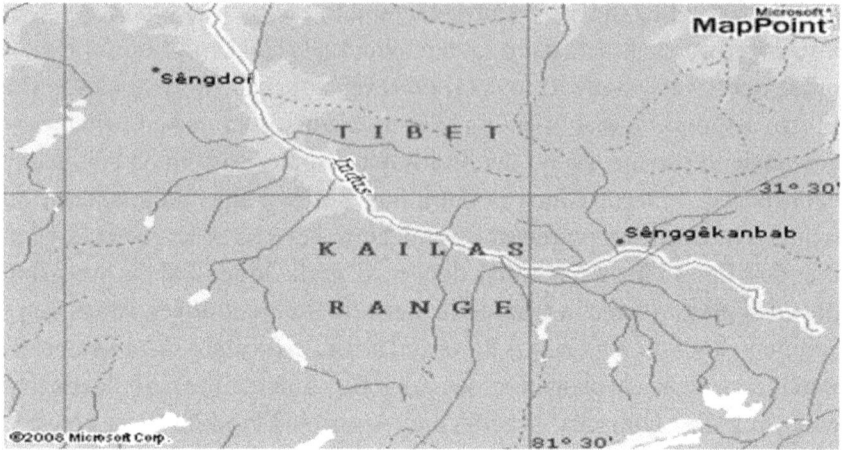

In the **Indus** system, two rivers i.e the Indus and the Sutlej rivers originate from the Ngari region of the Tibetan plateau(Figure 54 & 55). The Indus river, the longest river (3180 kms) of the Indian sub-continent originates Northeast of Mount Kailash in Tibet.[59] It is known as the Sengge Zangbo (Tibetan) or the Shiquan He (Chinese) river, which means the lion river. However, other sources believe that the Indus river is the confluence of the Sengge and the Gar rivers that flow through the Nganglong Kangri and Gangdise Shan mountain ranges.[60] Indus river enters India through the Ladakh region of Jammu & Kashmir state and flows into Baltistan and Gilgit in the Northern areas just South of the Karakoram range.

Figure 55: Origin of the Sutlej in Tibet, China

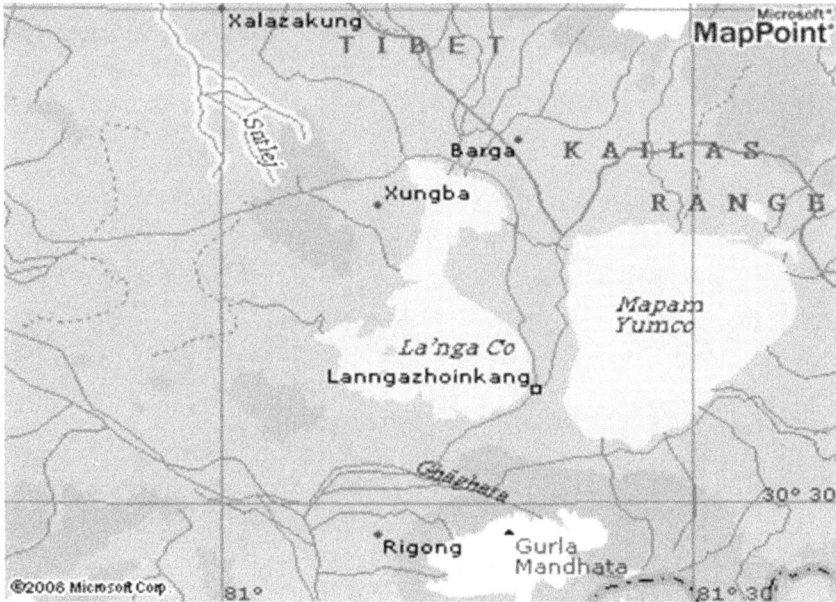

The **Sutlej** river, which is the longest tributary of the Indus river system, also originates from around the area of Lake Mansarovar[61] / Mount Kailash [62] in Tibet, China. It is known in Tibetan as Langqen Zangbo or the Xiangquan He river (in Chinese Xiang means elephant) and regarded as sacred as the Sengge river. The Sutlej enters India through the state of Himachal Pradesh.

The **Pare Chu** river, which was in news a few years ago, is a minor tributary of Sutlej. It originates just out side Spiti valley, flows about 30 km in Ladakh before entering Tibet where it runs another 85 km before re-entering India[63]

Figure 56 : Yarlung Tsangpo's Entry into Arunachal Pradesh, India

In the **Brahmaputra** river system (2,900 kms), the Yarlung Tsangpo is the best known of the tributaries of the Brahmaputra, originating in Tibet. It is referred to as the Mother River by Tibetans and is the largest river in Tibet. It originates in the Jima Yangzong glacier (near Mount Kailash)[64] at the Northern foot of the Eastern Himalayas, 63 kms South of Lake Manasarovar. It traverses around 1625 kms within Tibet before entering India through the state of Arunachal Pradesh. At an elevation of 4000 metres above sea level, it is the highest river in the world. Around 37% of Tibet's total population i.e 1 million, live in the area drained by the Yarlung Tsangpo and the region is home to Tibet's major cities and towns including Lhasa, Xigaze, Gyangze, Zetang and Bayi.

The Yarlung Tsangpo traverses in an almost straight line from West to East before reaching the junction of the Mainling and Medog counties in Tibet, where it bends sharply Southwards around the towering Gyalapering and Mount Namcha Barwa, creating the largest, U-shaped canyon in the world. Stretching 504.6 km, the canyon is 2268 meters deep on average, with the deepest point being 6009 meters. The last 260 kms that it traverses before entering India sees a drop in gradient of around 2200 metres.[65] A 38 gigawatt hydropower plant is under consideration that would be more than half as big as the 'Three Gorges Dam', with a capacity nearly as large as the UK's national grid. It enters Arunachal Pradesh, near Geling on the India-China border from which point it is known as the Siang river. The Siang flows about 400 kilometers through an amazing canyon before it meets with the Dibang river and the Lohit river in the plains of Assam at Kobo, South of Sadiya town. It is from this point, the confluence of three rivers, that the river is called Brahmaputra. The river traverses for 650 kms mostly in a Southerly direction before entering Bangladesh where it is known as the Jamuna[66].

The **Lohit** river is another tributary of the Brahmaputra which originates in Tibet, China in the Zayal Chu range and thereafter enters India through the state of Arunachal Pradesh at a point called Kibuthu, traverses for 200 kms before entering the plains of Assam and meeting up with Siang/Dihang and Dibang at Kobo[67]. Tempestuous and turbulent, and known as the river of blood, partly attributable to the laterite soil, it flows through the Mishmi Hills, to meet the Siang at the head of the Brahmaputra valley. It is called as Zayu Qu in Tibet.

The **Subansiri** is another major trans-border tributary of the Brahmaputra originating from the Western part of Mount Pororu (5059 m) in the Tibetan Himalayas. After flowing for 190 km through the Lhuntse county in Tibet, it enters India through the state of Arunachal Pradesh[68]. It continues for 200 km and enters into the plains of Assam through a gorge near Gerukamukh. It has a length of 520 km and drains a basin of 37,000 km^2.[69]

The **Parlung Zangbo,** which is referred to in Joint Statements between India and China on cooperation on trans-border rivers is not a trans-border river. Originating in the Lhunze County in Eastern Tibet, it has two main tributaries, which, after converging somewhere between the Menzhong Village and Zaqu River, empties itself into the Yarlung Tsangpo Grand Canyon. Therefore, it is an important tributary of the Yarlung Tsangpo or the Siang within Tibet[70].

Catchment or Drainage Area

Brahmaputra River System. India views the Ganga- Brahmaputra-Meghna basin as one basin since all three rivers merge in Bangladesh and discharge their waters through one channel into the Bay of Bengal forming largest river delta in the world (60,000 sq kms). According to official sources, the total area of the combined basin is 17,48,500 sq kms which makes it thirteenth largest river basin in the world[71]. In terms of the percentage share of the basin, the share of India is 63%, Bangladesh is 7%, Bhutan is 3%, Tibet (China) is 19% and Nepal is 8%. The Brahmaputra sub-basin extends over an area of 580,000 kms in Tibet (China), Bhutan, India and Bangladesh[72]. The drainage area of the Brahmaputra in Tibet is 2,03,000 sq kms **(50.51%)** and in India it is 1,94,413 sq kms **(33.52%)**.[73]

Indus River System. The Indus basin extends over an area of 11,65,500 sq kms in Tibet (China), India, Pakistan and Afghanistan[74] . It is bounded on the east by the Himalayas, on the west by the Sulaiman and Kirthar ranges, on the North by Karakoram and Haramosh ranges and on the South by the Arabian sea. India has 28 % of the catchment / drainage area, while Pakistan has 59 %. The combined share of Afghanistan and Tibet, China is 13 %. The drainage area lying in India is 321,289 sq kms which is nearly 9.8% of the total geographical area of the country. In India, the basin lies in the states of Jammu & Kashmir, Himachal Pradesh, Punjab, Rajasthan, Haryana and the Union Territory of Chandigarh.

Run-Off at Entry Point into India

Hydrological data for the Indus and Sutlej rivers at the points of entry into India are not available. However, Yarlung Tsangpo / Siang is estimated to have 160 bcms per annum at the entry point into India.

Existing Use of the Rivers in India

The Brahmaputra system contains more than 30% of the country's water resources. The total amount of water available in the Brahmaputra-Barak basin annually is 585.60 bcms,[75] yet, India utilizes around 21 bcms. It also has about 40% of the total hydropower potential (31,012 MW at 60% load factor), but only 3% of the potential has been tapped so far[76]. Similarly, the irrigation potential is also very high at about 4.2 million ha, but only 0.85 million ha i.e only 20% of the potential is being exploited[77]. Ground water is available at relatively shallow depths especially in the valleys of the Northeast, however only around 5% has been utilized so far as against the national average of 32%. The National Waterway 1 and 2 are on the Brahmaputra but this potential also remains largely unused.

Master Plan Part I is for main stream of Brahmaputra while Part II is for Barak river and its eight important tributaries. Both of these were approved by Government of India in 1997. As on 31 May 2011,Master Plan Part III had 34 plans already approved and 21 others in various other stages of processing[78]. Arunachal Pradesh itself has a hydropower potential of 56,000 MW and plans to construct 104 hydroelectric projects. Estimated income generated by these projects is around Rs 8,000 crore[79]. Around 20,000 MW are run-of-the-river projects; three major projects are planned on the Siang river, the Upper Siang project (11,000 MW), the Middle Siang project (1000 MW) and the Lower Siang project (1600 MW).

Indus river basin's hydropower potential is estimated to be 19,988 MW at 60% load factor. Out of 190 schemes identified in the basin, 18 schemes with a total installed capacity of 3,517 MW are in operation and 14 schemes with a total installed capacity of 5,626 MW are in various stages of completion. These 32 schemes account for 28% of the assessed potential of the basin[80]. Himachal Pradesh in which a major part of the Sutlej basin is located has identified the hydropower potential of the Sutlej basin as around 9700 MW. Of this around 3275 MW is already being generated; a major chunk of this comes from the Bhakra dam (1325 MW) and from the Nathpa Jhakri (1500 MW) project. The Nathpa Jhakri project in Kinnaur district is in operation since 2003 and is the largest run-of-the river project on the Sutlej river. The Khab hydroelectric project has been conceived as a run-of-river development to tap the hydroelectric potential of the upper reaches of river Sutlej as it enters into India. The project envisages the construction of 275 m high concrete gravity dam which would produce 1020 MW of electricity with a tentative construction cost of Rs 14,000 crores.[81] Therefore, it is clear that the existing use of both river systems in India is sub - optimal and major part of potential remains to be exploited.

Such is China's fixation on supply-side measures that China is to spend a staggering $290 billion under its current five-year plan on water-related infrastructure projects, including dams[82]. No nation is more vulnerable to China's re-engineering of transboundary flows than India because it alone receives nearly half of all river waters that leave Chinese territory. A total of 718 billion cubic meters of surface water flows out of Chinese territory yearly, of which 48.33% runs directly into India.[83] (Some additional Tibetan waters also flow to India via Nepal.) Bangladesh, on the other hand, has one of the world's highest dependency ratios with regard to cross-border inflows, receiving 91.3% of its water from India, although a sizable portion of that water originates in Tibet.

Whereas China continues to build giant dams and reroute rivers, trumpeting these projects as symbols of its engineering prowess, the public pressures generated by India's openness to democratic processes act as a brake on ambitious water projects that displace many people or flood vast areas. Still, given the growing gap between Asian water demand and supply, water disputes are almost as rife between India and its neighbours as they are between China and its neighbours. There are, however, two key differences. One, India has water pacts with all its riparian neighbours other than China. And two, its water-sharing treaties with Bangladesh and Pakistan contain dispute-settlement mechanisms. The issue that merits special emphasis is that the regions which are part of the major transboundary river basins between China and India are also the most militarized areas as also areas where territorial disputes are rife.

India's Prime Minister Narendra Modi may be waiting to see how China's experiment fares. His government appears to be reviving an old plan for its own National River Linking Project, a massive 9,320-mile scheme to redirect rivers to India's parched agricultural lands. While the plan has languished on drawing boards for years, Modi approved construction of the first link in July. Whether India could actually pull off such a vast engineering feat—and whether it's scientifically advisable—remains to be seen however it must be endeavoured with the Nations will as it has the capability to address multiple water related problems of the country.

Endnotes

1   Quenching the Dragon's Thirst The South-North Water Transfer Project—Old Plumbing for New China? By Carla Freeman

2   Jian Xie et al. (2009). *Addressing China's Water Scarcity: Recommendations for Selected Water Resource Management Issues.* The World Bank: xx-xxi.

3   Ibid.

4   Pomeranz, Kenneth, et al. "Himalayan Water Security: The Challenges for South and Southeast Asia." *asia policy* 16 (2013): 1-50. http://www.nbr.org/publications/asia_policy/free/ap16/Asia_Policy_16_WaterRoundtable_July2013.pdf

5   Maj Gen MKS Yadav,SM , Thesis submitted at National Defence College, New Delhi, 2011 on" Indo-China Trans-Border Rivers and Their Management"

6   Uttam Kumar Sinha (2012) Examining China's Hydro-Behaviour: Peaceful or Assertive?, Strategic Analysis, 36:1, 41-56, DOI: 10.1080/09700161.2012. http://dx.doi.org/10.1080/09700161.2012.628487

7   Ling Li, "Save China Through Water From Tibet", Beijing, November 2005.

8   Krishnan Ananth, "India China and Water Security", Published in "The Hindu" on 20 October 2009, http://www.thehindu.com/opinion/op-ed/article36468.ece, accessed on 30 Nov 2014.

9   The World Water Organization Website, http://www.theworldwater.org/world_water.php, accessed on 30 Nov 2014.

10 Czeslaw Tubilewicz, Editor, "Critical Issues in Contemporary China", Routledge-Taylor & Francis Group, August 2006, Chapter 5, "China' s Environmental Problems" by Richard Lois Edmonds, page 133.

11 Data and figures are from the Ministry of Water Resources, People's Republic of China, Annual Report 2007–2008, pp. 9–10, http://www.mwr.gov.cn/english/2007-2008.doc. 2007-2008   Annual Report, Ministry of Water Resources People's Republic of China

12 Ibid.

13 The CPC Central Committee and the State Council's Number 1 Document for 2011 (unofficial translation), at http://gain.fas.usdo.gov/Recent%20GAIN%.

14 Tubilewicz Czeslaw, Editor, "Critical Issues in Contemporary China",

Routledge – Taylor & Francis Group, August 2006, Chapter 5: "China's Environmental Problems" by Richard Louis Edmonds, page 134.

15 2030 Water Resources Group (Barilla Group, Coca-Cola Company, International Finance Corporation, McKinsey & Company, Nestlé S.A., New Holland Agriculture, SABMiller PLC, Standard Chartered Bank, and Syngenta AG), *Charting Our Water Future*(New York: 2030 Water Resources Group, 2009).

16 Ibid

17 Ibid,1

18 Zhengyin Qian, "Water Resources Development in China", China Water and Power Press, Beijing, 1994, Chapter 2, "History of Water Conservancy", page 43-93.

19 L. Berga. (2006). *Dams and Reservoirs, Societies and Environment in the 21st Century, Vol.1.* (London: Taylor and Francis): 27.

20 Interview notes, discussions with representatives of the Ministry of Water Resources (MWR), at MWR in Beijing, March 19, 2009.

21 Ibid,8

22 The Economic Times, PTI Dec 16, 2014, 01.03PM IST. China commissions its $80 billion water-diversion-project . http://articles.economictimes.indiatimes. com/2014-12-16/news/57112541_1_yangtze-danjiangkou-reservoir-water-quality

23 International Rivers, 2013. Available at: www.internationalrivers.org/

24 Zhang, Quanfa. "The South-to-North Water Transfer Project of China: Environmental Implications and Monitoring Strategy." *Journal of the American Water Resources Association*, Vol. 45.5, 2009: 1238-1247.

25 Meador, Michael R." Inter-basin Water Transfer: Ecological Concerns." *Fisheries*, Vol. 17.2, 1992: 17-22.

26 Fan, C. Cindy and Mingjie Sun. "Regional inequality in China, 1978-2006." Eurasian Geography and Economics, 49.1, 2008: 1-20.

27 "South-to-North Water Diversion Project, China", Website for the Water and Wastewater Industry, http://www.water-technology.net/projects/South_north/, accessed on 09 August 2014.

28 China successfully completes USD 80 billion water diversion project , The Economic Times, By PTI | 27 Dec, 2014, 06.11PM IST. http://economictimes. indiatimes.com/news/international/business/china-successfully-completes-usd-80-billion-water-diversion-project/articleshow/45660480.cms

29 **Dr. Crow-Miller Britt, Portland State University, United States,***Diverted opportunity: Inequality and what the South-North Water Transfer Project really means for China. POSTED ON MARCH 4, 2014 , GLOBAL WATER FORUM, WATER SECURITY*

30 National Group of China, ISRM, and National Society for Rock Mechanics and Engineering. (2009, December 3). "South-to-North Water Transfer Project." [Online]. Available: http://www.csrme.com/EN/News/2009-12/ EnableSite_ReadNews713509261259769600.html.

31 Weiluo Wang, "Water Resources and the Sino-Indian Strategic Partnership", http://www.hrichina.org/sites/default/files/oldsite/PDFs/CRF.1.2006/CRF-2006-1_Water.pdf, accessed on 09 August 2013

32 Li Ling in his book "Save China Through Water from Tibet" says that General Guo Kai was kept under detention during the Cultural Revolution (1966-76). One day, in the garbage heap, he came across geologist Weng Wenhao's "China Geography" in English. Intrigued by Weng's account of Tibet's hydrographic net, Guo began to wonder about possibilities of diverting Tibet's waters to solve the arid north. After his rehabilitation, he consulted experts in the Chinese Ministry of Water Resources as well as the Chinese Academy of Sciences and put forth his proposal.

33 "South-to-North Water Diversion Project, China", Website for the Water and Wastewater Industry, http://www.water-technology.net/projects/South_ north/, accessed on 09 August 2014.

34 Chellaney Brahma, From Arms Racing to "Dam Racing" in Asia How to Contain the Geopolitical Risks of the Dam-Building Competition Transatlantic Academy Paper Series, May 2012, Pg 3

35 International Commission on Large Dams, "Intranet," online data; and World Commission on Dams, "Dams and Water: Global Statistics," online data.

36 Ibid 30

37 T. P. Barnett, J. C. Adam, and D. P. Lettenmaier, "Potential Impacts of a Warming Climate on Water Availability in Snow- Dominated Regions," *Nature*, No. 438 (November 17, 2005), p. 306.

38 Y. Ding, S. Liu, J. Li, and D. Shangguan, "The Retreat of Glaciers in Response to Recent Climate Warming in Western China," *Annals of Glaciology* Vol. 43, No. 1 (2006), pp. 97-105

39 Chellaney Brahma ,Water, Power, and Competition in Asia, Posted on August 18, 2014, Asian Survey, Vol. 54, Number 4, pp. 621–650. ISSN0004-4687, electronic ISSN1533-838X. *(Copyright 2014 by the Regents of the University of California.)* http://chellaney.net/category/energy-environment/accessed *on 11/18/2014*

40 Walter W. Immerzeel, Ludovicus P. H. van Beek, and Marc F. P. Bierkens, "Climate Change Will Affect the Asian Water Towers," *Science*, Vol. 328, No. 5983 (June 11, 2010), pp. 1384- 85.

41 Food and Agriculture Organization, *Country Profile: Bangladesh*, 2010, Aquastat database.

42 Ibid, 5

43 Sharma Vishal, "Lakes Pose Threat to North India", Published in "Chandigarh Tribune" on 19 August 2006, http://www.tribuneindia.com/2006/20060820/cth1.htm#7, accessed on 18 August 2011.

44 Ibid

45 "China : Other Projects, Brahmaputra (Yarlung Tsangpo) River", Website "International Rivers", http://www.internationalrivers.org/china/china-other-projects, accessed on 09 August 2014.

46 Arpi Claude, "Diverting the Brahmaputra, Declaration of War?", Posted in Rediff.com on 23 October 2003, http://www.rediff.com/news/2003/oct/27spec.htm, accessed on 18 August 2011.

47 "Controversial Plan to Tap Tibetan Waters", Published in "The Southern Weekend" of 27 July 2006, Translated by Shao Da for China.org,cn on 08 August 2006, http://www.china.org.cn/english/MATERIAL/177295.htm, accessed on 09 August 2014.

48 Joseph Anil K, "No Plans to Divert the Brahmaputra: China", Posted in Rediff News on 22 November 2006 from Beijing, http://www.rediff.com/news/2006/nov/22china.htm, accessed on 10 August 2014.

49 Chellaney Brahma, "China aims for bigger share of South Asia's water lifeline", Published in "The Japan Times" on 26 June 2007, http://search.japantimes.co.j/cgi-bin/eo20070626bc.html, accessed on 09 August 2013.

50 Ibid, 5

51 Ibid,7

52 The estimated non-monsoon yield (October to April) is around 127 bcm. Thus, 18 bcms would amount to 1/7th of the total non-monsoon yield.

53 Ibid, 7

54 Mahanta Chandan, "Water Resources in the North East : State of the Knowledge Base", Background Paper No.2, August 2006, for World Bank Study "Development and Growth in Northeast India: The Natural Resources, Water, and Environment Nexus

55 Chellaney Brahma ,Water, Power, and Competition in Asia, Posted on August 18, 2014, Asian Survey, Vol. 54, Number 4, pp. 621–650. ISSN0004-4687, electronic ISSN1533-838X. *(Copyright 2014 by the Regents of the University of California.)* http://chellaney.net/category/energy-environment/accessed on 11/18/2014

56 Ibid

57 Shemin Ge, Mian Liu, Ning Lu, Jonathan W. Godt, and Gang Luo, "Did the Zipingpu Reservoir Trigger the 2008 Wenchuan Earthquake?" *Geophysical Research Letters* 36 (2009). Also see Richard Kerr and Richard Stone, "A Human Trigger for the Great Quake of Sichuan," *Science,* 323, no. 5912 (January 16, 2009); Sharon La Franiere, "Possible Link Between Dam and China Quake," *New York Times*, February 6, 2009; and Jordan Lite, "Great China Earthquake May Have Been Man-Made," *Scientific American*, February 3, 2009.

58 Durai Suchitra, "Issue of Utilisation, Development and Conservation of Common Water Resources between India and China", NDC, September 2008, http://www.ndc.in, accessed on 14 June 2014.

59 Xinhua News Agency, "Scientist finds new origin of Indus River", Published in "China Daily" on 21 October 2010, http://www2.chinadaily.com.cn/china/2010-10/21/content_11441098.htm, accessed on 30 July 2014

60 Indus River, Geography of India,Indianetzone, http://www.indianetzone.com/14/indus_river.htm, accessed on 31 July 2014.

61 Ibid

62 Himalayas : Himalayan Facts : Main Himalayan Rivers, http://www.

himalaya2000.com/himalayan-facts/himalayan-rivers.html, accessed on 31 July 2014 .

63 A High Walk Through Rupshu-Changthang", Posted on "India Profile", http://www.indiaprofile.com/adventure/changthang-treks.htm, accessed on 31 July 2014.

64 Origin of Brahmaputra River', Geography of India, Indianetzone, http://www.indianetzone.com/29/origin_brahmaputra_river.htm, accessed on 31 July 2014.

65 Singh Vijay P & Others, Editor, "The Brahmaputra Basin Water Resources", Chapter 13 on "Water Resources Planning" by Phukan SS, Pages 299-301.

66 "Origin of Brahmaputra River", Geography of India, Indianetzone, http://www.indianetzone.com/29/origin_brahmaputra_river.htm, accessed on 17 August 2014.

67 "Tributaries of Brahmaputra River", Geography of India, Indianetzone, http://indianetzone.com/29/tributaries_brahmaputra_river.htm, accessed on 31 October 2014.

68 There is very little published literature on the origins of the Subansiri in Tibet. Some Tibetan websites refer to the river as the *Tib Shipasha Chu*. Indian sources call it Bya Chu.

69 "The Subansiri River", Official Website of Dhemaji District, http://dhemaji.nic.in/floods/rivers.htm, accessed on 31 October 2014.

70 Durai Suchitra, "Issue of Utilisation, Development and Conservation of Common Water Resources between India and China", NDC, September 2008, http://www.ndc.in, accessed on 31 October 2014.

71 Chakravorty Roshni, Serageldin Ismail, "Sharing of River waters among India and its Neighbours in the 21st century:War or Peace?—The wars of the next century will be about water", https://www.mendeley.com/research/sharing-river-waters-among-india-neighbors-21st-century-war-peace-wars-next-century-about-water/,accessed on 17 August 2014.

72 Official Website of Central Water Commission, Government of India, http://www.cwc.nic.in/   http://www.cwc.nic.in/main/downloads/Water_Data_Complete_Book_2005.pdf, accessed on 31 July 2014.

73 Tuteja Ravi, "Status and Security Implications of Rivers Emanating fron Tibet and Flowing through India",Article No : 1019 posted at "Centre for Land

Warfare Studies" website on 12 October 2007, http://www.claws.in/index.php, accessed on 01 August 2014.

74   Indus River, Geography of India,Indianetzone, http://www.indianetzone. com/14/indus_river.htm, accessed on 31 July 2014.

75   Official Website of Central Water Commission, Government of India, http:// www.cwc.nic.in/, accessed on 31 August 2014.

76   Goswami Dulal C, Gauhati University, "Towards Sustainable Use of the Brahmaputra", Published in International Centre for Integrated Mountain Development (ICIMOD) Newsletter : Sustainable Mountain Development in the Greater Himalayan Region, No.50, Summer 2006

77   ibid

78   Official Website of Brahmaputra Board, http://brahmaputraboard.gov.in/, accessed on 31 December 2014.

79   Dutta Arnab Pratim, "State pulse : Arunachal Pradesh : Reservoir of dams", Published in "Central Chronicle" on 12 May 2008, http://environmentportal. in/news/state-pulse-arunachal-pradesh-reservoir-dams, accessed on 01 August 2014.

80   Official website of Central Water Commission, Government of India, http:// www.cwc.nic.in/regional/chandigarh/welcome.html

81   Report on Hydroelectric Projects in Himachal Pradesh, Chapter 2.3, http:// sjvn.nic.in/projects/rampurpdf/chap2_revised_4.pdf, accessed on 25 August 2014

82   Leslie Hook, "China: High and Dry," Financial Times, May 14, 2013.

83   FAO, Aquastat online database.

CHAPTER 5 : RECOMMENDATIONS FOR INDIA'S WATER SECURITY

"The future political impact of water scarcity may be devastating,"

– Former Canadian Prime Minister Jean Chrétien.

The Twenty First century brings with it an opportunity to be prepared for the wrath of geography as it unfolds the repercussions of mankind's relentless exploitation of natural resources. It is the time for taking timely corrective and enduring measures to contain the damage already done and subsequently sustain the ecology, yet meeting the aspirations of the world in the future .

Factors Impacting Water Security

Pressures on water resources are likely to worsen in response to population growth, shifts toward more meat-based diets, climate change, and other challenges[1]. Moreover, the world's water is increasingly becoming degraded in quality, raising the cost of treatment and threatening human and ecosystem health (Palaniappan et al. 2010).

On deliberate analysis it is clear that the lack of capacity related to water whether human, financial, institutional, technological, and service-provisioning amongst many factors is a major hurdle towards achieving water security. In many countries, such institutional frameworks, particularly those which allow for trans-sectoral decision- and policy -making, are often poorly developed [2]. Capacity development is needed at different levels and requires a cross-sectoral enabling environment that supports water security. Capacity is also needed at various levels, from individual to organisational and institutional, in order to reduce vulnerability to water insecurity, with poor capacity at various levels and across disciplines often cited as a major hurdle to the attainment of water security (UNW-DPC, UNESCO-IHP and BMU, 2009; UNEP, 2012). Policy-makers need to identify existing capacities, as well as gaps, in order to properly address the water security challenge. Such assessments need to be undertaken at both the institutional and relevant geographical (national, river basin, etc.) levels[3].

Increased capacity for water security depends on data availability on the quantity and quality of water resources, as well as financing for implementation of interventions. Sound management of water resources relies as much upon the knowledge of available water resources and their dynamics as well as on their uses and users. Such management can only be achieved with data of sufficient quality, which requires adequate human and financial resources. Better quality data and monitoring and reporting of water resources will lead to an increase in knowledge, which will support the ability to make informed decisions for enhancing water security through better water resources management[4] . Capacity development is a long-term process based on incentives, good governance, leadership, and knowledge management and transfer, which needs to be continuously adapted according to feedback and needs of the stake-holders. It is an organic learning process based on agreed norms, respect for value systems and fostering of self-esteem. For capacity development to be successful, it needs to integrate external inputs into national priorities, processes and systems, build upon existing capacities rather than create new ones, remain engaged under difficult circumstances, and, above all, remain accountable to the ultimate beneficiaries (OECD, 2006). Creation of an enabling environment and supporting policies for the use of unconventional water sources, such as wastewater management, for the redeployment, recovery and reuse of water for human and other competing uses, is needed[5]. There is enormous potential for wastewater to contribute to achieving water security, particularly in areas with acute levels of freshwater scarcity and increasing problems of water quality deterioration. Wastewater treatment and reuse, supported by relevant research and pertinent policy-level interventions, can transform this untapped resource from an environmental burden and health constraint into an economic asset that contributes to achieving water security while maintaining the health of people and the environment. Appropriate policies can guide the use of non-conventional water sources, including sufficient financial commitment for policy implementation and education of stakeholders, supported by increased collaboration between researchers, international organisations, governments, and water users

(Qadir *et al.*, 2006). Supporting policies, laws and infrastructures will create the right enabling environment to allow for increased capacity based on environmental potentials and limits and country- or region-specific needs (UNEP, 1993). These policies must be inter-disciplinary and pan institutional boundaries so that water resources management is integrated and sustained. There is a coordinated need for collaboration amongst agencies, international and national level trans-sectoral coordination, education and training to build institutional capacity and establishing a developed community to address water security challenges. Developed policies should include water planning, setting appropriate standards for water re-use, market-based reallocation, watershed management, and management of ecosystem services.

A Comprehensive Appraisal for India

On analysis, it appears that India's water crisis is rooted in three fundamental causes. The first is insufficient water per person as a result of population growth and rapid urbanisation. The total amount of usable water has been estimated to be between 700 to 1,200 billion cubic meters (BCM)[6]. With a population of 1.2 billion according to the 2011 census, India has barely 1,000 cubic meters of water per person, even using the higher estimate. The second cause is poor water quality resulting from insufficient and delayed investment in urban water-treatment facilities. The third problem is dwindling groundwater supplies due to over-extraction by farmers. This is because groundwater is an open-access resource and anyone can pump water from under his or her own land. The issue of seasonal and spatial variability of rains and snowfall lends further complexity to the problem. Considering the various issues there are many critical areas, the main concerns are the pressing need to increase irrigation and the difficulty of creating water-storage facilities.

The increasing stress on freshwater resources brought about by population growth and ever-changing demand of water use as well as for healthy eco-system, draws attention to the challenges ahead for planning and management of scarce water resources. Change in water use pattern is at times cause of conflicts among various stake holders not only at National/ State level, but even at local level. The mismatch between water resources and population, uneven distribution of rainfall in time and space as well as the fast growth of the social and economic development has lead to serious problems of water. Affected by industrialisation, urbanisation and global climate change, number of issues involved in managing water resources like competing demands; scope of increasing water productivity in different sectors; tools that enable most efficient use of available water; maintaining sustainable water quality have to be addressed in a coordinated and integrated manner for effective development and management of scarce water resources. India, as a large rapidly developing country, is facing more challenges of water resources, including flood and drought disasters, water scarcity and pollution as well as water and soil erosion A diagramatic holistic appraisal for outcome analysis is depicted in the figure below:-

Figure 57 - Holistic Appraisal Of Water Issues

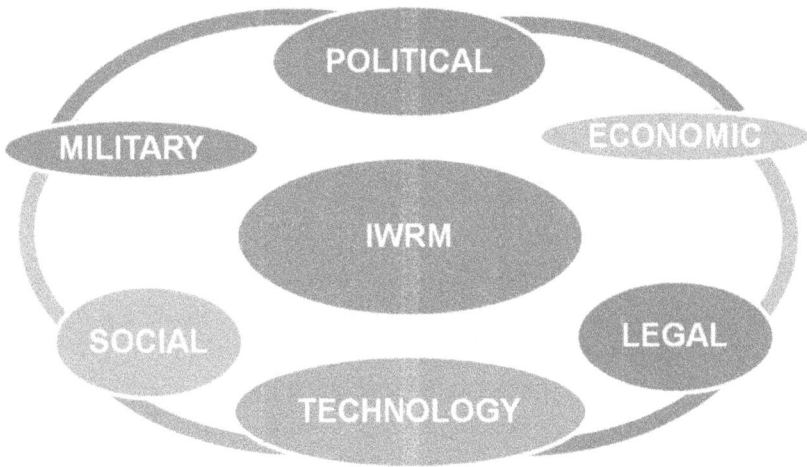

Political Measures

Water Governance

A key aspect for improved water management is water governance as it practically sets the 'rules of the game' for the way water is to be managed. It determines how, or whether, water resources are managed sustainably[7]. Good governance is a prerequisite to achieving water security, as the international community has long and repeatedly recognized. Poor water governance expressed through weak legislative and institutional arrangements, under investment, poorly enforced legislation, and inadequate accountability mechanisms, and corruption, resulting in loss of biodiversity through degradation and over-allocation of water resources, it further leads to weaker and less resilient livelihoods and economic growth. Policies, laws and institutions are the three pillars of water governance within a country and in a transboundary basin, where they are complemented by the agreements negotiated between basin countries. Governance mechanisms which are necessary for water security and include operating capacity, transparency, participation, accountability, and access to legal recourse.

Government policies concerning water and water-related sectors, including agriculture and energy, as well as environmental protection, can obviously exacerbate or alleviate pressures on water resources Such objectives are best achieved through formal agreements and processes at the national and international levels[8].

Some Relevant Recommendations for Water Governance

> Intergovernmental Organisations Lack Clear Leadership and Coordination.[9]

- Secure a sustainable funding source and a stronger mandate for coordinating intergovernmental organisations. The global nature of water-related challenges requires clear leadership and coordination. Intergovernmental agreements produced at world summits and forums require effective intergovernmental organisations like the UN to play the leading role in coordinating action. It (or any other intergovernmental mechanism established to coordinate action) must be given the resources and an empowered mandate to do so. This requires governments to fulfill pledges made at previous UN summits to ensure that financial resources are made available. It also requires political will from the United Nations.

- Promote greater collaboration to build understanding and coordinate action to effectively address the interlinked nature of the problems, it is imperative that water related action be led not from within a silo but rather with a deep understanding of the cross-sector issues—for example, taking into consideration development, energy, biodiversity, climate change, food security, and more. By instituting a process that brings together development agencies, civil society groups, and the private sector to define water-related goals and potential actions, the UN approach promotes better understanding, which can lead to more coordinated action and better outcomes.

➤ The role of nongovernmental actors is expanding. Global governance cannot be limited to merely governmental or intergovernmental processes. The rise and influence of a broad range of new actors, with their own sources of authority and power, are indicative of a more complicated global governance structure.

- Explore and develop guidelines and principles to help govern nongovernmental processes. As more parties become involved, effort is needed to better understand and define the roles and responsibilities of each in order to leverage unique capabilities.

- For entities that are actively engaging in areas that are in the traditional realm of governments, clear guidance as to how these new processes should interact with existing processes is needed.

➤ Water sector funding is inadequate and too narrowly focused. The international community, including the major economies and international organisations, has played a significant role in funding water sector improvements, especially in developing countries. Yet funding remains limited and too narrowly focused.

- Develop financing mechanisms to support ongoing operation and maintenance costs. Funding is needed to support ongoing operation and maintenance costs of water infrastructure. Available funding is insufficient to operate and maintain the existing infrastructure or to support the people and institutions needed to manage it effectively.

➤ New funders often fail to abide by environmental and social lending standards. For much of the twentieth century, the World Bank, the Asian Development Bank, intergovernmental agencies, and bilateral donors were the main funders of large-scale infrastructure in the developing world. In recent years, new economic realities and players have emerged. Commercial banks and energy and construction companies in the global South are playing an increasingly important role and are fundamentally changing water resource management. For instance, Pacific Environment's China program director, Kristen McDonald, and her colleagues reported in 2009 that Chinese financial institutions, state-owned enterprises, and private firms and other new players—predominantly energy and construction companies from Thailand, Vietnam, China, Russia, and Malaysia were involved in at least ninety-three major dam projects overseas. These had not adopted internationally accepted environmental and social lending standards and norms.

- Establish new lending standards and compliance strategies. New environmental and social lending standards are needed to ensure that lending promotes sustainable development objectives. The new players, along with civil society organisations, should be included in crafting and designing these new standards in order to ensure compliance.

➤ Knowledge and technology transfer efforts remain largely top-down. Over the past several decades, water-related knowledge and technological innovation have grown tremendously, with new techniques and ideas emerging from governmental bodies, independent research institutions, and academic bodies around the world. The challenge lies in getting this knowledge and technology to places that can implement them.

- Promote open-access knowledge transfer. Over the past few decades, there has been tremendous growth in the technologies available for transferring knowledge and information. Geospatial technologies, the Internet, and mobile devices are just a few of the technologies available to improve communication.

- Facilitate effective technology transfer by engaging local communities in the decision-making process. Empowering local communities to identify their water issues and solutions allows them to select an approach that more closely aligns with their social and cultural realities.

- Improve understanding and communication of risk and uncertainty. Some uncertainty inherent in hydrologic and water resource management systems is unavoidable. Yet the development of management practices and strategies relies heavily on future supply and demand predictions, which are fraught with uncertainty. Water resource managers around the world use various supply and demand predictions in their decision-making processes. A better understanding of the uncertainties and risks associated with them can lead to the development of more effective planning and management strategies that reflect these limitations.

➢ Data collection efforts are inadequate. Good data and ongoing monitoring activities are the cornerstones of effective water management and governance. We live in an information era, and vast amounts of water data are collected in different ways and at a variety of temporal and spatial scales, from local stream gauges to global satellites. Even when the data are collected, they are often not widely available or their quality is poor. Efforts are needed to improve the collection, compilation, and reporting of comprehensive water-related data.

  - Develop a centralized global water data portal. The rational management of water is predicated on the availability of comprehensive data. Capacity needs to be developed in all countries to collect, manage, and analyse water information. Some of the key data needed include precipitation, runoff, virtual water flows, groundwater levels, and overall water demand and supply.

  - Leverage new data collection technologies. New local data collection and monitoring efforts are emerging that engage stakeholders through crowdsourcing, or reporting of information through electronic devices.

➢ Lack of transparency and accountability limits the effectiveness of water sector investments and fosters corruption. The water sector lacks transparency and adequate participation from key stakeholders, especially in marginalised communities, and this in turn leads to an accountability deficit and can result in ineffective or inefficient management strategies and investments.

- Adopt new standards, codes, and best practices for water resource development and management to promote greater transparency and participation. Water resource development and management are guided by a series of standards, codes, and best practices. These standards, codes, and practices, which include both mandatory and voluntary initiatives, must provide a regulatory framework that brings about greater transparency, promotes participation and oversight to tackle corrupt practices, and develops best-practice guidance where regulatory frameworks are weak or poorly implemented.

- Promote capacity building and increase participation in water management. To bring about greater participation in water management and better implementation of frameworks that promote transparency, serious effort is needed to build the capacity of governmental officials and civil society groups, especially community-based organisations.

➢ There has been a failure to adopt broad-based agreements on transboundary watercourses. Many rivers, lakes, and groundwater aquifers are shared by two or more nations, and most of the planet's available freshwater crosses political borders, ensuring that politics inevitably intrude on water policy. As such, transboundary water management often requires the creation of international guidelines or specific agreements between riparian states.

- Adopting an effective international legal framework is a critical step in addressing future challenges. The 1997 United Nations Convention on the Law of the Non-Navigational Uses of International Watercourses which has since been ratified represents an important contribution to the strengthening of the rule of law regarding the protection and preservation of international watercourses, and must act as a precursor to the other similar conventions and documents being brought into force.

➢ Existing inter-basin agreements lack flexibility. Global climate change will pose a wide range of challenges to freshwater resources, altering water quantity, water quality, and system operations and imposing new governance complications. For countries whose watersheds and river basins lie wholly within their own political boundaries, adapting to increasingly severe climatic variability and changes will be difficult enough. When those water resources cross borders and implicate multiple political entities and actors, sustainable management of shared water resources in a changing climate will be especially difficult and will require active coordination, engagement, and participation of all the actors sharing the basin.

- Improve flexibility of existing inter-basin agreements. No two water treaties are the same. Each is developed under unique circumstances, addresses different concerns, and has a particular set of constraints. Additionally, climate change will affect each basin differently. As a result, each treaty must be evaluated to determine what flexibility mechanisms currently exist and where significant vulnerabilities remain. This process should be started before a problem arises so as to improve the atmosphere for cooperation and negotiation. Additionally, transboundary watershed countries should consider incorporating provisions into existing treaties to allow for greater flexibility in the face of change, including:-

- Creation of flexible allocation strategies and water quality criteria.

- Agreement on response strategies for extreme events, such as floods and drought.

- Development of clear amendment and review procedures to allow for changing hydrologic, social, and climatic conditions or in response to new scientific knowledge.

- Establishment of joint management institutions that can, for example, facilitate a climate vulnerability and adaptation assessment (Cooley and Gleick 2011).

Active interaction with neighbours and co riparians to secure India's interests. The following steps have been taken:-

➢ A large number of political initiatives and Memorandums of Understanding (MoUs) for bilateral cooperation have already been signed and a large number are in various stages of progress as on date, this constant endeavor and planning for anticipated changes both by nature and mankind have to be factored in to ensure India's national interests. Some recently signed MoUs signed by India are listed here[10]:-

➢ A Memorandum of Understanding on cooperation in the field of Water Resources Management between the Governments of India and Australia was signed on 10th November 2009 for a period of five years. Numerous meeting with the Joint Working Group (JWG) have taken this project to an advanced stage.

➢ The MoU on cooperation in Water Resources Development and Management between Ministry of Water Resources and Ministry of Agriculture and Animal Resources of Republic of Rwanda was signed on 22nd January, 2013 at New Delhi.

➢ Memorandum of Understanding on mutual cooperation in Water Resources Development and Management between the Governments of India and Iraq was signed on 23rd August, 2013 at New Delhi.

➢ A Memorandum of Understanding for cooperation in Water Resources Management between India and Iran was signed on 4th May 2013.

➢ A Memorandum of Understanding on cooperation in Water Resources Management and Development between Ministry of Water Resources, Government of India and Ministry of Energy and Water Resources of State of Israel has been finalized.

Concurrently, a sizeable effort is on in projects aided by various banks like the World Bank . The active role by the Ministry of Water Resources (MOWR) need to bring forth the issue of securing transboundary waters as well. The non cooperative stance of India's not so friendly neighbours lends further complexity to the situation, which needs constant monitoring. These actions, in pursuance of ensuring a cooperative stance, in all domains ranging from sharing waters, to sharing hydrological information/ data, sharing technologies and techniques, evolving refined management techniques etc both with other countries and organisations and within the country have to be an ongoing process. The issue before India in the coming years will be multi- dimensional: to manage its water resources better; cater for issues due to climate change and simultaneously to manage good riparian relations . There are no permanent solutions and remaining in step with the rapidly changing global and environmental dynamics will ensure India's national interests. Contingencies that are sure to arise whether due to natural events or trigerred by water sharing nations must be thought in detail and necessary infrastructure, plans and mitigating measures be put in place .

Economic Measures

Managing water as it has been done hitherto fore is no longer an option for most countries. The beginnings of change are under way and there is good reason to believe that water will be an important investment theme for governments, public, multilateral and private financial institutions in the coming decades. Although affordable solutions are in principle available to close the projected water supply-demand gaps for most countries and regions, institutional barriers, lack of awareness, and misaligned incentives may stand in the way of implementation, across both the private and public sectors. Overcoming these barriers will require persistent action and, in many cases, an integrated agenda of water sector transformation. One plausible way is the concept of "virtual water"—the water embedded in the production of food and other products—has been introduced as a way to evaluate the role of trade in distributing water resources[11]. That is by allowing those living in water-scarce regions to meet some of their water needs through the import of water-intensive goods, international trade can provide a mechanism to improve global water-use efficiency (Allan 1993).

Financial Support for Projects. There is wide agreement that water has suffered from chronic underinvestment. Financial institutions are likely to be an important actor in making up this shortfall. Investment opportunities span all sectors—the measures that in aggregate require the most capital vary in each country . In India, drip irrigation offers potential for lending and equity investments alike, the penetration of this technology will grow by 11 percent per year through 2030, requiring increased manufacturing capacity and credit for farmers.

Pricing and Subsidy. Governments have to use a variety of measures – incentives as well as sanctions, a mixture of persuasion and penalties. Economic incentives and market-based instruments should be considered in policy packages designed to change behaviour towards water and energy. They can greatly reinforce the impact of other types of measures, such as regulations, public awareness campaigns, exhortations and technological developments. This does not imply that the market should have the final word in allocating water resources and services. Pricing should be used sensitively with a view to its social and distributional impact. Pricing can, however, add a crucial boost to other water and energy policies. Economic instruments include prices, taxes, pollution charges, subsidies, and markets for buying and selling a service, a resource or the rights to use the service or resource. Economic pricing of water services can more closely reflect the economic cost of their provision; provide sufficient revenues for continued operation and maintenance; and avoid waste and distortions due to under-pricing.

Infrastructure. The world has more to lose than ever before from massive failure of critical infrastructure. The need to absorb latest events, treaties and the likely course, the water discourse is likely to follow will have to be a part of this large investment for infrastructure in all aspects of the drivers mentioned earlier. To improve efficiency and lower cost, various systems have been allowed to become hyper-dependent on one another. The failure of one weak link – whether from natural disaster, human error or terrorism – can create ripple effects across multiple systems and over wide geographical areas. The timely creation of infrastructural facilities keeping in mind the likely developments in the future is critical for all nations. In India where issues like large populations, depleting water availability , increased urbanisation ,climate change impacts are converging , it is time for implementing its plans with single minded purpose.

The agricultural water infrastructures are poorly developed and not likely to keep pace with the goals of national food and water security . India confronts a deepening water crisis, which is more acute than China's. Yet India's per capita capacity to store water for dry-season release (200 cubic meters yearly) is one of the world's lowest; it is 11 times lower than China's (2,200 cubic meters).[12] Since rain is concentrated in a few months and unevenly distributed across the country, it is imperative for India to develop the capacity to store and transport water. The first step is to increase local storage and recharge through watershed development. However, in the long run, dams are inevitable[13]. Global planning and analytical organisations providing insights into worldwide water issues forecast that India is likely to face a 50% deficit between water demand and supply by 2030.[14]

The 2030 Water Resources Group Study states that a particular basin or country would utilise a combination of three fundamental approaches to close the gap between demand-supply. Two of these focus on technical improvements, increasing supply and improving water productivity under a constant set of economic activities, while the third is tied to the underlying economic choices a country faces and involves actively reducing withdrawals by various activities. A progressive step would be a sustainable and cost-effective mix of these three solutions[15]. The figure below depicts what water in India costs against its availability to help policy makers decide on the courses of action .

Figure – 58 : India's Water Availability Cost Curve

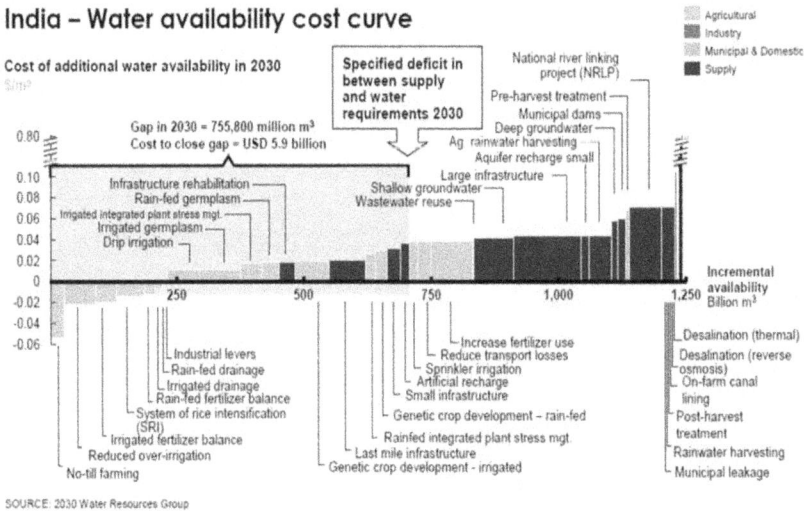

Source- Charting Our Water Future, Economic frameworks to inform decision-making; The 2030 Water Resources Group

Note: The width of the block represents the amount of additional water that becomes available from adoption of the measure. The height of the block represents its unit cost.

The model highlights the fact that in India, large measures if applied, would require to spend 5.9 Billion US Dollars to cover the deficiency gap of 755,800 Million m³ of water clearly specifying the deficit between supply and requirements in 2030 for decision making by policy makers.

Technology

Identifying and deliberating on existing and future technologies that should be taken into consideration when finding solutions for water in the future is a major challenge for global planners. Technology advancement in remote sensing, nanotechnology, salt water agriculture, desalination, and meat without animals are some technologies which provide opportunities for more efficient and effective water use and water purification[16]. There are numerous water technologies that merit attention for increasing the amount of water for drinking, agriculture, and manufacturing or which will allow us to use water more efficiently. The evidently important ones for water that matter significantly are analysed briefly in succeeding paragraphs. Innovation in water technology—in everything from supply (such as desalination) to industrial efficiency (such as more efficient water reuse) to agricultural technologies (such as crop protection and irrigation controls)—could play a major role in closing the supply-demand gap[17].

Remote Sensing

Remote sensing or multispectral imagery is an increasingly deployed technology with regards to water related resources and agriculture. Among many other drivers affecting water resources, multispectral imagery is among the more mature technologies. They may be used for identifying surface and sub surface water availability as also detecting leakage of canals from water storage locations.

Remote sensing has been deployed as a successful tool to help farmers with issues concerning soil wetness and watershed rehabilitation projects (Aubert, et al, 2010).Satellite imagery and analysis are currently commercially available. Possible developments that may have a potential effect on remote sensing's impact on water resources in the future include continual refinement of Geographic Information Systems (GIS) with the ability for real-time monitoring of agricultural crops and water quality and quantity. Remote sensing for water and agricultural analysis is already in place. Market forces and adoption of the technology by commercial and national entities is likely to continue to increase the diffusion of the technology. As the technology is refined and system integration packages come online improved water usage and pollution detection can improve the knowledge of water resources and their use[18] .Several developing countries are already using remote sensing; however, their use is not extended, and certainly the poor farmers do not have access to it presently. Additionally, the deep underground sensors that track water movements and quality to provide dynamic maps based on such information are likely to be game changers for the water monitoring systems .

Desalination

Currently most desalination plants that convert sea water into potable water are run using oil. The most popular form of desalination uses reverse osmosis which puts pressure on salt water so that the water goes through a membrane and the salt stays inside the membrane. As a result, there is a trade-off between water that exits through the filter and water that is expelled as waste. Another desalination strategy is to use the heat generated in the process of cooling nuclear power plants to distill water. Additionally, there are some small low-tech solar stills and large scale low tech solar stills can also provide an option for many developing countries. Desalination is likely to become more economical over the next ten years as membrane technology evolves. There is ongoing research on ceramic based membranes. Experts believe that nanotechnology can greatly increase the efficiency of the desalination process though there is a lack of consensus on when this will happen. There is significant interest in building wind driven desalination plants (Spang, 2006). Solar energy can drive reverse osmosis or solar humidification/dehumidification. Though these technologies have been around since the 1950s, they have not been cost effective (Wikipedia, 2010). However, this may change dramatically as water becomes scarce. As the need for high-quality water treatment increases, specifically for potable or high-quality industrial use or re-use, low pressure membrane technology could develop a market potential of up to 85 billion m^3 by 2030, 56 times its volume in 2005[19].

Nanotechnology

Nanotechnology is a promising technology in the application of sensors and many water purification and desalination processes. the application of nanotechnology for desalination, water reclamation, heavy metal extraction, and microbial purification is promising and likely to continue in making great strides in development. A major consideration for the feasibility of nanotechnology in water purification and desalination is the cost of industrial-scale raw material production.

Many of the fundamental discoveries in nanotechnology essentially improve upon the pre-existing methods for water purification. For example, membranes, catalysts, and other nano materials are able to provide increased filtration flow and increased catalytic reaction with lower energy costs.[20]. Nanotechnology is forecasted to become one of the fundamental enabling technologies for the 21st century. Nanotechnology is promising not only for improving water resource use through more efficient and effective filtration, purification and desalination methodologies, but also in sensing water quality measurements with real time monitoring and real time response capability (Rickerby, 2006).

Saline Agriculture

With abundant availability of saline water considering saline agriculture is natural. It has been sub optimally developed especially in developing countries and could reduce water stress for communities by allowing the communities to grow food, fiber, biofuel, and trees with saline or brackish water, freeing up potable water for drinking and other uses for which it is required. Today, only about 1% of the species of land plants can grow and reproduce in coastal or inland saline sites. (Rozema, 2008) Salinity can decrease crop yields for fresh water plants. (Munns, 2005). There are plants—known as halophytes—that do well in saline water. The challenge is that many deal with saline stress by concentrating salt in their tissues which makes them unsuitable for food, the seeds of halophytes don't necessarily have the same problem. However, they may be used for energy crops with potential for animal feed.

Social Measures

Agriculture. Agriculture accounts for approximately 3,100 BCM, or 71 percent of global water withdrawals today, without efficiency gains this will increase to 4,500 BCM by 2030 (a slight decline to 65 percent of global water withdrawals). The water challenge is therefore closely tied to food provision and trade. Centers of agricultural demand, also where some of the poorest subsistence farmers live, are primarily in India (projected withdrawals of 1,195 BCM in 2030), Sub-Saharan Africa (820 BCM), and China (420 BCM). It is predicted that demand for water for domestic use will decrease as a percentage of total, from 14 percent today to 12 percent in 2030, although it will grow in specific basins, especially in emerging markets[21].

More-developed countries have a much larger proportion of freshwater withdrawals for industry than less-developed countries, where agriculture dominates. Agriculture accounts for more than 90% of freshwater withdrawals in most of the world's least developed countries (LDCs) (FAO, 2011*a*). India's own agencies say it must nearly double its annual grain production to more than 450 million tons by 2050 to meet the demands of increasing prosperity and a growing population, or risk becoming a major food importer—a development that will disrupt the already tight international food markets.[22] Agricultural productivity is a fundamental part of the solution. In all of the case studies, agricultural water productivity measures contribute towards closing the water gap, increasing "crop per drop" through a mix of improved efficiency of water application and the net water gains through crop yield enhancement. These include the familiar technologies of improved water application, such as increased drip and sprinkler irrigation.

Figure 59: Example of Energy Efficiency Improvements

Direct Intervention	Indirect Intervention
Adoption and maintenance of fuel efficient engines	Improved water allocation and management of water demand
Precise water application	Improved surface water delivery to reduce the need for pumping
Precision farming for fertilizers	Provision of water services for multiple water use
Adoption of no till practices	Reduced water losses
Energy efficient buildings	Crop varieties and animal breeds that demand less input including multipurpose crops and perennials
Heat management of greenhouses	Redused soil erosion
Propeller design of fishing vessels	Use of bio-fertilizer
Use of high efficiency pumps (high cost)	Efficient machinery manufacture
	Identification of stock locations and markets by information and communication technology

Source: WWAP (United Nations World Water Assessment Programme). 2014. *The United Nations World Water Development Report 2014: Water and Energy.* Paris, UNESCO.

The annual rate of efficiency improvement in agricultural water use between 1990 and 2004 was approximately one percent across both rain-fed and irrigated areas, a similar rate of improvement is seen in the industry. Were agriculture and industry to sustain this rate to 2030, improvements in water efficiency would address only 20 percent of the supply-demand gap, leaving a large deficit to be filled.[23] Of the 140 MHa of net cultivated area in India, only around 60 MHa are irrigated. In order for Indian agriculture to grow at its targeted rate of 4% per year, it needs to increase the area irrigated, introduce new high-yield technology, or expand cultivable land. There is no scope to expand the cultivated area, which has remained around 140 MHa for the last two decades[24]. India must apply all measures in crop productivity including, no-till farming and improved drainage, utilisation of the best available germplasm or other seed development, optimizing fertilizer use, and application of crop stress management, including both improved practices (such as integrated pest management) and innovative crop protection technologies[25].

There are also lessons to be learned and applied within countries. In India itself, for example, depends on the Western half of the country for a significant share of its food production, a region less endowed with water than its Eastern counterpart, where water is abundant but productivity per unit of land and water is far lower than the national average[26]. With increased climate-related risks, it makes sense to secure production in areas less susceptible to variability. Yet increasing water and food productivity in the Eastern states is not only hindered by insufficient infrastructure and ineffective institutions; the current energy and food pricing, procurement, and distribution issues are also imbalanced in their provision of a level playing field for inter-regional competition. Western states are better endowed and better managed in each of these respects as compared to the Eastern states, where more than 80 percent of the population lives below the poverty line.[27]

Groundwater Depletion

Probably the single most serious problem in the entire field of water resources management, is the problem of groundwater depletion. Many of the most populous countries of the world i.e China, India, Pakistan, Mexico and nearly all of the countries of the Middle East and North Africa have literally been having a free ride over the past two or three decades by depleting their groundwater resources. The groundwater problem has two contradictory aspects.

> ➤ First, there is the rapid drawdown of fresh water aquifers mainly due to the worldwide explosion in the use of wells and pumps for irrigation and for domestic and industrial water supplies.

> ➤ Second, there is the opposite problem of rising water tables of saline and sodic water, and the pollution of aquifers by these and other toxic elements[28].

India, has more area irrigated by pump sets than by all the other surface irrigation systems combined. Pump irrigation from aquifers is the ideal form of irrigation. The water is stored underground, with no evaporation loss, and is instantly available when it is needed. But the extraction of water from aquifers in India exceeds recharge by a factor of two or more.[29] There is an urgent need to regulate withdrawals, ensure recharge of soil and advanced measures of irrigation.

A comprehensive World Bank study concluded that high-level policy reform in the shape of regulatory measures, economic instruments, or tradable groundwater extraction rights is simply not a credible way forward[30]. Instead, this report proposed that "bottom-up" community management may be the only hope. Other studies have supported this proposal[31], with particular focus on community level groundwater recharge and the use of communally managed alternatives to groundwater, such as small dams[32].

Figure 60 : A Summary of Enabling Factors for Transboundary Aquifer Cooperation

Enabling Factor (number of aquifers where present)	Description	Patterns of Influence
Existing legal mechanisms(100	Includes both binding and non-binding legal mechanisms, which place specific obligations on aquifer states	• Highly influential in North America, Europe and Africa • Plays a key role in cases of moderate cooperation
Existing regional institutions (16	Involves an institution charged with promoting cooperation and coordination on issues of regional importance. Institution demonstrate some specific focus on groundwater	• Global geographic influence • Strong influence in medium sized aquifers (10,000-1,000,000 km^2)where there are more than two aquifers states and in cases of low cooperation.
Funding mechanisms (12)	Either a aquifer state or the third party provided the funding for the joint project or institution	• Global geographic influence • Strong influence in large scale aquifers (<1000000 Km^2 and more than five aquifer states) • Noticeable influence on high cooperation events
High institutional capacity (8)	Organizations with the aquifer demonstrates the ability to deal with ground water governance issues related to monitoring, modelling and/or management	• Strongest in Europe and North America • Not critical to promoting any specific level or cooperation
Previous water cooperation (15)	Involves past interactions regarding water resources between atleast two or more aquifer states	• Critical in small sized aquifers (< 10,000 Km^2) • Significant influence on cases of low cooperation
Scientific research (7)	Research is conducted specifically for the assessment of transboundary impacts. Research provides significant new information to the aquifer states	• Influential in North and South America, also has some influence in Africa • Noticeable influence on low cooperation

Strong political will (8)	High ranking government official(s) indicated the prioritization of ground water management in the aquifer	• No geographic trend • Influential in high coopera-tion cases
Third party involvement (8)	There were significant contributions to cooperation from entities outside of the aquifer states governments	• Noticeable role in the global south • Highly influential for me-dium scale transboundary aquifers (10,000- 1,000,000 km^{2}) and 3-5 aquifer states

Source: Free Flow , Reaching Water Security Through Cooperation, Tudor Rose, UNESCO Publishing

Population

Global population is projected to reach 9.3 billion in 2050 (UNDESA, 2012). Population growth leads to increased water demand, reflecting growing needs for drinking water, health and sanitation, as well as for energy, food and other goods and services that require water for their production and delivery. Urban areas of the world, particularly those in developing countries, are expected to absorb all this population growth, at the same time drawing in some of the rural population. This intense urbanisation will increase demand for water supply, sanitation services and electricity for domestic purposes[33] . Urbanisation in India has spread rapidly in almost all areas barring a few. This trend raises higher demands on improving water quality and ensuring water supply and prevention of the floods in some cities with dense population and concentrated social properties. Urbanisation in India has occurred more slowly than in other developing countries and the proportion of the population in urban areas has been only 28 per cent based on the 2001 census. The pace of urbanisation is now set to accelerate as the country sets to a more rapid growth. Economic reform has already unleashed investment and growth offering its citizens rich opportunities. Surging growth and employment in cities will prove a powerful magnet. 300 million Indians currently live in towns and cities. Within 20-25 years, another 300 million people will get added to Indian towns and cities[34]. This urban expansion will happen at a speed quite unlike anything that India has seen before. It took nearly forty years for India's urban population to rise by 230 million. It could take only half the time to add the next 250 million. Immediate measures to cater for this have to be incorporated, if not well managed, this inevitable increase in India's urban population will place enormous stress on the system. Recent reports suggest that India spends $17 per capita per year in urban infrastructure, whereas the most benchmarks suggest a requirement $100. The investment required for building urban infrastructure in India, over the next 20 years, is estimated at approximately US$ 1 trillion. Expenditure on water must be planned for and utilised on priority in the overall context.

Figure 61 : Forecast Urban Population Growth- 2010 - 2050

Urban Population in 2050 compared with 2010:
Smaller   Larger but loss than double   Double or more, but less than fivefold   Fivefold or more

Climate Change

Climate change and variability further complicate the situation. Climate change adaptation is primarily about water, as stated for example by the Intergovernmental Panel on Climate Change (IPCC), which identifies water as the fundamental link through which climate change will impact humans and the environment (IPCC, 2008). In addition, water is critical for climate change mitigation, as many efforts to reduce carbon emissions such as carbon capture and storage rely on water availability for long-term success. Providing sufficient energy for all while radically reducing greenhouse gas emissions will require a paramount shift towards fossil-free energy use, very high energy efficiency, and equity. These goals may limit the availability of water resources for communities and ecosystems and result in a reduction of adaptive capacity for future change. Climate change mitigation requires effective adaptation to succeed. As per the IIPC, 2014

Adaptive water management techniques, including scenario planning, learning-based approaches, and flexible and low-regret solutions, can help create resilience to uncertain hydrological changes and impacts due to climate change , these must be adopted and developed in the Indian context.

Other measures which must be adopted by India in response would include:-

> Timelines must be identified, to achieve the target of protecting the lives and safety of assets.

> The flood / drought control and disaster reduction as well as water resources security system adapted to the socio-economic development and future trends should be set up.

> The risk management systems should be basically set up in coordination with various departments like Disaster Management etc.

> The adaptive management and the non-engineering construction should be strengthened by improving the flood and drought monitoring and forecasting and early warning system.

> Improving the management of emergency engineering system, combining the professional and social rescue teams for flood and drought emergencies, improving the material reserve system for the post-disaster reconstruction.

> Enhancing emergency management capabilities and improving plans for the extreme events.

> The reserves of water resources should be increased strategically by working out the water resources plans for specific circumstances in the specific period, setting up emergency water source to cater for the areas in different ways according to the conditions prevailing.

> Strict control over total groundwater extraction in areas where water is short and prohibiting deep extraction for strategically increasing the groundwater reserves.

> Measures for strengthening the ecological protection and water conservation of water conservation zones and constructing the backbone water projects to increase water storage capacity of river

basins must be instituted.

> Temperature increases and glacial melt will provide more water in the short-term[35]. Predictions indicate that the quantity of run-off water from melting glaciers will rise until at least 2050. Coupled with increased precipitation, more run-off water will lead to increased flooding events, these must be planned for in great detail.

There are some mitigation measures that must be acted upon on priority. Major users of coal like China and India need to curb it's usage. China has committed to reducing its CO2 emissions by 40 to 45 per cent per unit of GDP below 2005 levels by 2020[36], through a reduction in fossil fuel use. It planned to cut energy consumption by more than 3.9 per cent in 2014, resulting in a predicted decrease in coal consumption of 220 million tonnes. In India, the National Action Plan on Climate Change was established in 2008[37]. The Plan sets the goal of improving water use efficiency by 20 per cent, through pricing and other measures. Other targets which it must set include the conservation of biodiversity, the re-afforestation of six million hectares of degraded forest lands, the support of climate adaptation measures in agriculture and gaining a better understanding of climate science, impacts and challenges. Although India, is making critical mitigation announcements, only following through from policy to action will make a difference.. Strengthening cooperation on climate change adaptation and mitigation across the Sino- Indian border is a paramount issue for a positive water future in the region. India must keep pace with China's positive approach to climate change impacts. Yet China still remains one of the only nations without any institutionalised water sharing agreement with downstream countries.

The Water – Energy Linked Issue

Water and energy are tightly interlinked and highly interdependent. Choices made in one domain will have a direct and indirect consequences on the other, positive or negative. The form of energy production being pursued determines the amount of water required to produce that energy. At the same time, the availability and allocation of freshwater resources determine how much (or how little) water can be secured for energy production. Decisions made for water use and management and for energy production can have significant, multifaceted and wide reaching impacts on each other – and these impacts often carry a mix of both positive and negative repercussions.

Future Scenario for Energy. In spite of the uncertainties, coal is expected to remain the backbone fuel for electricity generation globally through to 2035. Although its use for this purpose will continue to rise in absolute terms, its share in the total generation is expected to fall while the share of gas increases slightly (IEA, 2012a). Oil-fired power generation is also likely to diminish, due in part to increased competition for oil from the transportation sector. Adaptive measures must be taken in the following.

- **Nuclear.** Output is expected to grow in absolute terms, driven by expanded generation in China, Korea, India and Russia, but its share in the global electricity mix is expected to fall slightly over time In Canada and the USA, the competitiveness of nuclear power is being challenged by the growth of relatively inexpensive natural gas. India must develop technology and explorations for the same.

- **Hydropower.** Hydroelectricity is currently the largest renewable source for power generation in the world, meeting 16% of global electricity needs in 2010 (IEA, 2012a). Hydropower, when associated with water storage in reservoirs, can store energy over weeks, months, seasons or years. In India ,while 32.08 thousand-mega watt (MW) i.e. about 21.6% of country's total hydroelectric potential (148.7 thousand MW identified capacity as per reassessment study) has been developed as on 31.03.2010, about 14.3 thousand MW (i.e. about 9.6%) was under development. Contrary to the highest potential assessed in North Eastern Region, the potential actually tapped in this region is lowest. This must be developed to the extent feasible giving utmost priority to the lagging regions of North- Eastern states in an early time frame. It is a power which can be used more rapidly than any other generation source, hydropower (and pumped storage) can contribute to the stability of the electrical system by providing the full range of ancillary services required for the high penetration of variable renewable energy sources, such as wind and solar (IRENA, 2012b).

Military Measures

Securing areas of potential conflict especially those bordering with Pakistan (PoK) and China as also those areas where the issue of territorial disputes remains unresolved ie Arunachal Pradesh, Pakistan occupied Kashmir (PoK), Aksai Chin (Figure 62). These areas are a confluence of social unrest, military confrontation and also are strategically important either directly being rich in water and other resources or by enabling use or access to such critical resources. Key areas must be identified and secured. Likely impact of climate change and glaciers melting will require adaptive measures for both holding and maintaining strategically important areas , these have to be considered in detail and plans prepared for the same.

Figure 62 :Likely Areas of Conflict

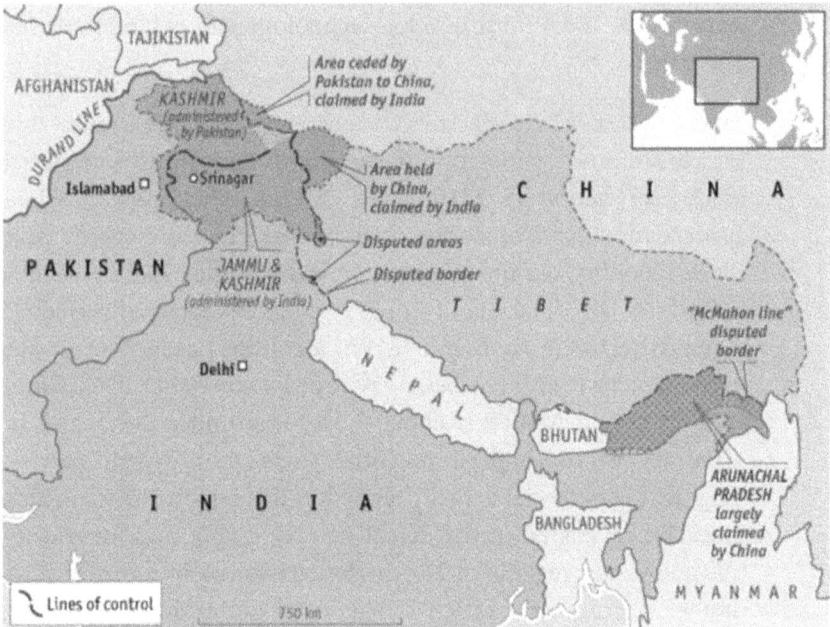

Legal Measures

Legal Instruments. As the 1997 U.N. Watercourse Convention (which sets rules on shared water resources to establish an international water law) (Annexure 1) has come into force, with the ratification process being completed[38]. India being amongst the non-signatories will need to convey its apprehensions clearly. For India, it is an opportune time for deliberate analysis and decided action. The national interests must be met and the following issues be conveyed with regard to India's objections to the convention earlier[39] : -

- Article 3. Regarding this Article, India must convey that a Framework Convention should not be prescriptive but should leave states free to evolve and implement mutually agreeable terms in relation to specific international watercourses as the article fails to reflect the principle of freedom adequately, autonomy and the right of states to conclude international agreements without being fettered by the UN Framework Convention.

- Article 5. With reference to 'Equitable and Reasonable Utilisation and Participation' is not clear and is unambiguous with the term "sustainable utilisation". It must seek clarifications and not accept being vague and difficult to implement.

- Article 32 . Could be relevant to countries that are part of political and economic regional integration of states(European Union). In India's case providing compensation for non-nationals claiming recompense for alleged transboundary injury is un- implementable.

- Article 33 . For settlement of disputes mandates India must state clearly that the parties should be left free to choose any acceptable procedure for securing an amicable settlement through mutual consent.

After the announcement by USA and China in November 2014 that both countries will curb their greenhouse gas emissions over the next two decades, India will need to bolster support from other nations now. Before committing with the details required for the Global Climate Summit in Paris, India will perforce have to put forth the figures as INDCs after a thorough and detailed analysis in harmony with policy implications. The impact on future use of water, fuel, technologies and resultant pollution etc will be significant. It has to be so calibrated that it adequately supports the progressive economic and development trajectory that India is predicted to follow in the coming decades .

A major reason for adhering and giving tremendous clout to to global institutions is the large quantum of funds being received from agencies like World bank etc. by countries for construction , maintenance and improvements of water related facilities. With the emerging growth and resultant clout of the Chinese economy, it is a matter of time when an indirect control of such institutions by the Chinese will either aid some nations or hinder some nations, India needs to plan and execute mid and long term strategies to ensure that her interests are safeguarded in this milieu.

India must clearly discern and define its position, as an ill-considered coerced response will leave it with severe restrictions without having harnessed the full potential for its development and economic growth. India must , therefore, ensure her own security of national interests before committing to similar targets as it has yet to create the basic infrastructure and development objectives to ensure its economic progress in the decades ahead.

Internal Measures

Integrated Management of Water Resources.

- India's Twelfth Five-Year Plan (2012–17) has focused attention on a large number of issues. The plan puts great emphasis on aquifer mapping, watershed development, involvement of NGOs, and efficiency in developing irrigation capacity, this must be progressed further.

- Since water is a state subject in the federal constitution, state governments must play a large role in these efforts. At the same time, many active NGOs should assist in enforcing compliance with environmental obligations through the right to information act, active and competitive media, and growing awareness on water issues.

- Identify accountabilities for water resources management

The responsibility and appraisal system for most stringent water resources management must be further improved and also the main indicators for water development, conservation and protection must be introduced into comprehensive assessment system of local economic and social development. India must introduce the comprehensive evaluation system of the local economic and social development.

- Regional tensions prevail in conditions of inadequate water. Continuously evolving integrated water management is required for increased availability and to ease such tensions.

- Coordination between government ministries is a problem in India, as is the lack of coordination between central government and the local level. Measures to enhance coordination between relevant ministries connected to water, such as those for agriculture or mining, and ensure that policy on water is coordinated with land, urban development, environment, agriculture and energy policies amongst others.

- It must improve water resources monitoring system. The facilities for measuring and monitoring water- taking, drainage and sewage outlet into the rivers and lakes should be further improved. The monitoring and measuring capacity for the major rivers and groundwater for quantity and quality monitoring and capacity-building should be strengthened to enhance monitoring capability.

- Management of water by the communities at the local level is an enabling process. Hierarchical approaches often fail to meet actual needs. It would facilitate a more holistic understanding and encourage a focus on sustainability, as well as a collaborative approach towards water.

- Survey, assessment and reporting system for water resources must be coordinated and developed.

The investigation and assessment of drinking water sources in rural areas must be carried out. The identification of rural drinking water source protected areas and the scope of protection should be promoted. The monitoring and evaluation system of water regime, soil moisture and ecological information should be strengthened .

Water Governance. Some key issues critical for establishing good water governance which will benefit water stressed India effectively are summarised here[40] :-

- Establishing the river basin and/or the aquifer system, as appropriate, as the basic bio-geographic unit for water management, requiring coordination and cooperation between political units across national and international borders.

- In areas where important groundwater aquifers do not coincide with river basins, special attention should be given to the coordination and cooperation over these aquifers, particularly in establishing mechanisms and incentives that move away from unsustainable groundwater pumping to the sustainable management of groundwater resources.

- Reconciling the security of water rights with risk, uncertainty of resource availability and supply, and sustainability through measures such as the periodical review of permits, avoidance of monopolisation, and transfer of negative externalities.

- Pursuing efficiency gains and providing for dispute resolution mechanisms, in order to offer equity and flexibility in the allocation of water rights among competing uses.

- Prioritising the environment and vital human rights in water allocation policies, laws and decision-making processes, including requirements to assess and manage environmental flows.

- Integrating water resources management of surface and underground waters with land and biological resources governance.

- Empowering water users and other stakeholders to take on greater responsibility, access relevant information and administrative and judicial remedies, and participate in decision-making processes regarding water management and allocation.

- Accounting for customary water allocation systems, rights and practices at the local level, where these exist.

- Strengthening risk management of water-related natural hazards, including the use of early warning systems.

- Protecting freshwater ecosystems of high conservation value from infrastructure development, including the designation and management of protected areas.

Agriculture. Agriculture needs to grow by at least 4% per year if India is to sustain its targeted economic growth rate (above 8%). With 8% growth, demand for agricultural products will increase. The expansion of irrigation makes it possible to double-crop more land or technical progress increases per-hectare output[41]. Increase agricultural productivity by rationally expanding irrigation or by other means, to remain in step with India's future economic growth. Food production and the water it requires are a key part of the water challenge. In India, where agriculture plays the most important role in the least-cost solution, aggregate agricultural income could increase by $83 billion by 2030 from operational savings and increased revenues, if the full potential of agricultural measures is implemented.[42]

Water Shed Development. Emphasis throughout the country on watershed development is imperative. Necessary measures cited in the National Water Policy must be applied and evolved further. The concept of local watershed or basin-wide management, linked to issues such as conservation and environmental projection, also provides scope for cross-regional dialogue and knowledge- sharing. Enhance and expand existing cross-regional dialogues both on local approaches (such as watershed management) and on macro-level basin-wide management. Moreover, it can be undertaken at the local level all over the country and can be accomplished in a relatively short time

Urban Water Management. Poor, inefficient and leaky distribution networks leading to large amounts of "unaccounted water" should be immediately attended to both for quality and quantity.

Ground Water. The central and state governments should empower local groups with knowledge, understanding, and real-time information on the status of groundwater so as to manage extraction in a cooperative way. This problem can only be managed by a cooperative agreement among the users of the aquifer, who should know how much can be extracted without depleting the resource. The state can monitor and provide this information. . Even with full groundwater recharge, water harvesting, and recycling, there will still be a need to store water in reservoirs; otherwise, this water will drain into the sea during monsoon floods. Creating natural and artificial lakes and ponds etc will also help recharge the aquifers in addition to being an eco- friendly storage measure.

Increase Water Storage. India must educate people about the need for dams to store water. The environmentalists and other groups who oppose dams should be engaged in a dialogue to work out alternatives and build a consensus. Despite some objections, there remains a critical need for storage dams because climate change will increase the availability of water while greatly altering its distribution. These must be planned in detail in concert with the National River Linking Project.

Pollution Control. The government should strengthen state pollution control boards to enforce effluent standards. The technical and human resources currently available to the boards are inadequate to effectively monitor activities, enforce regulations, and convict violators. In addition, adequate sewage treatment facilities must be constructed. Many cities treat only a part, and some no more than half, of the effluent.

Water Pricing. Authorities need to charge a proper price for water so that local sewage work operators have the income and resources to sufficiently maintain treatment plants. If necessary, India should work with private firms to modernize urban water-distribution systems. Enhance understanding of the nexus between food, energy and water to enable pricing of electricity, and ideally water, to better reflect social and environmental costs.

Best Practices Application. Learning from successful projects with government, scientific think tanks and community participation is a plausible method, particularly where micro-conservation techniques like rainwater harvesting are concerned.

Demand Vis A Vis Supply Based Model Of Water Management. The most effective collaborative approaches focus on water usage and thereby demand rather than simply water supply. Both aspects are to be pursued with equal intensity.

The financial implications of this challenge are also clear. Historically, the focus for most countries in addressing the water challenge has been to consider additional supply, in many cases through energy-intensive measures such as desalination. However, in many cases desalination—even with expected efficiency improvements—is vastly more expensive than traditional surface water supply infrastructure, which in turn is often much more expensive than efficiency measures, such as irrigation scheduling in agriculture. These efficiency measures can result in a net increase in water availability, and even net cost savings when operating savings of the measures outweigh annualized capital costs[43] .

Reduce Demand For Water. By 2030, demand in **India** will grow to almost 1.5 trillion m³, driven by domestic demand for rice, wheat, and sugar for a growing population, a large proportion of which is moving toward a middle-class diet. Against this demand, India's current water supply is approximately 740 billion m³. As a result, most of India's river basins could face severe deficit by 2030 unless concerted action is taken, with some of the most populous—including the Ganga, the Krishna, and the Indian portion of the Indus—facing the biggest absolute gap[44].

- Incentivise the cultivation of less water-intensive crops.

- Encourage less water-intensive methods of irrigation through pricing and/or through the promotion of cost-efficient technologies.

- Enhance the availability of data of demand to assist guide policy-making

Supply Of Water .Take Measures to ensure good quality and quantity in supply of water :-

- Focus on local rainwater-harvesting projects.

- Build storages like dams, lakes, reservoirs and ponds to enable maximum storage of seasonally and spatially available water from rivers ,rains etc.

Co-riparians must focus on the demand of water, rather than only to its supply side:-

- Develop and enhance cooperative frameworks for better understanding of challenges and opportunities.

- Collaborative addressing of issues like climate change; tourism; urbanisation; energy; environment and health; fisheries; food, agriculture; groundwater management; disasters management and ecology; sanitation and water-borne diseases; navigation.

Data collection, accuracy and data-sharing to be a constantly evolving process .

- It is evident that management and passing of data and information is vital. Mitigation of transboundary water tensions and improved domestic water management would be largely facilitated with greater awareness within and between countries .

- Data-sharing is vital, especially during and for the prevention of floods and droughts. Streamline processes and timelines by which flood and drought data is transmitted to relevant agencies.

Water – Energy- Nexus. A coherent and considered policy which provides adequate government cum public response to the inter-connectedness of the water, energy , food and related domains – requires numerous actions. Together these actions will make up the *enabling environment* necessary to bring about the changes needed for the sustainable and mutually compatible development of water and energy[45]. The international community can bring actors together and catalyse support for national, subnational and local governments as well as utility providers, who have a major role in how the water–energy nexus plays out at the national and local levels. Some amongst these are listed below :-

- Creating legal and institutional frameworks to promote this coherence.

- Ensuring reliable data and statistics to take ,monitor and analyse decisions.

- Developing coherent national policies affecting the different but inter connected domains.

- Developing awareness and involvement through education, training and public information media.

- Research and Development for technological and other scientific or social solutions.

- Adequate funding and cost effective programme development.

- Moderating demand and supply equations for all these interconnected facets.

- Improving the efficiency and sustainability with which water and energy are used and finding win–win options that create savings of both.

Revisit existing treaties and agreements or focus parallel discussions on emerging issues. Ensure treaties address technological advances, environmental factors and climate change. Ensure new treaties have built-in third party or mutually agreed arbitration clauses.

Build the capacity of water policy-makers and international negotiators at national, state and provincial level in the country.

External Factors: Transboundary Issues

A deliberate and dispassionate appraisal elucidates the fact that domestic water management and transboundary water relations are inseparable parts of the same problem. Clearly there is a need for aligning the transboundary water perspective with the domestic . Considering the geo-political imperatives in and around India has to be a vital step to address the water challenges in the region, it is as important to adopt sensible riparian policies and water management schemes as is to ensure that the systems are ecologically balanced and sustainable. With a sizeable quantum of water coming into India from across her border it is important to ensure that these transboundary waters continue to flow and are optimally utilised.

For this the governance has to be effective, countries need to develop their own water governance capacity through transparent, coherent and cost-efficient policies, laws and institutions. The cooperation and collaboration amongst nations sharing transboundary waters is a prerequisite. The issue of 'Political Will' is also a common problem both in domestic water management and in transboundary water relations. Whether due to internal compulsions or poor understanding of the subject, lack of political commitment has been responsible for numerous stalled cross-border projects, such as those between India and Nepal, Pakistan and even Bangladesh. India must ensure these issues are suitably addressed.

Water is the common factor for many global issues be it agriculture, climate change energy, and urban development. It can surely act as a panacea for cooperation as well, holding the key to global sustainability – but this requires deeper commitment from all. As population globally grows and the fresh water resources shrink, riparian relations will be sensitive. Many of the existing treaties may have to be evaluated afresh and new treaties based on current hydrological knowledge will need to be framed. The environmental reality of India being a upper, middle and lower riparian is likely to be the pivot for India's riparian politics. Large increase of population, limited coordinated management of water resources and climatic factors, point to India becoming water stressed by 2025 and water scarce by 2050.

China

It has been seen over the years that China tends to be unilaterally acting on waters in its own interests and as a trend does not sign water sharing treaties with any of its co riparians. Chinas unilaterally dominates over the headwaters of the Brahmaputra and Sutlej rivers which flow into India as also the Indus that flows through Ladakh before it enters Baltistan in POK. China has already implemented the South North Water Transfer Project along the Eastern and Middle routes, with the Western Route now in its sights. It plans to divert the waters of the Yarlung-Tasangpo (Brahmaputra) for its Great Western River Diversion Project (GWRDP) from near the great bend.. It has made numerous river based projects on all its transboundary rivers including a barrage on the river Sutlej and a 6400MW Senge-Tsangpo dam on the Indus. Although India and China have had some basic levels of cooperation on water issues like the exchange of data, etc. these need to be taken forward. India has taken steps to take these to a higher level of hydrological cooperation with China. Some recent developments in this domain are listed below:-

- During the Prime Minister's visit to China in October 2013, both side signed a separate "Memorandum of Understanding on Strengthening Cooperation on Trans-Border Rivers" on 23rd October 2013, in which inter alia the scope of provision of hydrological information of three hydrological stations has also been enhanced to start from May 15th instead of June 1st to October 15th of the relevant year, from 2014. Not a significant step but a movement all the same.

- In accordance with the MoU for 'Strengthening Cooperation on Trans-border Rivers' signed on 23rd October 2013, the two sides revised the Implementation Plan upon the provision of hydrological information of Yaluzangbu / Brahmaputra signed on 30th May, 2013 for providing of hydrological information changing the data provision period from 1st June- 15th October every year to 15th May- 15th October of relevant year, from 2014, during the 8th meeting of India-China Expert Level Mechanism on transborder rivers held at New Delhi from June 24-27, 2014. This revised IP was signed in Beijing on June 30, 2014 during the Visit of the Honourable Vice President of India to China.

- Memorandum of Understanding has been signed during the visit of the Chinese Premier to India in April 2005 for supply of hydrological information in respect of River Sutlej (Langquin Zangbu) in flood season. Chinese side is providing hydrological information in respect of their Tsada station on river Sutluj (Langquin Zangbu). The new MoU upon provision of hydrological information of Sutlej/Langqen Zangbo River in flood season by China to India with a validity of five years has been signed with China on 16th December, 2010 during the visit of Hon'ble Prime Minister of China to India.

India considering its geo-political realities must take a few essential steps. Some recommendations in brief are as follows:-

- India, must raise its lower riparian concerns with China continually in bilateral and global forums. With the ratification of the UN Convention on the Law of the Non-navigational Uses of International Watercourses, 1997, the concept of 'equality', 'no harm' and 'community of co-riparian states' must be debated over and brought to the table. Due deliberations are critical, as what India seeks as a lower riparian from China, will be expected from it by Pakistan as an upper riparian. For China, with no water treaties with any of the South Asian nations any riparian cooperation clearly lies in building dams to generate electricity, on the rivers flowing from Tibet and safeguarding against natural or mankind induced calamities.

- Global major events in context of climate change are either commenced or on the anvil. The announcement by USA and China in November 2014 that both countries will curb their greenhouse gas emissions over the next two decades and the EU also committing to reducing carbon-dioxide emissions by 40% from 1990 levels by 2030. These emission cuts are not deep enough to avoid exceeding the 2°C increase from the present temperatures of the earth, but they represent a significant change in tone and are an indication of momentum and cooperation from key players in the negotiations. This step by China is likely to be implemented by China seeking to develop large scale hydro-electric power projects on the rivers of the Tibetan Plateau as a normal and now legitimate means of reducing its carbon footprint. Its actions are more likely to be globally acceptable, India will have to set targets for its essential immediate, mid-term and long term objectives and ensure these steps are translated into action within the windows of opportunity available. The flows of the Brahmaputra and Barak, Subhansiri, Indus, and the Sutlej are likely to be altered both by China's likely activities and also by increased temperatures and global warming. India must develop the maximum possible hydro-electric power projects from the identified potential of the Brahmaputra Basin on priority. The simultaneous actions to create water storages wherever feasible to ensure availability in case of reduced supplies of water. The storages have to be so created that they could subsequently in a later phase, be a part of the National River Linking Project. The progress of the National River Linking Project itself must be developed on an equally urgent priority.

- Certain Measures that India has already initiated must now gain momentum , The recommended steps are :-

  ➤ Seek joint basin management of the Brahmaputra with India , China and Bangladesh .

  ➤ Raise global awareness on the criticality of these waters emanating from the Tibetan Plateau .

  ➤ India's must take initiatives for seeking broader-coalition on the Ganges-Brahmaputra-Meghna (GBM) river system involving Nepal, Bangladesh and Bhutan to convince China to accept a river-basin approach. Akin to the Mekong Sub-regional Cooperation (also referred to as the Lancang-Mekong River) .

> ➤ India and China do not have any bilateral treaty and are not part of any international treaty on water sharing. The user's right principle is the likely way forward. Both Brahmaputra and Barak have vast volumes of water as also the natural hydrological gradient allows the lower riparians, to harness the hydro-electric potential of the rivers in the lower reaches despite China's diversion plans on the rivers. In addition the larger quantity of water of the Brahmaputra is from the catchment areas within India's geographical boundaries these must be harnessed in the most suitable manner and as soon as possible.

- Pakistan is not likely to counter any of China's activities on the rivers, however , India must apply global pressures and seek coordination with Bangladesh and Nepal, as co-riparian states in actively countering China's water diversion plans. However , India must also learn the nuances of large water transfer projects for use in the National River Interlinking Project.

- India must learn from the Chinese existing arrangements with Kazakhstan and Russia on the Irtysh and Ili rivers and see how these countries are dealing with China to develop an insight into China's intentions and approach.

- Projects in the North Eastern states particularly Arunachal Pradesh should be accorded a priority. Delays on account of weather and environmental issues should not be allowed to interfere with the pace and tempo of progress.

- A deliberate plan to achieve the following steps must be put in place :-

  > ➤ Prepare for self sufficiency from water collected in catchment areas in India's geographical limits .Ensure by diplomatic and military actions that the security of these territorial areas is factored into the boundary resolution actions .

  > ➤ Build and operationalise maximum hydroelectric storage dams for actualizing the hydroelectric potential of the transboundary rivers as expeditiously as feasible.

➢ Concurrently, monitor and utilize the transboundary aquifers of the region to augment its requirements. Geographical areas where such tranboundary aquifers exist must be secured and their strategic value be given due importance.

➢ Climate change is likely to result in a phase of large increase of water because of melting glaciers especially in the Eastern Himalayas .Water storage and diversion projects must be planned to mitigate this issue and to optimally put this water to gainful use. The interlinking of rivers project in India will be of critical significance in this action.

➢ Ensure that global pressure is applied to restrict China's relentless pollution resulting in global warming and resultant glacial melt. The significance of the U.S.- China Cooperation: The Joint Agreement on Climate Change and Clean Energy in December 2014 should be understood[46]. It actually creates a legitimate argument for China to pursue large scale hydroelectric projects and water diversions to meet its water requirements.

Bhutan

India's cooperation with Bhutan on water issues is a successful model. Bhutan's geo-strategic locationplays a vital role in checking China's unilateral approach.

The "Comprehensive Scheme for Establishment of Hydro-meteorological and Flood Forecasting Network on rivers Common to India and Bhutan" scheme is in operation. The network consists of 44 Hydro-meteorological/ meteorological stations located in Bhutan and being maintained by the Royal Government of Bhutan with funding from India. The data received from these stations are utilized in India by the Central Water Commission for formulating flood forecasts[47]. The matter relating to problem of floods created by the rivers originating from Bhutan and coming to India was taken up with the Royal Government of Bhutan. Five meetings of Joint Group of Expert (JGE) have been held so far on flood management to discuss and assess the probable causes and effects of the recurring floods and erosion in the Southern foothills of Bhutan and adjoining plains in India. The collaborative efforts of both countries in mutually benefiting schemes is appositive and must be maintained. This should be continued and improved continuously.

A few measures which should be sustained are as follows:-

- India should continue to build upon the successes of hydro-cooperation with Bhutan. The commitment to achieve a target of 10,000 MW of hydroelectricity by 2020 is a step in the right direction. As explained earlier, the relations between India and Bhutan are structured in reciprocity.

- Bhutan's hydro electric power potential is significant, the projects must be suitably progressed by India to meet its own growing energy requirements. The Punasangchhu-I project , Punasangchhu-II (1200MW). Mangdechhu (1200MW), and Sankosh (4000MW) are steps in the right direction. The contract for these dams are also being executed by Indain companies , this is a mutually beneficial partnership and must be maintained with suitable actions.

Diplomatic Initiatives

For the rest of South Asia, with whom India has varying degrees of strained relationships, ties with Bhutan have always been a welcome respite. Government officials say they hope the rest of South Asia can learn from the India-Bhutan model, pointing out that Nepal's hydro-electric potential at 88,000 Mw is about three times of Bhutan, at 23,760 Mw[48].

The visit to Bhutan by Prime Minister Shri Narendra Modi was highly significant as it is his first visit abroad after he was sworn-in as the Prime Minister of India on 26 May 2014 in New Delhi. The visit reinforces the tradition of regular high-level exchanges between the two countries and upholds and strengthens the special and unique age-old friendship between Bhutan and India[49]. Prime Minister Shri Narendra Modi unveiled the Foundation Stone of the 600 Megawatt Kholongchu Hydropower Project which is a Joint Venture project between the Indian and Bhutanese PSUs, SJVNL and Druk Green Power Corporation. The construction of the Project which is located in Trashiyangtse in Eastern Bhutan is likely to commence soon.

Nepal

India and Nepal have had a long history of cooperation on water issues dotted with frequent misunderstandings and accusations. India needs to bring about a change in mindset of Nepal policy makers by investing in long-term relationships . Numerous bilateral mechanisms exist devoted to different aspects of water management. Nepal grudges India about the unequal benefits from water sharing between the nations. Issues like inadequate financial assistance , technical support and even sovereignty. India must assuage the justifiable aspirations of Nepal's concerns possibly by fair technological, financial and developmental assistance. Patient and fair handling of the issues will be required. The scope of bilateral cooperation must be enhanced. The importance of important tributaries of Ganga which flow into India from Nepal is critical for ecosystem sustenance as also for the large demand of water in the belt. The hydropower potential of Nepal must be utilized to maintain a steady relationship based on a fair and balanced system.. The renewed approach should be structured to achieve mutual benefits not a myopic focus on hydropower generation alone. Some factors which merit attention are as follows :-

- The seismic vulnerability of the areas make the terrain unsuitable for building large dams and large storages. India's must identify areas for a win- win strategy. Some plausible spheres could be:-

  ➢ To assist in flood management and control;

  ➢ Prevention of sediment, inundation and soil erosion; and irrigation which benefit both countries

- The Kosi and Gandak treaties should be reconsidered and the application of modern and contemporary technology, management tools and a mutually beneficial arrangement be arrived at.

Bangladesh

As per numerous water experts the Indo-Bangladesh Ganges Treaty, 1996 has been more than generous towards Bangladesh. However, Bangladesh still continues to complain against the inadequacy of the treaty and demands more water. Bangladesh has to be engaged being an important lower riparian in all domains. India must safeguard her own interest and negotiate with caution. The numerous issues raised by Bangladesh include :-

- Concern about the sharing of the Teesta River waters.

- Tipaimukh dam and the Indian project for interlinking of the waters.

Some basic actions that will give Bangladesh a reassurance and confidence are listed below:-

- The consultative and technical knowledge based framework must form the basis of this riparian relationship between the two. Cooperative arrangements based on water sharing and not on water rights is the way forward as is the case in any long term sustaining relationship.

- Climate change and deteriorating environmental conditions will be the main drivers of this relationship .

- It is likely that Bangladeshi efforts to meet Indian concerns would give them greater negotiating space specially over the sharing of waters, one of the primary Bangaldesh's concerns vis-à-vis India.

The ups and downs in the Teesta talks are proof that there is no easy approach. Bangladesh is keen that India comes to an early agreement not just on Teesta but also on all the major rivers that crisscross the two states. The West Bengal government in fact has been insisting that India should link security issues with water issues and make it conditional on Bangladesh to accept that before India agrees to any mutually acceptable solution of water sharing . India as the upper riparian should ensure that the equitable principles are fairly adhered to without undermining its own requirements.

Pakistan

The Indus Water Treaty has been generous towards Pakistan. The clauses of the treaty also impede hydroelectric and agricultural development in Jammu & Kashmir. India should make a considered proposal to Pakistan for revision of the treaty including the important issues of Jammu and

Kashmir as also the likely impacts of climate change which are not well factored in the existing treaty.

As the treaty does not have an exit clause it should not be abrogated, it is better to seek a renegotiation as permissible by International law and the Article XII of the IWT. In the eventuality of an unprecedented crisis or violation by Pakistan, India must be prepared for the contingency of unilaterally abrogating the treaty. Concurrent to the above mentioned activities India must create assets and dams to optimally utilise the waters of the Eastern and Western rivers going to Pakistan as permitted by the present treaty. India must also deliberate on the relevant suggestions made by numerous studies and committees over the years on the utilisation of the waters of the Eastern rivers.

Geographical areas occupied illegitimately and administered by Pakistan and China are being used by both countries for developing their assets , this control will extend to important water resources as well. Measures to restrict these and maintaining a controlling mechanism for these waters must be developed.

The following should from part of the Grand National Strategy to effectively develop the Western rivers of the IWT to our strategic advantage :-

(a) **Completion of Kishenganga Project.** Pakistan is in the process of construction of a hydro-electric project on Neelum river (downstream from Kishanganga). As per IWT, the nation having an existing project has priority rights over the water. Pakistan completion of Neelam-Jhelum project may spell trouble for own Kishanganga project. Pakistan fears that once India's Kishenganga project is complete it will have a devastating effect on the Pakistan's own hydro-power plans, the local economy and on the ecology. The Indian project will curb water flow to the Pakistani project to some extent besides affecting the local flora and fauna due to diversion of water from its original course. The project may also affect 133,209 hectares of agricultural land in the Neelum Valley and the Muzaffarabad district.

(b) **Completion of Projects on Chenab River.** Pakistan has often used the provisions of the Treaty to raise objections to the projects proposed by the Indian side and permitted under the Treaty. The completion of the planned projects would give a strategic edge to India wherein it has the capacity to withhold water for more than a month as also release it at will. However, the downstream projects must have the capability to handle more water that is being released from major upstream reservoirs like the Baglihar.

(c) **Identify Hydro-electric Power Projects on Indus and Jhelum.** India as a nation is perpetually short of power. Jammu and Kashmir has a potential of developing up to 20,000MW of power which is in the interests of the state and India. So in addition to giving storage capacity on these rivers, it will enhance power generation in the nation.

(d) **Domestic Purpose Clause.** As per IWT, it is permitted to use the water of the Western rivers for domestic purpose. This clause needs to be exploited to the maximum. For example, Baglihar is located on the Western side of the Seoj Dhar Mountain Range. The city of Jammu and its agricultural plains are located on the South Eastern side of the same range. A tunnel through this range can take away water from Chenab to Jammu, leaving Pakistani Sialkot completely dry. India has a full right to undertake this as one of the provisions of the IWT states that water could be used for the welfare of people of J & K. By creating a tunnel, India would be simply acting in the interests of the people of J&K. Loss of Chenab water cannot be replaced by diverting the Jhelum river water from the Mangla reservoir without upsetting the Sindhi interests. But an option for the same and preliminary planning for this and other such projects must be carried out.

(e) **Re-negotiation of the IWT.** India should call Pakistan's bluff and suggest renegotiation of the treaty in line with current political, economic, environmental and geo-political realities. That will test Pakistan's sincerity about "resolving' the water issue between the two countries. In the meanwhile, India should go ahead with the construction of the planned projects. India should also identify storage projects which are in accordance with the Treaty provisions. Many in India feel that the allocation of 80 % of waters to Pakistan and 20 % to India was an unfair settlement which was accepted by India as a goodwill gesture. The flip side to this is the other school of thought which is that at the time of partition, the territory that went to India was using less than 10 % of this water. Both sides feel aggrieved about the treaty. As the degree of dissatisfaction with the treaty has arisen, re-negotiation of the treaty as per the current geo strategic realities is a viable option.

(f) **Issues of Jammu and Kashmir.** There is a strong sense of grievance in Jammu and Kashmir that the treaty has made it very difficult for the state to derive any benefit by way of irrigation, hydro-electric power or navigation from the rivers that flow through it but stand allocated to Pakistan. The Government of India is attempting to address the issue but the objections from Pakistan are proving to be a stumbling block. The people of Jammu and Kashmir are vehemently against the IWT, which according to them has overlooked the interests of the locals of the state. Kashmir annually loses approximately US$1.3 billion on account of the prohibitions of the IWT by virtue of which the state cannot store water for irrigation purposes. An estimated 1.37 MHa of land is also devoid of irrigation facilities in Jammu and Kashmir due to restrictions imposed by the water treaty. India cannot afford to alienate the people of Jammu and Kashmir who have an equal right of access to natural resources for their development. Hence India has two options in this regard:-

(i) Renegotiate the treaty so that the interests of the locals of Jammu and Kashmir is not compromised.

(ii) Create adequate storage for irrigation purposes to ensure that the rights and the progress of the people of Jammu and Kashmir is not compromised.

(iii) Pakistan claims to champion the cause of the Kashmiri. It is in India's interests to expose the Pakistani doublespeak wherein it is blocking all India's initiatives for the welfare of the people of Kashmir. Either of the two measures suggested above will expose Pakistan's so called stand of 'Championing the Kashmiri cause' as any opposition would amount to sidelining the Kashmiri interest.

(g) **Coercive Water Diplomacy.** During the three wars (1965, 1971 and 1999) India had not even held out the water threat. International obligations apart, at times of conflict it is but natural to use all means at the disposal of a state to ensure victory.

(h) **Derecognise IWT.** Even though there is no exit clause in the treaty, the threat to unilaterally end the treaty must from part of the national strategy. All structural and operational facilities must continue to be developed keeping within the provisions of the IWT to make it realistic option.

(j) **Expose Shortcoming in Pakistan's Internal Water Politics.**
The internal river politics of Pakistan is also Punjab centric wherein the people of the Occupied Kashmir and Sindh do not benefit in a major way from the link canals and irrigation systems as the people of Punjab. It serves India's purposes to acquaint the people of Jammu and Kashmir of this fact. The global attention to self-defeating internal mismanagement of the available water resources in Pakistan will also convey that the criticalities that exist are manageable if suitable measure are taken on time.

(k) **Face The Problem.** There is an urgent need for Global and Indian think tanks, domain experts and scholars to actively pursue these critical issues and pressurize governments to take timely action to face and address this issue .

(l) On a priority India must take all actions to complete the resume and complete the construction of Tulbul Navigation Project. India has ramped up its hydroelectricity projects in recent years to try to boost its woefully inadequate power supplies. The government has a total of 45 projects either already completed or in the proposal stage on the Western rivers, some as large as 1000 megawatt and many as small as 2 and 3 megawatt[50].

India has always pursued the idea of joint development of river basins with some neighbouring countries. Environment, IWRM and climate change should be given priority in bilateral cooperation. India should propose a basin-oriented approach involving Nepal, Bhutan, Bangladesh, China and India to improve water management[51]. As a key player in South

Asia, India should think in terms of enabling Bhutan to export power to Bangladesh so as to allay the fears of a single buyer monopoly. It necessitates the path of prudent national water management and sensible co-riparian relations to secure freshwater supply in the long-term.

Endnotes

1 Heather Cooley, Newsha Ajami, Mai-Lan Ha, Veena Srinivasan, Jason Morrison, Kristina Donnelly, and Juliet Christian-Smith ,*Global Water Governance in the Twenty-First Century, The World's Water Volume 8,* pg 1 http://islandpress.org/worlds-water-volume-8

2 Water Security and the Global Water Agenda, A UN- Water Analytical Brief; United Nations University, Institute for Water, Environment & Health , 2013. http://www.unwater.org/downloads/watersecurity_analyticalbrief.pdf

3 Ibid

4 Ibid

5 Ibid

6 Interview of *Kirit S. Parikh, in* India's water crisis: causes and cures, *Produced by The National Bureau of Asian Research for the Senate India Caucus,* August 2013

7 Free Flow , Reaching Water Security Through Cooperation, Tudor Rose, UNESCO Publishing. http://digital.tudor-rose.co.uk/free-flow/files/assets/common/downloads/publication.pdf

8 India's National Water Policy, 2012; Government of India, Ministry of Water Resources India, Pages 3 and 5 http://wrmin.nic.in/writereaddata/NationalWaterPolicy/NWP2012Eng6495132651.pdf

9 Ibid ,1

10 Bilateral Cooperation, Government of India, Ministry of Water Resources India. http://wrmin.nic.in/forms/list.aspx?lid=345&Id=4

11 Ibid, 1

12 Chellaney Brahma, *Water, Peace, and War,* p. 287.

13 Ibid, 6

14 Chellaney Brahma , Water, Power, and Competition in Asia. Asian Survey, Vol. 54, Number 4, pp. 621–650 Posted on August 18, 2014,

15 2030 Water Resources Group (Barilla Group, Coca-Cola Company, International Finance Corporation, McKinsey & Company, Nestlé S.A., New Holland Agriculture, SABMiller PLC, Standard Chartered Bank, and Syngenta AG), *Charting Our Water Future*(New York: 2030 Water Resources Group, 2009),

16 Foster W, Exploring alternative futures of the World Water System., Building a second generation of World Water Scenarios , Driving force: Technology,

2010

17 Ibid , 15

18 Kao, H. M., Ren, H., Lee, C. S., Chang, C. P., Yen, J. Y., and Lin, T. H. "Determination of shallow water depth using optical satellite images." International Journal of Remote Sensing. 2009, 6241-6260.

19 Ibid,15

20 Fleischer, Torsten and Grunwald, Armin. "Making nanotechnology developments sustainable. A role for technology assessment?" Journal of Cleaner Production. 2007. 889-898.

21 Ibid,15

22 Commission for Integrated Water Resource Development, *Integrated Water Resource Development: A Plan for Action*, vol. 1 (New Delhi: Commission for Integrated Water Resource Development, Ministry of Water Resources, 1999); National Water Development Agency, Indian Ministry of Water Resources, "The Need," <http://goo.gl/bIuvm>.

23 Ibid ,15

24 Ibid, 6

25 Ibid ,15

26 Tushaar Shah and Uma Lele , GWP Technical Committee members, Climate Change, Food and Water Security in South Asia: Critical Issues and Cooperative Strategies in an Age of Increased Risk and Uncertainty A Global Water Partnership (GWP) and International Water Management Institute (IWMI) Workshop, 23-25 February 2011, Colombo, Sri Lanka pg 36

27 Saxena, N.C. (2010) Personal Communication with Uma Lele.

28 Seckler D, Barker R,Upali A et al, Water Scarcity in The Twenty first Century, 2010,Pg 40.

29 Ibid

30 Ibid

31 Ibid , 27

32 Paul Wyrwoll, India's Groundwater Crisis. posted on July 30,2012 IN DEVELOPMENT , WATER SECURITY, , Australian National University, Australia

33 WWAP (United Nations World Water Assessment Programme). 2014. *The United Nations World Water Development Report 2014: Water and Energy*. Paris, UNESCO. http://www.unesco.org/new/en/natural-sciences/

environment/water/wwap/wwdr/2014-water-and-energy/

34 The Planning Commission Approach to the 12th Plan :The Challenges of Urbanisation in India. http://12thplan.gov.in/12fyp_docs/17.pdf

35 IPCC, 2014: Summary for policymakers. In: *Climate Change 2014: Impacts, Adaptation, and Vulnerability. Part A: Global and Sectoral Aspects. Contribution of Working Group II to the Fifth Assessment Report of the Intergovernmental Panel on Climate Change* [Field, C.B., V.R. Barros, D.J. Dokken, K.J. Mach, M.D. astrandrea, T.E. Bilir, M. Chatterjee, K.L. Ebi, Y.O. Estrada, R.C. Genova, B. Girma, E.S. Kissel, A.N. Levy, S. MacCracken, P.R. Mastrandrea, and L.L. White (eds.)]. Cambridge University Press, Cambridge, United Kingdom and New York, NY, USA, pp. 1-32.

36 An interview with Jennifer L. Turner on , U.S.-China Cooperation: The Significance of the Joint Agreement on Climate Change and Clean Energy , Wilson Center NOW; Dec 04, 2014 http://www.wilsoncenter.org/article/us-china-cooperation-the-significance-the-joint-agreement-climate-change-and-clean-energy

37 Center For Climate Change and Energy Solutions. http://www.c2es.org/international/key-country-policies/india/climate-plan-summary

38 International Water Law Project (IWLP), Status of the Watercourses Convention, http://www.internationalwaterlaw.org/documents/intldocs/watercourse_status.html

39 Theme Paper on Transboundary Waters, World Water Day 2009 , Central Water Commission , Government Of India Ministry Of Water Resources. http://www.cwc.nic.in/main/downloads/Theme%20Paper%20WWD-2009.pdf

40 Ibid, 2

41 *Ibid,6*

42 Ibid, 15

43 Ibid

44 Ibid

45 Ibid

46 Ibid

47 Ministry for Water Resources, River Development and Ganga Rejuvenation, Government of India. http://wrmin.nic.in/forms/list.aspx?lid=350&Id=4

48 Bhutan king shows the way in South Asia, Business Standard, New Delhi ,January 28, 2013. http://www.business-standard.com/article/

international/bhutan-king-shows-the-way-in-south-asia-113012800096_1. html

49 Bhutan-India Joint Press Statement on the State Visit of Prime Minister of India Shri Narendra Modi to the Kingdom of Bhutan from 15-16 June 2014, Embassy of India, Thimpu, Bhutan. http://www.indianembassythimphu.bt/pages.php?id=96

50 Mandhana Niharika ,Water Wars: Why India and Pakistan Are Squaring Off Over Their Rivers, Time, Monday, Apr. 16, 2012. http://content.time.com/ time/world/article/0,8599,2111601,00.html

51 Water Security For India: The External Dynamics; *Institute for Defence Studies and Analyses Task Force Report, 2010.* http://www.indiaenvironmentportal. org.in/files/book_WaterSecurity.pdf

UN Convention on the Law of the Non-navigational Uses of International Watercourses

Adopted by the UN General Assembly in resolution 51/229 of 21 May 1997

The Parties to the present Convention,

Conscious of the importance of international watercourses and the non-navigational uses thereof in many regions of the world,

Having in mind Article 13, paragraph 1 (a), of the Charter of the United Nations, which provides that the General Assembly shall initiate studies and make recommendations for the purpose of encouraging the progressive development of international law and its codification,

Considering that successful codification and progressive development of rules of international law regarding non-navigational uses of international watercourses would assist in promoting and implementing the purposes and principles set forth in Articles 1 and 2 of the Charter of the United Nations,

Taking into account the problems affecting many international watercourses resulting from, among other things, increasing demands and pollution,

Expressing the conviction that a framework convention will ensure the utilisation, development, conservation, management and protection of international watercourses and the promotion of the optimal and sustainable utilisation thereof for present and future generations

Affirming the importance of international cooperation and good neighbourliness in this field,

Aware of the special situation and needs of developing countries,

Recalling the principles and recommendations adopted by the United Nations Conference on Environment and Development of 1992 in the Rio Declaration and Agenda 21,

Recalling also the existing bilateral and multilateral agreements regarding the non-navigational uses of international watercourses,

Mindful of the valuable contribution of international organisations, both governmental and non-governmental, to the codification and progressive development of international law in this field,

Appreciative of the work carried out by the International Law Commission on the law of the non-navigational uses of international watercourses,

Bearing in mind United Nations General Assembly resolution 49/52 of 9 December 1994,

Have agreed as follows:

PART I. INTRODUCTION

Article 1: Scope of the present Convention

1. The present Convention applies to uses of international watercourses and of their waters for purposes other than navigation and to measures of protection, preservation and management related to the uses of those watercourses and their waters.

2. The uses of international watercourses for navigation is not within the scope of the present Convention except insofar as other uses affect navigation or are affected by navigation.

Article 2: Use of Terms

For the purposes of the present Convention:

(a) "Watercourse" means a system of surface waters and groundwaters constituting by virtue of their physical relationship a unitary whole and normally flowing into a common terminus;

(b) "International watercourse" means a watercourse, parts of which are situated in different States;

(c) "Watercourse State" means a State Party to the present Convention in whose territory part of an international watercourse is situated, or a Party that is a regional economic integration organization, in the territory of one or more of whose Member States part of an international watercourse is situated;

(d) "Regional economic integration organization" means an organization constituted by sovereign States of a given region, to which its member States have transferred competence in respect of matters governed by this Convention and which has been duly authorized in accordance with its internal procedures, to sign, ratify, accept, approve or accede to it.

Article 3: Watercourse Agreements

1. In the absence of an agreement to the contrary, nothing in the present Convention shall affect the rights or obligations of a watercourse State arising from agreements in force for it on the date on which it became a party to the present Convention.

2. Notwithstanding the provisions of paragraph 1, parties to agreements referred to in paragraph 1 may, where necessary, consider harmonizing such agreements with the basic principles of the present Convention.

3. Watercourse States may enter into one or more agreements, hereinafter referred to as "watercourse agreements", which apply and adjust the provisions of the present Convention to the characteristics and uses of a particular international watercourse or part thereof.

4. Where a watercourse agreement is concluded between two or more watercourse States, it shall define the waters to which it applies. Such an agreement may be entered into with respect to an entire international watercourse or any part thereof or a particular project programme or use except insofar as the agreement adversely affects, to a significant extent, the use by one or more other watercourse States of the waters of the watercourse, without their express consent.

5. Where a watercourse State considers that adjustment and application of the provisions of the present Convention is required because of the characteristics and uses of a particular international watercourse, watercourse States shall consult with a view to negotiating in good faith for the purpose of concluding a watercourse agreement or agreements.

6. Where some but not all watercourse States to a particular international watercourse are parties to an agreement, nothing in such agreement shall

affect the rights or obligations under the present Convention of watercourse States that are not parties to such an agreement.

Article 4: Parties to Watercourse Agreements

1. Every watercourse State is entitled to participate in the negotiation of and to become a party to any watercourse agreement that applies to the entire international watercourse, as well as to participate in any relevant consultations.

2. A watercourse State whose use of an international watercourse may be affected to a significant extent by the implementation of a proposed watercourse agreement that applies only to a part of the watercourse or to a particular project, programme or use is entitled to participate in consultations on such an agreement and, where appropriate, in the negotiation thereof in good faith with a view to becoming a party thereto, to the extent that its use is thereby affected.

PART II. GENERAL PRINCIPLES

Article 5: Equitable and Reasonable Utilisation and Participation

1. Watercourse States shall in their respective territories utilize an international watercourse in an equitable and reasonable manner. In particular, an international watercourse shall be used and developed by watercourse States with a view to attaining optimal and sustainable utilisation thereof and benefits therefrom, taking into account the interests of the watercourse States concerned, consistent with adequate protection of the watercourse.

2. Watercourse States shall participate in the use, development and protection of an international watercourse in an equitable and reasonable manner. Such participation includes both the right to utilize the watercourse and the duty to cooperate in the protection and development thereof, as provided in the present Convention.

Article 6: Factors Relevant to Equitable and Reasonable Utilisation

1. Utilisation of an international watercourse in an equitable and reasonable manner within the meaning of article 5 requires taking into account all

relevant factors and circumstances, including:

(a) Geographic, hydrographic, hydrological, climatic, ecological and other factors of a natural character;

(b) The social and economic needs of the watercourse States concerned;

(c) The population dependent on the watercourse in each watercourse State;

(d) The effects of the use or uses of the watercourses in one watercourse State on other watercourse States;

(e) Existing and potential uses of the watercourse;

(f) Conservation, protection, development and economy of use of the water resources of the watercourse and the costs of measures taken to that effect;

(g) The availability of alternatives, of comparable value, to a particular planned or existing use.

2. In the application of article 5 or paragraph 1 of this article, watercourse States concerned shall, when the need arises, enter into consultations in a spirit of cooperation.

3. The weight to be given to each factor is to be determined by its importance in comparison with that of other relevant factors. In determining what is a reasonable and equitable use, all relevant factors are to be considered together and a conclusion reached on the basis of the whole.

Article 7: Obligation Not to Cause Significant Harm

1. Watercourse States shall, in utilizing an international watercourse in their territories, take all appropriate measures to prevent the causing of significant harm to other watercourse States.

2. Where significant harm nevertheless is caused to another watercourse State, the States whose use causes such harm shall, in the absence of agreement to such use, take all appropriate measures, having due regard for the provisions of articles 5 and 6, in consultation with the affected State, to eliminate or mitigate such harm and, where appropriate, to discuss the question of compensation.

Article 8: General Obligation to Cooperate

1. Watercourse States shall cooperate on the basis of sovereign equality, territorial integrity, mutual benefit and good faith in order to attain optimal utilisation and adequate protection of an international watercourse.

2. In determining the manner of such cooperation, watercourse States may consider the establishment of joint mechanisms or commissions, as deemed necessary by them, to facilitate cooperation on relevant measures and procedures in the light of experience gained through cooperation in existing joint mechanisms and commissions in various regions.

Article 9: Regular Exchange of Data and Information

1. Pursuant to article 8, watercourse States shall on a regular basis exchange readily available data and information on the condition of the watercourse, in particular that of a hydrological, meteorological, hydrogeological and ecological nature and related to the water quality as well as related forecasts.

2. If a watercourse State is requested by another watercourse State to provide data or information that is not readily available, it shall employ its best efforts to comply with the request but may condition its compliance upon payment by the requesting State of the reasonable costs of collecting and, where appropriate, processing such data or information.

3. Watercourse States shall employ their best efforts to collect and, where appropriate, to process data and information in a manner which facilitates its utilisation by the other watercourse States to which it is communicated.

Article 10: Relationship Between Different Kinds of Uses

1. In the absence of agreement or custom to the contrary, no use of an international watercourse enjoys inherent priority over other uses.

2. In the event of a conflict between uses of an international watercourse, it shall be resolved with reference to articles 5 to 7, with special regard being given to the requirements of vital human needs.

PART III. PLANNED MEASURES

Article 11: Information Concerning Planned Measures

Watercourse States shall exchange information and consult each other and, if necessary, negotiate on the possible effects of planned measures on the condition of an international watercourse.

Article 12: Notification Concerning Planned Measures with Possible Adverse Effects

Before a watercourse State implements or permits the implementation of planned measures which may have a significant adverse effect upon other watercourse States, it shall provide those States with timely notification thereof. Such notification shall be accompanied by available technical data and information, including the results of any environmental impact assessment, in order to enable the notified States to evaluate the possible effects of the planned measures.

Article 13: Period for Reply to Notification

Unless otherwise agreed:

(a) A watercourse State providing a notification under article 12 shall allow the notified States a period of six months within which to study and evaluate the possible effects of the planned measures and to communicate the findings to it;

(b) This period shall, at the request of a notified State for which the evaluation of the planned measures poses special difficulty, be extended for a period of six months.

Article 14: Obligations of the Notifying State During the Period for Reply

During the period referred to in article 13, the notifying State:

(a) Shall cooperate with the notified States by providing them, on request, with any additional data and information that is available and necessary for an accurate evaluation; and

(b) Shall not implement or permit the implementation of the planned measures without the consent of the notified States.

Article 15: Reply to Notification

The notified States shall communicate their findings to the notifying State as early as possible within the period applicable pursuant to article 13. If a notified State finds that implementation of the planned measures would be inconsistent with the provisions of articles 5 or 7, it shall attach to its finding a documented explanation setting forth the reasons for the finding.

Article 16: Absence of Reply to Notification

1. If, within the period applicable pursuant to article 13, the notifying State receives no communication under article 15, it may, subject to its obligations under articles 5 and 7, proceed with the implementation of the planned measures, in accordance with the notification and any other data and information provided to the notified States.

2. Any claim to compensation by a notified State which has failed to reply within the period applicable pursuant to article 13 may be offset by the costs incurred by the notifying State for action undertaken after the expiration of the time for a reply which would not have been undertaken if the notified State had objected within that period.

Article 17: Consultations and Negotiations Concerning Planned Measures

1. If a communication is made under article 15 that implementation of the planned measures would be inconsistent with the provisions of articles 5 or 7, the notifying State and the State making the communication shall enter into consultations and, if necessary, negotiations with a view to arriving at an equitable resolution of the situation.

2. The consultations and negotiations shall be conducted on the basis that each State must in good faith pay reasonable regard to the rights and legitimate interests of the other State.

3. During the course of the consultations and negotiations, the notifying State shall, if so requested by the notified State at the time it makes the communication, refrain from implementing or permitting the

implementation of the planned measures for a period of six months unless otherwise agreed.

Article 18: Procedures in the Absence of Notification

1. If a watercourse State has reasonable grounds to believe that another watercourse State is planning measures that may have a significant adverse effect upon it, the former State may request the latter to apply the provisions of article 12. The request shall be accompanied by a documented explanation setting forth its grounds.

2. In the event that the State planning the measures nevertheless finds that it is not under an obligation to provide a notification under article 12, it shall so inform the other State, providing a documented explanation setting forth the reasons for such finding. If this finding does not satisfy the other State, the two States shall, at the request of that other State, promptly enter into consultations and negotiations in the manner indicated in paragraphs 1 and 2 of article 17.

3. During the course of the consultations and negotiations, the State planning the measures shall, if so requested by the other State at the time it requests the initiation of consultations and negotiations, refrain from implementing or permitting the implementation of those measures for a period of six months unless otherwise agreed.

Article 19: Urgent Implementation of Planned Measures

1. In the event that the implementation of planned measures is of the utmost urgency in order to protect public health, public safety or other equally important interests, the State planning the measures may, subject to articles 5 and 7, immediately proceed to implementation, notwithstanding the provisions of article 14 and paragraph 3 of article 17.

2. In such case, a formal declaration of the urgency of the measures shall be communicated without delay to the other watercourse States referred to in article 12 together with the relevant data and information.

3. The State planning the measures shall, at the request of any of the States referred to in paragraph 2, promptly enter into consultations and negotiations with it in the manner indicated in paragraphs 1 and 2 of article 17.

PART IV. PROTECTION, PRESERVATION AND MANAGEMENT

Article 20: Protection and Preservation of Ecosystems

Watercourse States shall, individually and, where appropriate, jointly, protect and preserve the ecosystems of international watercourses.

Article 21: Prevention, Reduction and Control of Pollution

1. For the purpose of this article, "pollution of an international watercourse" means any detrimental alteration in the composition or quality of the waters of an international watercourse which results directly or indirectly from human conduct.

2. Watercourse States shall, individually and, where appropriate, jointly, prevent, reduce and control the pollution of an international watercourse that may cause significant harm to other watercourse States or to their environment, including harm to human health or safety, to the use of the waters for any beneficial purpose or to the living resources of the watercourse. Watercourse States shall take steps to harmonize their policies in this connection.

3. Watercourse States shall, at the request of any of them, consult with a view to arriving at mutually agreeable measures and methods to prevent, reduce and control pollution of an international watercourse, such as:

(a) Setting joint water quality objectives and criteria;

(b) Establishing techniques and practices to address pollution from point and non-point sources;

(c) Establishing lists of substances the introduction of which into the waters of an international watercourse is to be prohibited, limited, investigated or monitored.

Article 22: Introduction of Alien or New Species

Watercourse States shall take all measures necessary to prevent the introduction of species, alien or new, into an international watercourse which may have effects detrimental to the ecosystem of the watercourse resulting in significant harm to other watercourse States.

Article 23: Protection and Preservation of the Marine Environment

Watercourse States shall, individually and, where appropriate, in cooperation with other States, take all measures with respect to an international watercourse that are necessary to protect and preserve the marine environment, including estuaries, taking into account generally accepted international rules and standards.

Article 24: Management

1. Watercourse States shall, at the request of any of them, enter into consultations concerning the management of an international watercourse, which may include the establishment of a joint management mechanism.

2. For the purposes of this article, "management" refers, in particular, to:

(a) Planning the sustainable development of an international watercourse and providing for the implementation of any plans adopted; and

(b) Otherwise promoting the rational and optimal utilisation, protection and control of the watercourse.

Article 25: Regulation

1. Watercourse States shall cooperate, where appropriate, to respond to needs or opportunities for regulation of the flow of the waters of an international watercourse.

2. Unless otherwise agreed, watercourse States shall participate on an equitable basis in the construction and maintenance or defrayal of the costs of such regulation works as they may have agreed to undertake.

3. For the purposes of this article, "regulation" means the use of hydraulic works or any other continuing measure to alter, vary or otherwise control the flow of the waters of an international watercourse.

Article 26: Installations

1. Watercourse States shall, within their respective territories, employ their best efforts to maintain and protect installations, facilities and other works

related to an international watercourse.

2. Watercourse States shall, at the request of any of them which has reasonable grounds to believe that it may suffer significant adverse effects, enter into consultations with regard to:

(a) The safe operation and maintenance of installations, facilities or other works related to an international watercourse; and

(b) The protection of installations, facilities or other works from willful or negligent acts or the forces of nature.

PART V. HARMFUL CONDITIONS AND EMERGENCY SITUATIONS

Article 27: Prevention and mitigation of harmful conditions

Watercourse States shall, individually and, where appropriate, jointly, take all appropriate measures to prevent or mitigate conditions related to an international watercourse that may be harmful to other watercourse States, whether resulting from natural causes or human conduct, such as flood or ice conditions, water-borne diseases, siltation, erosion, salt-water intrusion, drought or desertification.

Article 28: Emergency situations

1. For the purposes of this article, "emergency" means a situation that causes, or poses an imminent threat of causing, serious harm to watercourse States or other States and that results suddenly from natural causes, such as floods, the breaking up of ice, landslides or earthquakes, or from human conduct, such as industrial accidents.

2. A watercourse State shall, without delay and by the most expeditious means available, notify other potentially affected States and competent international organisations of any emergency originating within its territory.

3. A watercourse State within whose territory an emergency originates shall, in cooperation with potentially affected States and, where appropriate, competent international organisations, immediately take all practicable measures necessitated by the circumstances to prevent, mitigate and

eliminate harmful effects of the emergency.

4. When necessary, watercourse States shall jointly develop contingency plans for responding to emergencies, in cooperation, where appropriate, with other potentially affected States and competent international organisations.

PART VI. MISCELLANEOUS PROVISIONS

Article 29: International watercourses and installations in time of armed conflict

International watercourses and related installations, facilities and other works shall enjoy the protection accorded by the principles and rules of international law applicable in international and non-international armed conflict and shall not be used in violation of those principles and rules.

Article 30: Indirect Procedures

In cases where there are serious obstacles to direct contacts between watercourse States, the States concerned shall fulfill their obligations of cooperation provided for in the present Convention, including exchange of data and information, notification, communication, consultations and negotiations, through any indirect procedure accepted by them.

Article 31: Data and Information Vital to National Defence or Security

Nothing in the present Convention obliges a watercourse State to provide data or information vital to its national defence or security. Nevertheless, that State shall cooperate in good faith with the other watercourse States with a view to providing as much information as possible under the circumstances.

Article 32: Non-discrimination

Unless the watercourse States concerned have agreed otherwise for the protection of the interests of persons, natural or juridical, who have suffered or are under a serious threat of suffering significant transboundary harm as a result of activities related to an international watercourse, a watercourse

State shall not discriminate on the basis of nationality or residence or place where the injury occurred, in granting to such persons, in accordance with its legal system, access to judicial or other procedures, or a right to claim compensation or other relief in respect of significant harm caused by such activities carried on in its territory.

Article 33: Settlement of disputes

1. In the event of a dispute between two or more Parties concerning the interpretation or application of the present Convention, the Parties concerned shall, in the absence of an applicable agreement between them, seek a settlement of the dispute by peaceful means in accordance with the following provisions.

2. If the Parties concerned cannot reach agreement by negotiation requested by one of them, they may jointly seek the good offices of, or request mediation or conciliation by, a third party, or make use, as appropriate, of any joint watercourse institutions that may have been established by them or agree to submit the dispute to arbitration or to the International Court of Justice.

3. Subject to the operation of paragraph 10, if after six months from the time of the request for negotiations referred to in paragraph 2, the Parties concerned have not been able to settle their dispute through negotiation or any other means referred to in paragraph 2, the dispute shall be submitted, at the request of any of the parties to the dispute, to impartial fact-finding in accordance with paragraphs 4 to 9, unless the Parties otherwise agree.

4. Fact-finding Commission shall be established, composed of one member nominated by each Party concerned and in addition a member not having the nationality of any of the Parties concerned chosen by the nominated members who shall serve as Chairman.

5. If the members nominated by the Parties are unable to agree on a Chairman within three months of the request for the establishment of the Commission, any Party concerned may request the Secretary-General of the United Nations to appoint the Chairman who shall not have the nationality of any of the parties to the dispute or of any riparian State of the watercourse concerned. If one of the Parties fails to nominate a member within three months of the initial request pursuant to paragraph 3, any

other Party concerned may request the Secretary-General of the United Nations to appoint a person who shall not have the nationality of any of the parties to the dispute or of any riparian State of the watercourse concerned. The person so appointed shall constitute a single-member Commission.

6. The Commission shall determine its own procedure.

7. The Parties concerned have the obligation to provide the Commission with such information as it may require and, on request, to permit the Commission to have access to their respective territory and to inspect any facilities, plant, equipment, construction or natural feature relevant for the purpose of its inquiry.

8. The Commission shall adopt its report by a majority vote, unless it is a single-member Commission, and shall submit that report to the Parties concerned setting forth its findings and the reasons therefore and such recommendations as it deems appropriate for an equitable solution of the dispute, which the Parties concerned shall consider in good faith.

9. The expenses of the Commission shall be borne equally by the Parties concerned

10. When ratifying, accepting, approving or acceding to the present Convention, or at any time thereafter, a Party which is not a regional economic integration organization may declare in a written instrument submitted to the Depositary that, in respect of any dispute not resolved in accordance with paragraph 2, it recognizes as compulsory ipso facto and without special agreement in relation to any Party accepting the same obligation:

(a) Submission of the dispute to the International Court of Justice; and/or

(b) Arbitration by an arbitral tribunal established and operating, 'unless the parties to the dispute otherwise agreed, in accordance with the procedure laid down in the annex to the present Convention.

A Party which is a regional economic integration organization may make a declaration with like effect in relation to arbitration in accordance with subparagraph (b).

PART VII. FINAL CLAUSES

Article 34: Signature

The present Convention shall be open for signature by all States and by regional economic integration organisations from 21 May 1997 until 20 May 2000 at United Nations Headquarters in New York.

Article 35: Ratification, Acceptance, Approval or Accession

1. The present Convention is subject to ratification, acceptance, approval or accession by States and by regional economic integration organisations. The instruments of ratification, acceptance, approval or accession shall be deposited with the Secretary-General of the United Nations.

2. Any regional economic integration organization which becomes a Party to this Convention without any of its member States being a Party shall be bound by all the obligations under the Convention. In the case of such organisations, one or more of whose member States is a Party to this Convention, the organization and its member States shall decide on their respective responsibilities for the performance of their obligations under the Convention. In such cases, the organization and the member States shall not be entitled to exercise rights under the Convention concurrently.

3. In their instruments of ratification, acceptance, approval or accession, the regional economic integration organisations shall declare the extent of their competence with respect to the matters governed by the Convention. These organisations shall also inform the Secretary-General of the United Nations of any substantial modification in the extent of their competence.

Article 36: Entry into Force

1. The present Convention shall enter into force on the ninetieth day following the date of deposit of the thirty-fifth instrument of ratification, acceptance, approval or accession with the Secretary-General of the United Nations.

2. For each State or regional economic integration organization that ratifies, accepts or approves the Convention or accedes thereto after the deposit of the thirty-fifth instrument of ratification, acceptance, approval or accession, the Convention shall enter into force on the ninetieth day after

the deposit by such State or regional economic integration organization of its instrument of ratification, acceptance, approval or accession.

3. For the purposes of paragraphs 1 and 2, any instrument deposited by a regional economic integration organization shall not be counted as additional those deposited by States.

Article 37: Authentic Texts

The original of the present Convention, of which the Arabic, Chinese, English, French, Russian and Spanish texts are equally authentic, shall be deposited with the Secretary-General of the United Nations.

IN WITNESS WHEREOF the undersigned plenipotentiaries, being duly authorized thereto, have signed this Convention.

DONE at New York, this _____ day of one thousand nine hundred and ninety-seven.

ANNEX

ARBITRATION

Article 1

Unless the parties to the dispute otherwise agree, the arbitration pursuant to article 33 of the Convention shall take place in accordance with articles 2 to 14 of the present annex.

Article 2

The claimant party shall notify the respondent party that it is referring a dispute to arbitration pursuant to article 33 of the Convention. The notification shall state the subject matter of arbitration and include, in particular, the articles of the Convention, the interpretation or application of which are at issue. If the parties do not agree on the subject matter of the dispute, the arbitral tribunal shall determine the subject matter.

Article 3

1. In disputes between two parties, the arbitral tribunal shall consist of three members. Each of the parties to the dispute shall appoint an arbitrator and the two arbitrators so appointed shall designate by common agreement the third arbitrator, who shall be the Chairman of the tribunal. The latter shall not' be a national of one of the parties to the dispute or of any riparian State of the watercourse concerned, nor have his or her usual place of residence in the territory of one of these parties or such riparian State, nor have dealt with the case in any other capacity.

2. In disputes between more than two parties, parties in the same interest shall appoint one arbitrator jointly by agreement.

3. Any vacancy shall be filled in the manner prescribed for the initial appointment.

Article 4

1. If the Chairman of the arbitral tribunal has not been designated within two months of the appointment of the second arbitrator, the President of the International Court of Justice shall, at the request of a party, designate the Chairman within a further two-month period.

2. If one of the parties to the dispute does not appoint an arbitrator within two months of receipt of the request, the other party may inform the President of the International Court of Justice, who shall make the designation within a further two-month period.

Article 5

The arbitral tribunal shall render its decisions in accordance with the provisions of this Convention and international law.

Article 6

Unless the parties to the dispute otherwise agree, the arbitral tribunal shall determine its own rules of procedure.

Article 7

The arbitral tribunal may, at the request of one of the Parties, recommend essential interim measures of protection.

Article 8

1. The parties to the dispute shall facilitate the work of the arbitral tribunal and, in particular, using all means at their disposal, shall:

(a) Provide it with all relevant documents, information and facilities; and

(b) Enable it', when necessary, to call witnesses or experts and receive their evidence.

2. The parties and the arbitrators are under an obligation to protect the confidentiality of any information they receive in confidence during the proceedings of the arbitral tribunal.

Article 9

Unless the arbitral tribunal determines otherwise because of the particular circumstances of the case, the costs of the tribunal shall be borne by the parties to the dispute in equal shares. The tribunal shall keep a record of all its costs, and shall furnish a final statement thereof to the parties.

Article 10

Any Party that has an interest of a legal nature in the subject matter of the dispute which may be affected by the decision in the case, may intervene in the proceedings with the consent of the tribunal.

Article 11

The tribunal may hear and determine counterclaims arising directly out of the subject matter of the dispute.

Article 12

Decisions both on procedure and substance of the arbitral tribunal shall be taken by a majority vote of its members.

Article 13

If one of the parties to the dispute does not appear before the arbitral tribunal or fails to defend its case, the other party may request the tribunal to continue the proceedings and to make its award. Absence of a party or a failure of a party to defend its case shall not constitute a bar to the proceedings. Before rendering its final decision, the arbitral tribunal must satisfy itself that the claim is well founded in fact and law.

Article 14

1. The tribunal shall render its final decision within five months of the date on which it is fully constituted unless it finds it necessary to extend the time limit for a period which should not exceed five more months.

2. The final decision of the arbitral tribunal shall be confined to the subject matter of the dispute and shall state the reasons on which it is based'. It shall contain the names of the members who have participated and the date of the final decision. Any member of the tribunal may attach a separate or dissenting opinion to the final decision.

3. The award shall be binding on the parties to the dispute. It shall be without appeal unless the parties to the dispute have agreed in advance to an appellate procedure.

4. Any controversy which may arise between the parties to the dispute as regards the interpretation or manner of implementation of the final decision may be submitted by either party for decision to the arbitral tribunal which rendered it.

STATUS OF SIGNATORIES

THE UN CONVENTION ON NON – NAVIGATIONAL USES OF WATER, 1997

Participant	Signature (S)	Ratification (R)	Acceptance (A)	Accession (a)	Approval (AA)
Benin	-	-	-	5 July 2012	-
Burkina Faso	-	-	-	22 March 2011	-
Chad	-	-	-	26 September 2012	-
Côte d'Ivoire	25 September 1998	25 February 2014	-	-	-
Denmark	-	-	-	30 April 2012	-
Finland	31 October 1997	-	23 January 1998	-	-
France	-	-	-	24 February 2011	-
Germany	13 August 1998	15 January 2007	-	-	-
Greece	-	-	-	2 December 2010	-
Guinea-Bissau	-	-	-	19 May 2010	-

Participant	Signature (S)	Ratification (R)	Acceptance (A)	Accession (a)	Approval (AA)
Hungary	20 July 1999				26 January 2000
Iraq				9 July 2001	
Ireland				**20 December 2013**	
Italy				**30 November 2012**	
Jordan	17 April 1999	22 June 1999			
Lebanon				25 May 1999	
Libyan Arab Jamahiriya				14 June 2005	
Luxembourg	14 October 1997	**8 June 2012**			
Montenegro				**24 September 2013**	
Morocco				13 April 2011	
Namibia	19 May 2000	29 August 2001			
Netherlands	9 March 2000		9 January 2001		
Niger				**20 February 2013**	

Participant	Signature (S)	Ratification (R)	Acceptance (A)	Accession (a)	Approval (AA)
Nigeria		27 September 2010			
Norway	30 September 1998	30 September 1998			
"State of Palestine"				**2 January 2015**	
Paraguay	25 August 1998				
Portugal	11 November 1997	22 June 2005			
Qatar				28 February 2002	
South Africa	13 August 1997	26 October 1998			
Spain				24 September 2009;	
Sweden				15 June 2000	
Syrian Arab Republic	11 August 1997	2 April 1998			
Tunisia	19 May 2000	22 April 2009			

Participant	Signature (S)	Ratification (R)	Acceptance (A)	Accession (a)	Approval (AA)
United Kingdom of Great Britain & Northern Ireland				**13 December 2013**	
Uzbekistan				4 September 2007	
Venezuela (Bolivarian Republic of)	22 September 1997				
Vietnam					**19 May 2014**
Yemen	17 May 2000				

Source: International Water Law Project http://www.internationalwaterlaw. org/documents/intldocs/watercourse_status.html

DECLARATIONS AND RESERVATIONS (Unless otherwise indicated, the declarations and reservations were made upon ratification, acceptance, approval or accession.)

Denmark - 30 April 2012

"Declaration: Until further notice, the Convention shall not apply to the Faroe Islands and Greenland."

Hungary

"Declaration: The Government of the Republic of Hungary declares itself bound by either of the two means for the settlement of disputes (International Court of Justice, arbitration), reserving its right to agree on the competent body of jurisdiction, as the case may be."

Montenegro

"Declaration: Montenegro declares that in respect of any dispute not resolved in accordance with Article 33 paragraph 2 of the said Convention, Montenegro recognizes as compulsory ipso facto, and without special agreement in relationship to any party accepting the same obligation: 1. Submission of the dispute to the International Court of Justice; and/or 2. Arbitration by an arbitral tribunal established and operating, unless the parties to the dispute otherwise agreed, in accordance with the procedure laid down in the annex to the present Convention.""

Netherlands - 17 February 2010

"Declaration: The Kingdom of the Netherlands declares, in accordance with paragraph 10 of Article 33 of the United Nations Convention on the Law of the Non-Navigational Uses of International Watercourses, that it accepts both means of dispute settlement referred to in that paragraph as compulsory in relation to any Party accepting one or both means of dispute settlement."

Syrian Arab Republic

"Reservation: The acceptance by the Syrian Arab Republic of this Convention and its ratification by the Government shall not under any circumstances be taken to imply recognition of Israel and shall not lead to its entering into relations therewith that are governed by its provisions."

OBJECTIONS (Unless otherwise indicated, the objections were made upon ratification, acceptance approval or accession.)

Israel - 15 July 1998

"Declaration: In regard to the reservation made by the Syrian Arab Republic upon ratification:

In view of the Government of the State of Israel such reservation, which is explicitly of a political nature, is incompatible with the purposes and objectives of this Convention and cannot in any way affect whatever obligations are binding upon the Syrian Arab Republic under general international treaty law or under particular conventions. The Government of the State of Israel will, in so far as concerns the substance of the matter, adopt towards the Syrian Arab Republic an attitude of complete reciprocity."

GOVERNMENT OF INDIA
Ministry of Water Resources

NATIONAL WATER POLICY (2012)

1. PREAMBLE

1.1   A scarce natural resource, water is fundamental to life, livelihood, food security and sustainable development. India has more than 18 % of the world's population, but has only 4% of world's renewable water resources and 2.4% of world's land area. There are further limits on utilisable quantities of water owing to uneven distribution over time and space. In addition, there are challenges of frequent floods and droughts in one or the other part of the country. With a growing population and rising needs of a fast developing nation as well as the given indications of the impact of climate change, availability of utilisable water will be under further strain in future with the possibility of deepening water conflicts among different user groups. Low consciousness about the scarcity of water and its life sustaining and economic value results in its mismanagement, wastage, and inefficient use, as also pollution and reduction of flows below minimum ecological needs. In addition, there are inequities in distribution and lack of a unified perspective in planning, management and use of water resources. The objective of the National Water Policy is to take cognizance of the existing situation, to propose a framework for creation of a system of laws and institutions and for a plan of action with a unified national perspective.

1.2   The present scenario of water resources and their management in India has given rise to several concerns, important amongst them are;

(i)   Large parts of India have already become water stressed. Rapid growth in demand for water due to population growth, urbanisation and changing lifestyle pose serious challenges to water security.

(ii)   Issues related to water governance have not been addressed adequately. Mismanagement of water resources has led to a critical situation in many parts of the country.

(iii) There is wide temporal and spatial variation in availability of water, which may increase substantially due to a combination of climate change, causing deepening of water crisis and incidences of water related disasters, i.e., floods, increased erosion and increased frequency of droughts, etc.

(iv) Climate change may also increase the sea levels. This may lead to salinity intrusion in ground water aquifers / surface waters and increased coastal inundation in coastal regions, adversely impacting habitations, agriculture and industry in such regions.

(v) Access to safe water for drinking and other domestic needs still continues to be a problem in many areas. Skewed availability of water between different regions and different people in the same region and also the intermittent and unreliable water supply system has the potential of causing social unrest.

(vi) Groundwater, though part of hydrological cycle and a community resource, is still perceived as an individual property and is exploited inequitably and without any consideration to its sustainability leading to its over-exploitation in several areas.

(vii) Water resources projects, though multi-disciplinary with multiple stakeholders, are being planned and implemented in a fragmented manner without giving due consideration to optimum utilisation, environment sustainability and holistic benefit to the people.

(viii) Inter-regional, inter-State, intra-State, as also inter-sectoral disputes in sharing of water, strain relationships and hamper the optimal utilisation of water through scientific planning on basin/sub-basin basis.

(ix) Grossly inadequate maintenance of existing irrigation infrastructure has resulted in wastage and under-utilisation of available resources. There is a widening gap between irrigation potential created and utilized.

(x) Natural water bodies and drainage channels are being encroached upon, and diverted for other purposes. Groundwater recharge zones are often blocked.

(xi) Growing pollution of water sources, especially through industrial effluents, is affecting the availability of safe water besides causing environmental and health hazards. In many parts of the country, large stretches of rivers are both heavily polluted and devoid of flows to support aquatic ecology, cultural needs and aesthetics.

(xii) Access to water for sanitation and hygiene is an even more serious problem. Inadequate sanitation and lack of sewage treatment are polluting the water sources.

(xiii) Low consciousness about the overall scarcity and economic value of water results in its wastage and inefficient use.

(xiv) The lack of adequate trained personnel for scientific planning, utilizing modern techniques and analytical capabilities incorporating information technology constrains good water management.

(xv) A holistic and inter-disciplinary approach at water related problems is missing.

(xvi) The public agencies in charge of taking water related decisions tend to take these on their own without consultation with stakeholders, often resulting in poor and unreliable service characterized by inequities of various kinds.

(xvii) Characteristics of catchment areas of streams, rivers and recharge zones of aquifers are changing as a consequence of land use and land cover changes, affecting water resource availability and quality.

1.3 Public policies on water resources need to be governed by certain basic principles, so that there is some commonality in approaches in dealing with planning, development and management of water resources. These basic principles are:

(i) Planning, development and management of water resources need to be governed by common integrated perspective considering local, regional, State and national context, having an environmentally sound basis, keeping in view the human, social and economic needs.

(ii) Principle of equity and social justice must inform use and allocation of water.

(iii) Good governance through transparent informed decision making is crucial to the objectives of equity, social justice and sustainability. Meaningful intensive participation, transparency and accountability should guide decision making and regulation of water resources.

(iv) Water needs to be managed as a common pool community resource held, by the state, under public trust doctrine to achieve food security, support livelihood, and ensure equitable and sustainable development for all.

(v) Water is essential for sustenance of eco-system, and therefore, minimum ecological needs should be given due consideration.

(vi) Safe Water for drinking and sanitation should be considered as pre-emptive needs, followed by high priority allocation for other basic domestic needs (including needs of animals), achieving food security, supporting sustenance agriculture and minimum eco-system needs. Available water, after meeting the above needs, should be allocated in a manner to promote its conservation and efficient use.

(vii) All the elements of the water cycle, i.e., evapo-transpiration, precipitation, runoff, river, lakes, soil moisture, and ground water, sea, etc., are interdependent and the basic hydrological unit is the river basin, which should be considered as the basic hydrological unit for planning.

(viii) Given the limits on enhancing the availability of utilisable water resources and increased variability in supplies due to climate change, meeting the future needs will depend more on demand management, and hence, this needs to be given priority, especially through (a) evolving an agricultural system which economizes on water use and maximizes value from water, and (b) bringing in maximum efficiency in use of water and avoiding wastages.

(ix) Water quality and quantity are interlinked and need to be managed in an integrated manner, consistent with broader environmental management approaches inter-alia including the use of economic incentives and penalties to reduce pollution and wastage.

(x) The impact of climate change on water resources availability must be factored into water management related decisions. Water using activities need to be regulated keeping in mind the local geo climatic and hydrological situation.

2. WATER FRAMEWORK LAW

2.1 There is a need to evolve a National Framework Law as an umbrella statement of general principles governing the exercise of legislative and/ or executive (or devolved) powers by the Centre, the States and the local governing bodies. This should lead the way for essential legislation on water governance in every State of the Union and devolution of necessary authority to the lower tiers of government to deal with the local water situation.

2.2 Such a framework law must recognize water not only as a scarce resource but also as a sustainer of life and ecology. Therefore, water, particularly, groundwater, needs to be managed as a community resource held, by the state, under public trust doctrine to achieve food security, livelihood, and equitable and sustainable development for all. Existing Acts may have to be modified accordingly.

2.3 There is a need for comprehensive legislation for optimum development of inter-

State rivers and river valleys to facilitate inter-State coordination ensuring scientific planning of land and water resources taking basin/sub-basin as unit with unified perspectives of water in all its forms (including precipitation, soil moisture, ground and surface water) and ensuring holistic and balanced development of both the catchment and the command areas. Such legislation needs, inter alia, to deal with and enable establishment of basin authorities, comprising party States, with appropriate powers to plan, manage and regulate utilisation of water resource in the basins.

3. USES OF WATER

3.1 Water is required for domestic, agricultural, hydro-power, thermal power, navigation, recreation, etc. Utilisation in all these diverse uses of water should be optimized and an awareness of water as a scarce resource should be fostered.

3.2 The Centre, the States and the local bodies (governance institutions) must ensure access to a minimum quantity of potable water for essential health and hygiene to all its citizens, available within easy reach of the household.

3.3 Ecological needs of the river should be determined, through scientific study, recognizing that the natural river flows are characterized by low or no flows, small floods (freshets), large floods, etc., and should accommodate developmental needs. A portion of river flows should be kept aside to meet ecological needs ensuring that the low and high flow releases are proportional to the natural flow regime, including base flow contribution in the low flow season through regulated ground water use.

3.4 Rivers and other water bodies should be considered for development for navigation as far as possible and all multipurpose projects over water

bodies should keep navigation in mind right from the planning stage.

3.5 In the water rich Eastern and north Eastern regions of India, the water use infrastructure is weak and needs to be strengthened in the interest of food security.

3.6 Community should be sensitized and encouraged to adapt first to utilisation of water as per local availability of waters, before providing water through long distance transfer. Community based water management should be institutionalized and strengthened.

4. ADAPTATION TO CLIMATE CHANGE

4.1 Climate change is likely to increase the variability of water resources affecting human health and livelihoods. Therefore, special impetus should be given towards mitigation at micro level by enhancing the capabilities of community to adopt climate resilient technological options.

4.2 The anticipated increase in variability in availability of water because of climate change should be dealt with by increasing water storage in its various forms, namely, soil moisture, ponds, ground water, small and large reservoirs and their combination. States should be incentivized to increase water storage capacity, which inter-alia should include revival of traditional water harvesting structures and water bodies.

4.3 The adaptation strategies could also include better demand management, particularly, through adoption of compatible agricultural strategies and cropping patterns and improved water application methods, such as land leveling and/or drip / sprinkler irrigation as they enhance the water use efficiency, as also, the capability for dealing with increased variability because of climate change. Similarly, industrial processes should be made more water efficient.

4.4 Stakeholder participation in land-soil-water management with scientific inputs from local research and academic institutions for evolving different agricultural strategies, reducing soil erosion and improving soil fertility should be promoted. The specific problems of hilly areas like sudden run off, weak water holding capacity of soil, erosion and sediment transport and recharging of hill slope aquifers should be adequately addressed.

4.5 Planning and management of water resources structures, such as, dams, flood embankments, tidal embankments, etc., should incorporate coping strategies for possible climate changes. The acceptability criteria in regard to new water resources projects need to be re-worked in view of the likely climate changes

5. ENHANCING WATER AVAILABLE FOR USE

5.1 The availability of water resources and its use by various sectors in various basin and States in the country need to be assessed scientifically and reviewed at periodic intervals, say, every five years. The trends in water availability due to various factors including climate change must be assessed and accounted for during water resources planning.

5.2 The availability of water is limited but the demand of water is increasing rapidly due to growing population, rapid urbanisation, rapid industrialisation and economic development. Therefore, availability of water for utilisation needs to be augmented to meet increasing demands of water. Direct use of rainfall, desalination and avoidance of inadvertent evapo-transpiration are the new additional strategies for augmenting utilisable water resources.

5.3 There is a need to map the aquifers to know the quantum and quality of ground water resources (replenishable as well as non-replenishable) in the country. This process should be fully participatory involving local communities. This may be periodically updated.

5.4 Declining ground water levels in over-exploited areas need to be arrested by introducing improved technologies of water use, incentivizing efficient water use and encouraging community based management of aquifers. In addition, where necessary, artificial recharging projects should be undertaken so that extraction is less than the recharge. This would allow the aquifers to provide base flows to the surface system, and maintain ecology.

5.5 Inter-basin transfers are not merely for increasing production but also for meeting basic human need and achieving equity and social justice. Inter-basin transfers of water should be considered on the basis of merits of each case after evaluating the environmental, economic and social impacts of such transfers.

5.6 Integrated Watershed development activities with groundwater perspectives need to be taken in a comprehensive manner to increase soil moisture, reduce sediment yield and increase overall land and water productivity. To the extent possible, existing programs like MGNREGA may be used by farmers to harvest rain water using farm ponds and other soil and water conservation measures.

6. DEMAND MANAGEMENT AND WATER USE EFFICIENCY

6.1 A system to evolve benchmarks for water uses for different purposes, i.e., water footprints, and water auditing should be developed to promote and incentivize efficient use of water. The 'project' and the 'basin' water use efficiencies need to be improved through continuous water balance and water accounting studies. An institutional arrangement for promotion, regulation and evolving mechanisms for efficient use of water at basin/sub-basin level will be established for this purpose at the national level.

6.2 The project appraisal and environment impact assessment for water uses, particularly for industrial projects, should, inter-alia, include the analysis of the water footprints for the use.

6.3 Recycle and reuse of water, including return flows, should be the general norm.

6.4 Project financing should be structured to incentivize efficient and economic use of water and facilitate early completion of ongoing projects.

6.5 Water saving in irrigation use is of paramount importance. Methods like aligning cropping pattern with natural resource endowments, micro irrigation (drip, sprinkler, etc.), automated irrigation operation, evaporation-transpiration reduction, etc., should be encouraged and incentivized. Recycling of canal seepage water through conjunctive ground water use may also be considered.

6.6 Use of very small local level irrigation through small bunds, field ponds, agricultural and engineering methods and practices for watershed development, etc, need to be encouraged. However, their externalities, both positive and negative, like reduction of sediments and reduction of water availability, downstream, may be kept in view.

6.7 There should be concurrent mechanism involving users for monitoring if the water use pattern is causing problems like unacceptable depletion or building up of ground waters, salinity, alkalinity or similar quality problems, etc., with a view to planning appropriate interventions.

7. WATER PRICING

7.1 Pricing of water should ensure its efficient use and reward conservation.

Equitable access to water for all and its fair pricing, for drinking and other uses such as sanitation, agricultural and industrial, should be arrived at through independent statutory Water Regulatory Authority, set up by each State, after wide ranging consultation with all stakeholders.

7.2   In order to meet equity, efficiency and economic principles, the water charges should preferably / as a rule be determined on volumetric basis. Such charges should be reviewed periodically.

7.3   Recycle and reuse of water, after treatment to specified standards, should also be incentivized through a properly planned tariff system.

7.4   The principle of differential pricing may be retained for the pre-emptive uses of water for drinking and sanitation; and high priority allocation for ensuring food security and supporting livelihood for the poor. Available water, after meeting the above needs, should increasingly be subjected to allocation and pricing on economic principles so that water is not wasted in unnecessary uses and could be utilized more gainfully.

7.5   Water Users Associations (WUAs) should be given statutory powers to collect and retain a portion of water charges, manage the volumetric quantum of water allotted to them and maintain the distribution system in their jurisdiction. WUAs should be given the freedom to fix rates subject to floor rates determined by WRAs.

7.6   The over-drawal of groundwater should be minimized by regulating the use of electricity for its extraction. Separate electric feeders for pumping ground water for agricultural use should be considered.

8. CONSERVATION OF RIVER CORRIDORS, WATER BODIES AND INFRASTRUCTURE

8.1 Conservation of rivers, river corridors, water bodies and infrastructure should be undertaken in a scientifically planned manner through community participation. The storage capacities of water bodies and water courses and/or associated wetlands, the flood plains, ecological buffer and areas required for specific aesthetic, recreational and/or social needs may be managed to the extent possible in an integrated manner to balance the flooding, environment and social issues as per prevalent laws through planned development of urban areas, in particular.

8.2   Encroachments and diversion of water bodies (like rivers, lakes, tanks, ponds, etc.) and drainage channels (irrigated area as well as urban area drainage) must not be allowed, and wherever it has taken place, it should be restored to the extent feasible and maintained properly.

8.3 Urban settlements, encroachments and any developmental activities in the protected upstream areas of reservoirs/water bodies, key aquifer recharge areas that pose a potential threat of contamination, pollution, reduced recharge and those endanger wild and human life should be strictly regulated.

8.4 Environmental needs of Himalayan regions, aquatic eco-system, wet lands and embanked flood plains need to be recognized and taken into consideration while planning.

8.5 Sources of water and water bodies should not be allowed to get polluted. System of third party periodic inspection should be evolved and stringent punitive actions be taken against the persons responsible for pollution.

8.6 Quality conservation and improvements are even more important for ground waters, since cleaning up is very difficult. It needs to be ensured that industrial effluents, local cess pools, residues of fertilizers and chemicals, etc., do not reach the ground water.

8.7 The water resources infrastructure should be maintained properly to continue to get the intended benefits. A suitable percentage of the costs of infrastructure development may be set aside along with collected water charges, for repair and maintenance. Contract for construction of projects should have inbuilt provision for longer periods of proper maintenance and handing over back the infrastructure in good condition.

8.8 Legally empowered dam safety services need to be ensured in the States as well as at the Centre. Appropriate safety measures, including downstream flood management, for each dam should be undertaken on top priority.

9. PROJECT PLANNING AND IMPLEMENTATION

9.1 Considering the existing water stress conditions in India and the likelihood of further worsening situation due to climate change and other factors, water resources projects should be planned as per the efficiency benchmarks to be prescribed for various situations.

9.2 Being inter-disciplinary in nature, water resources projects should be planned considering social and environmental aspects also in addition to techno-economic considerations in consultation with project affected and beneficiary families. The integrated water resources management with emphasis on finding reasonable and generally acceptable solutions for most of the stakeholders should be followed for planning and management of water resources projects.

9.3   Considering the heavy economic loss due to delay in implementation of projects, all clearances, including environmental and investment clearances, be made time bound.

9.4   Concurrent monitoring at project, State and the Central level should be undertaken for timely interventions to avoid time and cost over-runs.

9.5   All components of water resources projects should be planned and executed in a pari-passu manner so that intended benefits start accruing immediately and there is no gap between potential created and potential utilized.

9.6   Local governing bodies like Panchayats, Municipalities, Corporations, etc., and Water Users Associations, wherever applicable, should be involved in planning of the projects. The unique needs and aspirations of the Scheduled caste and Scheduled Tribes, women and other weaker sections of the society should be given due consideration.

9.7   All water resources projects, including hydro power projects, should be planned to the extent feasible as multi-purpose projects with provision of storage to derive maximum benefit from available topology and water resources.

10. MANAGEMENT OF FLOOD AND DROUGHT

10.1   While every effort should be made to avert water related disasters like floods and droughts, through structural and non-structural measures, emphasis should be on preparedness for flood / drought with coping mechanisms as an option. Greater emphasis should be placed on rehabilitation of natural drainage system.

10.2   Land, soil, energy and water management with scientific inputs from local, research and scientific institutions should be used to evolve different agricultural strategies and improve soil and water productivity to manage droughts. Integrated farming systems and non-agricultural developments may also be considered for livelihood support and poverty alleviation.

10.3   In order to prevent loss of land eroded by the river, which causes permanent loss, revetments, spurs, embankments, etc., should be planned, executed, monitored and maintained on the basis of morphological studies. This will become increasingly more important, since climate change is likely to increase the rainfall intensity, and hence, soil erosion.

10.4   Flood forecasting is very important for flood preparedness and should be expanded extensively across the country and modernized using real time data acquisition system and linked to forecasting models. Efforts should be towards developing physical models for various basin sections, which should be linked to each other and to medium range weather forecasts to enhance lead time.

10.5   Operating procedures for reservoirs should be evolved and implemented in such a manner to have flood cushion and to reduce trapping of sediment during flood season. These procedures should be based on sound decision support system.

10.6   Protecting all areas prone to floods and droughts may not be practicable; hence, methods for coping with floods and droughts have to be encouraged.

Frequency based flood inundation maps should be prepared to evolve coping strategies, including preparedness to supply safe water during and immediately after flood events. Communities need to be involved in preparing an action plan for dealing with the flood/ drought situations.

10.7   To increase preparedness for sudden and unexpected flood related disasters, dam/embankment break studies, as also preparation and periodic updating of emergency action plans / disaster management plans should be evolved after involving affected communities. In hilly reaches, glacial lake outburst flood and landslide dam break floods studies with periodic monitoring along with instrumentation, etc., should be carried out.

11. WATER SUPPLY AND SANITATION

11.1   There is a need to remove the large disparity between stipulations for water supply in urban areas and in rural areas. Efforts should be made to provide improved water supply in rural areas with proper sewerage facilities. Least water intensive sanitation and sewerage systems with decentralized sewage treatment plants should be incentivized.

11.2   Urban and rural domestic water supply should preferably be from surface water in conjunction with groundwater and rainwater. Where alternate supplies are available, a source with better reliability and quality needs to be assigned to domestic water supply. Exchange of sources between uses, giving preference to domestic water supply should be possible. Also, reuse of urban water effluents from kitchens and bathrooms, after primary treatment, in flush toilets should be encouraged, ensuring no human contact.

11.3   Urban domestic water systems need to collect and publish water accounts and water audit reports indicating leakages and pilferages, which should be reduced taking into due consideration social issues.

11.4   In urban and industrial areas, rainwater harvesting and de-salinization, wherever techno-economically feasible, should be encouraged to increase availability of utilisable water. Implementation of rainwater harvesting should include scientific monitoring of parameters like hydrogeology, groundwater contamination, pollution and spring discharges.

11.5   Urban water supply and sewage treatment schemes should be integrated and executed simultaneously. Water supply bills should include sewerage charges.

11.6   Industries in water short regions may be allowed to either withdraw only the make up water or should have an obligation to return treated effluent to a specified standard back to the hydrologic system. Tendencies to unnecessarily use more water within the plant to avoid treatment or to pollute ground water need to be prevented.

11.7 Subsidies and incentives should be implemented to encourage recovery of industrial pollutants and recycling / reuse, which are otherwise capital intensive.

12. INSTITUTIONAL ARRANGEMENTS

12.1   There should be a forum at the national level to deliberate upon issues relating to water and evolve consensus, co-operation and reconciliation amongst party States. A similar mechanism should be established within each State to amicably resolve differences in competing demands for water amongst different users of water, as also between different parts of the State.

12.2   A permanent Water Disputes Tribunal at the Centre should be established to resolve the disputes expeditiously in an equitable manner. Apart from using the "good offices" of the Union or the State Governments, as the case may be, the paths of arbitration and mediation may also to be tried in dispute resolution.

12.3   Water resources projects and services should be managed with community participation. For improved service delivery on sustainable basis, the State Governments / urban local bodies may associate private sector in public private partnership mode with penalties for failure, under regulatory control on prices charged and service standards with full accountability to democratically elected local bodies.

12.4 Integrated Water Resources Management (IWRM) taking river basin / sub-basin as a unit should be the main principle for planning, development and management of water resources. The departments / organisations at Centre / State Governments levels should be restructured and made multi-disciplinary accordingly.

12.5   Appropriate institutional arrangements for each river basin should be developed to collect and collate all data on regular basis with regard to rainfall, river flows, area irrigated by crops and by source, utilisations for various uses by both surface and ground water and to publish water accounts on ten daily basis every year for each river basin with appropriate water budgets and water accounts based on the hydrologic balances. In addition, water budgeting and water accounting should be carried out for each aquifers.

12.6   Appropriate institutional arrangements for each river basin should also be developed for monitoring water quality in both surface and ground waters.

12.7   States should be encouraged and incentivized to undertake reforms and progressive measures for innovations, conservation and efficient utilisation of water resources.

13. TRANS-BOUNDARY RIVERS

13.1 Even while accepting the principle of basin as a unit of development, on the basis of practicability and easy implementability, efforts should be made to enter into international agreements with neighbouring countries on bilateral basis for exchange of hydrological data of international rivers on near real time basis.

13.2 Negotiations about sharing and management of water of international rivers should be done on bilateral basis in consultative association with riparian States keeping paramount the national interest. Adequate institutional arrangements at the Center should be set up to implement international agreements.

14. DATABASE AND INFORMATION SYSTEM

14.1   All hydrological data, other than those classified on national security consideration, should be in public domain. However, a periodic review for further declassification of data may be carried out. A National Water Informatics Center should be established to collect, collate and process hydrologic data regularly from all over the country, conduct the preliminary processing, and maintain in open and transparent manner on a GIS platform.

14.2   In view of the likely climate change, much more data about snow and glaciers, evaporation, tidal hydrology and hydraulics, river geometry changes, erosion, sedimentation, etc. needs to be collected. A programme of such data collection needs to be developed and implemented.

14.3   All water related data, like rainfall, snowfall, geo-morphological, climatic, geological, surface water, ground water, water quality, ecological, water extraction and use, irrigated area, glaciers, etc., should be integrated with well defined procedures and formats to ensure online updation and transfer of data to facilitate development of database for informed decision making in the management of water.

15. RESEARCH AND TRAINING NEEDS

15.1   Continuing research and advancement in technology shall be promoted to address issues in the water sector in a scientific manner. Innovations in water resources sector should be encouraged, recognized and awarded.

15.2   It is necessary to give adequate grants to the States to update technology, design practices, planning and management practices, preparation of annual water balances and accounts for the site and basin, preparation of hydrologic balances for water systems, benchmarking and performance evaluation.

15.3 It needs to be recognized that the field practices in the water sector in advanced countries have been revolutionized by advances in information technology and analytical capabilities. A re-training and quality improvement programme for water planners and managers at all levels in India, both in private and public sectors, needs to be undertaken.

15.4   An autonomous center for research in water policy should also be established to evaluate impacts of policy decisions and to evolve policy directives for changing scenario of water resources.

15.5 To meet the need of the skilled manpower in the water sector, regular training and academic courses in water management should be promoted. These training and academic institutions should be regularly updated by developing infrastructure and promoting applied research, which would help to improve the current procedures of analysis and informed decision making in the line departments and by the community. A national campaign for water literacy needs to be started for capacity building of different stakeholders in the water sector.

16. IMPLEMENTATION OF NATIONAL WATER POLICY

16.1   National Water Board should prepare a plan of action based on the National Water Policy, as approved by the National Water Resources Council, and to regularly monitor its implementation.

16.2   The State Water Policies may need to be drafted/revised in accordance with this policy keeping in mind the basic concerns and principles as also a unified national perspective.

Appendix 4

2/18/2015   AQUASTAT database Database Query Results

| E - External data   I - AQUASTAT estimate |
| K - Aggregate data   L - Modelled data |
| Click for details |
| Click on green cells for metadata |

aquastat   English

India

	Latest value(s)	
Total area *(1000 ha)*	328 726E	*(2012)*
Arable land *(1000 ha)*	156 200E	*(2012)*
Cultivated area (arable land + permanent crops) *(1000 ha)*	169 000E	*(2012)*
% of total country area cultivated *(%)*	51.41E	*(2012)*
Total population *(1000 inhab)*	1 252 140E	*(2013)*
Rural population *(1000 inhab)*	851 504E	*(2013)*
Urban population *(1000 inhab)*	400 636E	*(2013)*
Population density *(inhab/km2)*	376.2E	*(2012)*
Long-term average precipitation in depth *(mm/yr)*	1 083E	*(2014)*
Long-term average precipitation in volume *(10^9 m3/yr)*	3 560E	*(2012)*
National Rainfall Index (NRI) *(mm/yr)*	1 502E	*(2000)*
Surface water produced internally *(10^9 m3/yr)*	1 404I	*(2014)*
Groundwater produced internally *(10^9 m3/yr)*	432	*(2014)*
Overlap between surface water and groundwater *(10^9 m3/yr)*	390I	*(2014)*
Total internal renewable water resources (IRWR) *(10^9 m3/yr)*	1 446I	*(2014)*
Total internal renewable water resources per capita *(m3/inhab/yr)*	1 155K	*(2014)*
Surface water: entering the country (natural) *(10^9 m3/yr)*	635.2I	*(2014)*
Surface water: inflow not submitted to treaties (actual) *(10^9 m3/yr)*	635.2I	*(2014)*
Surface water: inflow submitted to treaties (actual) *(10^9 m3/yr)*	0I	*(2014)*
Surface water: inflow secured through treaties (actual) *(10^9 m3/yr)*	0	*(2014)*
Surface water: accounted inflow (actual) *(10^9 m3/yr)*	635.2I	*(2014)*
Surface water: total flow of border rivers (natural) *(10^9 m3/yr)*	0	*(2014)*
Surface water: total flow of border rivers (actual) *(10^9 m3/yr)*	0	*(2014)*
Surface water: accounted flow of border rivers (natural) *(10^9 m3/yr)*	0	*(2014)*
Surface water: accounted flow of border rivers (actual) *(10^9 m3/yr)*	0	*(2014)*
Surface water: accounted part of border lakes (natural) *(10^9 m3/yr)*	0	*(2014)*
Surface water: accounted part of border lakes (actual) *(10^9 m3/yr)*	0	*(2014)*
Surface water: total entering and bordering the country (natural) *(10^9 m3/yr)*	635.2I	*(2014)*
Surface water: total entering and bordering the country (actual) *(10^9 m3/yr)*	635.2I	*(2014)*
Surface water: leaving the country (natural) *(10^9 m3/yr)*	1 385I	*(2014)*
Surface water: outflow not submitted to treaties (actual) *(10^9 m3/yr)*	1 142I	*(2014)*
Surface water: outflow submitted to treaties (actual) *(10^9 m3/yr)*	243I	*(2014)*
Surface water: outflow secured through treaties (actual) *(10^9 m3/yr)*	170.3I	*(2014)*
Surface water: total external renewable (actual) *(10^9 m3/yr)*	464.9I	*(2014)*
Groundwater: entering the country (natural) *(10^9 m3/yr)*	0	*(2014)*
Groundwater: entering the country (actual) *(10^9 m3/yr)*	0	*(2014)*
Groundwater: leaving the country (natural) *(10^9 m3/yr)*	0	*(2014)*
Groundwater: leaving the country (actual) *(10^9 m3/yr)*	0I	*(2014)*
Water resources: total external renewable (natural) *(10^9 m3/yr)*	635.2I	*(2014)*
Water resources: total external renewable (actual) *(10^9 m3/yr)*	464.9I	*(2014)*
Total renewable surface water (natural) *(10^9 m3/yr)*	2 039I	*(2014)*
Total renewable surface water (actual) *(10^9 m3/yr)*	1 869I	*(2014)*
Total renewable groundwater (natural) *(10^9 m3/yr)*	432	*(2014)*
Total renewable groundwater (actual) *(10^9 m3/yr)*	432	*(2014)*
Overlap: between surface water and groundwater *(10^9 m3/yr)*	390I	*(2014)*
Total renewable water resources (natural) *(10^9 m3/yr)*	2 081I	*(2014)*
Total renewable water resources (actual) *(10^9 m3/yr)*	1 911I	*(2014)*
Dependency ratio *(%)*	30.52I	*(2014)*
Total renewable water resources per capita (actual) *(m3/inhab/yr)*	1 526K	*(2014)*
Exploitable: regular renewable surface water *(10^9 m3/yr)*	690	*(2003)*
Exploitable: irregular renewable surface water *(10^9 m3/yr)*		

Exploitable: total renewable surface water *(10^9 m3/yr)*		
Exploitable: regular renewable groundwater *(10^9 m3/yr)*	398.7	*(2004)*
Total exploitable water resources *(10^9 m3/yr)*	1 089	*(2003)*
Total dam capacity *(km3)*	224	*(2005)*
Dam capacity per capita *(m3/inhab)*	193.3K	*(2005)*
Agricultural water withdrawal *(10^9 m3/yr)*		
Industrial water withdrawal *(10^9 m3/yr)*		
Municipal water withdrawal *(10^9 m3/yr)*	56	*(2010)*
Total water withdrawal *(10^9 m3/yr)*	761	*(2010)*
Irrigation water withdrawal *(10^9 m3/yr)*		
Irrigation water requirement *(10^9 m3/yr)*	370.8L	*(2006)*
Agricultural water withdrawal as % of total water withdrawal *(%)*	90.41	*(2010)*
Industrial water withdrawal as % of total water withdrawal *(%)*	2.234	*(2010)*
Municipal water withdrawal as % of total withdrawal *(%)*	7.359	*(2010)*
Total water withdrawal per capita *(m3/inhab/yr)*	615.4K	*(2010)*
Fresh surface water withdrawal (primary and secondary) *(10^9 m3/yr)*	396.5	*(2010)*
Fresh groundwater withdrawal (primary and secondary) *(10^9 m3/yr)*	251	*(2010)*
Total freshwater withdrawal (primary and secondary) *(10^9 m3/yr)*	647.5I	*(2010)*
Desalinated water produced *(10^9 m3/yr)*	0.0006I	*(2010)*
Direct use of treated municipal wastewater *(10^9 m3/yr)*		
Direct use of agricultural drainage water *(10^9 m3/yr)*	113.5I	*(2010)*
Produced municipal wastewater *(10^9 m3/yr)*	15.45	*(2011)*
Collected municipal wastewater *(10^9 m3/yr)*		
Treated municipal wastewater *(10^9 m3/yr)*	4.416	*(2011)*
Number of municipal wastewater treatment facilities *(-)*	270	*(2011)*
Capacity of the municipal wastewater treatment facilities *(10^9 m3/yr)*	4.573	*(2011)*
Not treated municipal wastewater *(10^9 m3/yr)*	11.03	*(2011)*
Treated municipal wastewater discharged (secondary water) *(10^9 m3/yr)*		
Not treated municipal wastewater discharged (secondary water) *(10^9 m3/yr)*	9.66	*(2008)*
Direct use of treated municipal wastewater *(10^9 m3/yr)*		
Direct use of treated municipal wastewater for irrigation purposes *(10^9 m3/yr)*		
Direct use of not treated municipal wastewater for irrigation purposes *(10^9 m3/yr)*	1.23	*(1985)*
Area equipped for irrigation by direct use of treated municipal wastewater *(1000 ha)*	1.32	*(1988)*
Area equipped for irrigation by direct use of not treated municipal wastewater *(1000 ha)*	7.5	*(1988)*
Freshwater withdrawal as % of total actual renewable water resources *(%)*	33.88I	*(2010)*

CSV (Tables)   CSV (Flat)   Provide data
« New search

Appendix 5

TREATY BETWEEN THE GOVERNMENT OF THE PEOPLE'S REPUBLIC OF BANGLADESH AND THE GOVERNMENT OF THE REPUBLIC OF INDIA ON SHARING OF THE GANGA/GANGES WATERS AT FARAKKA

THE GOVERNMENT OF THE PEOPLE'S REPUBLIC OF BANGLADESH AND THE GOVERNMENT OF THE REPUBLIC OF INDIA,

DETERMINED to promote and strengthen their relations of friendship and good neighbourliness,

INSPIRED by the common desire of promoting the well-being of their peoples,

BEING desirous of sharing by mutual agreement the waters of the international rivers flowing through the territories of the two countries and of making the optimum utilisation of the water resources of their region in the fields of flood management, irrigation, river basin development and generation of hydro-power for the mutual benefit of the peoples of the two countries,

RECOGNISING that the need for making an arrangement for sharing of the Ganga/Ganges waters at Farakka in a spirit of mutual accommodation and the need for a solution to the long-term problem of augmenting the flows of the Ganga/Ganges are in the mutual interests of the peoples of the two countries,

BEING desirous of finding a fair and just solution without affecting the rights and entitlements of either country other than those covered by this Treaty, or establishing any general principles of law or precedent,

HAVE AGREED AS FOLLOWS:

ARTICLE – I

The quantum of waters agreed to be released by India to Bangladesh will be at Farakka.

ARTICLE – II

i)   The sharing between India and Bangladesh of the Ganga/Ganges waters at Farakka by ten day periods from the 1st January to the 31st May every year will be with reference to the formula at Annexure I and an indicative schedule giving the implications of the sharing arrangement under Annexure I is at Annexure II.

ii) The Indicative schedule at Annexure-II, as referred to in sub-para (i) above, is based on 40 years (1949-1988) 10-day period average availability of water at Farakka. Every effort would be made by the upper riparian to protect flows of water at Farakka as in the 40-years average availability as mentioned above.

iii) In the event flow at Farakka falls below 50,000 cusecs in any 10-day period, the two Governments will enter into immediate consultations to make adjustments on an emergency basis, in accordance with the principles of equity, fair play and no harm to either party.

ARTICLE - III

The waters released to Bangladesh at Farakka under Article I shall not be reduced below Farakka except for reasonable uses of waters, not exceeding 200 cusecs, by India between Farakka and the point on the Ganga/Ganges where both its banks are in Bangladesh.

ARTICLE - IV

A Committee consisting of representatives nominated by the two Governments in equal numbers (hereinafter called the Joint Committee) shall be constituted following the signing of this Treaty. The Joint Committee shall set up suitable teams at Farakka and HardingeBridge to observe and record at Farakka the daily flows below Farakka Barrage, in the FeederCanal, and at the Navigation Lock, as well as at the HardingeBridge.

ARTICLE - V

The Joint Committee shall decide its own procedure and method of functioning.

ARTICLE - VI

The Joint Committee shall submit to the two Governments all data collected by it and shall also submit a yearly report to both the Governments. Following submission of the reports the two Governments will meet at appropriate levels to decide upon such further actions as may be needed.

ARTICLE - VII

The Joint Committee shall be responsible for implementing the arrangements contained in this Treaty and examining any difficulty arising out of the implementation of the above arrangements and of the operation of Farakka Barrage. Any difference or dispute arising in this regard, if not resolved by the Joint Committee, shall be referred to the Indo-Bangladesh Joint Rivers Commission. If the difference or dispute still remains unresolved, it shall be referred to the two Governments which shall meet urgently at the appropriate level to resolve it by mutual discussion.

ARTICLE - VIII

The two Governments recognise the need to cooperate with each other in finding a solution to the long-term problem of augmenting the flows of the Ganga/Ganges during the dry season.

ARTICLE - IX

Guided by the principles of equity, fairness and no harm to either party, both the Governments agree to conclude water sharing Treaties/Agreements with regard to other common rivers.

ARTICLE - X

The sharing arrangement under this Treaty shall be reviewed by the two Governments at five years interval or earlier, as required by either party and needed adjustments, based on principles of equity, fairness, and no harm to either party made thereto, if necessary. It would be open to either party to seek the first review after two years to assess the impact and working of the sharing arrangement as contained in this Treaty.

ARTICLE - XI

For the period of this Treaty, in the absence of mutual agreement on adjustments following reviews as mentioned in Article X, India shall release downstream of Farakka Barrage, water at a rate not less than 90% (ninety percent) of Bangladesh's share according to the formula referred to in Article II, until such time as mutually agreed flows are decided upon.

ARTICLE - XII

This Treaty shall enter into force upon signature and shall remain in force for a period of thirty years and it shall be renewable on the basis of mutual consent.

IN WITNESS WHEREOF the undersigned, being duly authorised thereto by the respective Governments, have signed this Treaty.

DONE at New Delhi on 12th December, 1996 in Hindi, Bangla and English languages. In the event of any conflict between the texts, the English text shall prevail.

Signed   Signed

(SHEIKH HASINA)   (H.D.DEVE GOWDA)
PRIME MINISTER   PRIME MINISTER
PEOPLE'S REPUBLIC OF   REPUBLIC OF INDIA
BANGLADESH

****

ANNEXURE - I

Availability at Farakka	Share of India	Share of Bangladesh
70,000 cusecs or less	50%	50%
70,000 cusecs-75,000 cusecs	Balance of flow	35,000 cusec
75,000 cusecs or more	40,000 cusecs	Balance of flow

Subject to the condition that India and Bangladesh each shall receive guaranteed 35,000 cusecs of water in alternate three 10-day periods during the period March 11 to May 10.

ANNEXURE - II

Schedule

(Sharing of waters at Farakka between January 01 and May 31 every year)

If actual availability corresponds to average flows of the period 1949 to 1988, the implication of the formula in Annex-I for the share of each side is:

Period		India's share (Cusecs)	Bangladesh's share (Cusecs)
January			
1 – 10	107,516	40,000	67,516
11 – 20	97,673	40,000	57,673
21 – 31	90,154	40,000	50,154
February			
1 – 10	86,323	40,000	46,323
11 – 20	82,859	40,000	42,859
21 – 31	79,106	40,000	39,106
March			
1 – 10	74,419	39,419	35,000*
11 – 20	68,931	33,931	35,000*
21 – 31	64,688	35,000*	29,688

April			
1 – 10	63,180	28,180	35,000*
11 – 20	62,633	35,000*	27,633
21 – 31	60,992	25,922	35,000*
May			
1 – 10	67,351	35,000*	32,351
11 – 20	73,590	38,590	35,000
21 – 31	81,854	40,000	41,854

(* Three ten day periods during which 35,000 cusecs shall be provided)

5.0.10 Gazette Notifications

Nil

5.0.11 Publications

Nil

BIBLIOGRAPHY

1. A High Walk Through Rupshu -Changthang", Posted on "India Profile", http://www.indiaprofile.com/adventure/changthang-treks. htm, accessed on 31 July 2014.

2. A Systems Approach to Water Resources, by Robert Pirani of Regional Plan Association. http://www.america2050.org/upload/2009/10/ Systems_Approach_to_Water_Resources.pdf

3. Aaron T.Wolf, Shared Waters: Conflict and Cooperation, 2007, http://www.transboundarywaters.orst.edu/publications/abst_docs/ wolf_2007_shared_waters.pdf

4. Agreement between The Government Of India And The Royal Government Of Bhutan Regarding The Chukha Hydro-Electric Project , 23 March 1974, New Delhi,

5. Akhtar, Shaheen. "Emerging Challenges to Indus Waters Treaty". Institute of Regional Studies, Islamabad. http://www.irs.org.pk/ PublFocus.htm#_ftn1

6. Amber Brown and Marty D. Matlock, A Review of Water Scarcity Indices and Methodologies, White Paper 106 (Tempe, AZ: The Sustainability Consortium, 2011), http://www.sustainabilityconsortium.org/wp-content/themes/sustainability/assets/pdf/whitepapers/2011_Brown_ Matlock_Water-Availability-Assessment-Indices-and-Methodologies-Lit-Review.pdf.

7. An interview with Jennifer L. Turner on, U.S.-China Cooperation: The Significance of the Joint Agreement on Climate Change and Clean Energy, Wilson Center NOW; Dec 04, 2014 http://www. wilsoncenter.org/article/us-china-cooperation-the-significance-the-joint-agreement-climate-change-and-clean-energy

8. Annual Report- 2007-2008, Ministry of Water Resources People's Republic of China

9. Aquastat Pakistan Water Overview' FAO. 2010 Version http://www. fao.org/nr/water/aquastat/countries/pakistan/index.stm

10. Arpi Claude, "Diverting the Brahmaputra, Declaration of War?", Posted in Rediff.com on 23 October 2003, http://www.rediff.com/news/2003/oct/27spec.htm, accessed on 18 August 2014.

11. Article by Mr Ranaswamy R Iyer, honorary research professor at the Centre for Policy Research (CPR) New Delhi and member SAPANA(South Asian Policy Analysis Network) titled 'Indus and Baglihar: An Overview' in Volume VI SAPNA report.

12. Article by Mr Shahid Husain former secretary of water and power, Government of Pakistan, member SAPANA titled 'Pakistan's Perspective' in SAPANA Vol VI pg 136-150.

13. Article titled 'Indus Basin River System - Flooding and Flood Mitigation' by H. Rehman and A. Kamal, Federal Flood Commission, Ministry of Water and Power, Islamabad, Pakistan.

14. Asad Sarwar Quereshi et al., "Challenges and Prospects of Sustainable Groundwater Management in the Indus Basin, Pakistan," Water Resources Management 24, no.8 (2010); FAO, "Pakistan country profile".

15. Asia Pacific Centre For Security Studies May 2006. www.apcss.org article titled 'Spotlight on Indus River Diplomacy: India, Pakistan, and the Baglihar Dam Dispute' by Robert G. Wirsing And Christopher Jasparro.

16. Asia Times Online,www.atimes.com article written by Mr Haroon Mirani 13 Jan 2009.

17. Asia's Worsening Water Crisis- Posted on March 17, 2012. Chellaney, Brahma.:http://chellaney.net/2012/03/17/asias-worsening-water-crisis/. Survival | vol. 54 no. 2 | April–May 2012 | pp. 143–156, Asian Survey, Vol. 54, Number 4, pp. 621–650. ISSN0004-4687, electronic ISSN1533-838X. (Copyright 2014 by the Regents of the University of California.)

18. Asit K. Biswas (2008) Integrated Water Resources Management: Is It Working?, International Journal of Water Resources Development,

19. Avoiding Water Wars: Water Scarcity and Central Asia's Growing Importance for Stability in Afghanistan and Pakistan" Prepared for the Committee on Foreign Relations United States Senate, 22 February 2011.

20. B. G. Verghese, Fuss Over Indus-I: India's Rights Are Set Out in the Treaty, The Tribune (Chandigarh), 25 May 2005.

21. BBC, News on Science and Environment, 13 February 2015,   http://www.bbc.com/news/science-environment-31456369

22. Beyond the Indus Water Treaty: A Perspective on Kashmir's "Power" Woes http://www.idsa.in/idsacomments/BeyondtheIndusWaterTreaty_aanant_020212 . Arpita Anant - IDSA COMMENT February 2, 2012

23. Bhutan king shows the way in South Asia, Business Standard, New Delhi   , January 28, 2013 http://www.business-standard.com/article/international/bhutan-king-shows-the-way-in-south-asia-113012800096_1.html

24. Bhutan-India Joint Press Statement   on the State Visit of Prime Minister of India Shri Narendra Modi to the Kingdom of Bhutan from 15-16 June 2014, Embassy of India, Thimpu, Bhutan http://www.indianembassythimphu.bt/pages.php?id=96

25. Bilateral Cooperation, Government of India, Ministry of Water Resources India. http://wrmin.nic.in/forms/list.aspx?lid=345&Id=4

26. Case Study of Transboundary Dispute Resolution: the Indus Water Treaty.   Authors:AaronT.Wolf1andJoshua.T.Newton.http://www.transboundarywaters.orst.edu/research/case_studies/Documents/indus.pdf

27. Cécile Levacher, Strategic Analysis Paper, Future Direction International. 29 May 2014, Global Food and Water Security Research Programme Climate Change in the Tibetan Plateau Region: Glacial Melt and Future Water Security

28. Center For Climate Change and Energy Solutions. http://www.c2es.org/

29. Central water commission website www.cwc.com

30. Chakravorty Roshni, Serage ldin Ismail, "Sharing of River waters among India and its Neighbours in the 21st century: War or Peace?—The wars of the next century will be about water", https://www.mendeley.com/research/sharing-river-waters-among-india-neighbors-21st-century-war-peace-wars-next-century-about-water/,accessed on 17 August 2014.

31. Chellaney Brahma , From Arms Racing to "Dam Racing" in Asia How

to Contain the Geopolitical Risks of the Dam-Building Competition Transatlantic Academy Paper Series, May 2012, Pg 3

32. Chellaney Brahma ,Water, Power, and Competition in Asia, Posted on August 18, 2014, Asian Survey, Vol. 54, Number 4, pp. 621–650. ISSN0004-4687, electronic ISSN1533-838X. (Copyright 2014 by the Regents of the University of California.)http://chellaney.net/category/energy-environment/accessed on 18 November , 2014

33. Chellaney Brahma, "China aims for bigger share of South Asia's water lifeline", Published in "The Japan Times" on 26 June 2007, http://search.japantimes.co.j/cgi-bin/eo20070626bc.html, accessed on 09 August 2013.

34. Chellaney Brahma, Water, Peace, and War, p. 287.

35. Chellaney, Brahma ,Asia's Worsening Water Crisis- Posted on March 17, 2012..:. Survival | vol. 54 no. 2 | April–May 2012 | pp. 143–156, DOI: 10.1080/00396338.2012.672806

36. China : Other Projects, Brahmaputra (Yarlung Tsangpo) River", Website "International Rivers", http://www.internationalrivers.org/china/china-other-projects, accessed on 09 August 2014.

37. China successfully completes USD 80 billion water diversion project, The Economic Times, By PTI | 27 Dec, 2014, 06.11PM IST.http://economictimes.indiatimes.com/news/international/business/china-successfully-completes-usd-80-billion-water-diversion-project/articleshow/45660480.cms

38. China's Water Resources and Hydropower Planning and Design General Institute, Presentation at the ESCAP Ad Hoc Expert Group Meeting on Water-Use Efficiency Planning, Bangkok, 26–28 October 2004.

39. Cleveland, H. The Management of Water Resources, Science, Aug. 4, 1978.

40. Commission for Integrated Water Resource Development, Integrated Water Resource Development: A Plan for Action, vol. 1 (New Delhi: Commission for Integrated Water Resource Development, Ministry of Water Resources, 1999); National Water Development Agency, Indian Ministry of Water Resources, "The Need," <http://goo.gl/bIuvm

41. Connecting The Drops .An Indus Basin Roadmap for Cross-Border

Water Research, Data Sharing, and Policy Coordination.Indus Basin Working Group   http://www.stimson.org/images/uploads/research-pdfs/connecting_the_drops_stimson.pdf

42. Controversial Plan to Tap Tibetan Waters", Published in "The Southern Weekend" of 27 July 2006, Translated by Shao Da for China.org,cn on 08 August 2006, http://www.china.org.cn/english/MATERIAL/177295. htm, accessed on 09 August 2014.

43. Coping with Water: Q&A with FAO Director-General Dr. Jacques Diouf', UN Food and Agriculture Organization, 22 March 2007.

44. Czeslaw Tubilewicz, Editor, "Critical Issues in Contemporary China", Routledge-Taylor & Francis Group, August 2006, Chapter 5, "China's Environmental Problems" by Richard Lois Edmonds, page 133.

45. Daniel Wild, Carl-Johan Francke, Pierin Menzli and Urs Schön, Water: A Market of the Future (Zurich: Sustainable Asset Management, 2007).

46. Data and figures are from the Ministry of Water Resources, People's Republic of China, Annual Report 2007–2008, pp. 9–10, at http://www.mwr.gov.cn/english/2007-2008.doc.

47. De Silva Ranashinghe, Sergei. 'Pakistan's Food and Water Crisis more Detrimental to Security than Extremism.' Future Directions International (FDI), 18 March 2011. http://www.futuredirections. org.au/admin/uploaded_pdf/1300424386-   DI%20Strategic%20 Analysis%20 Paper%20-%2018%20March%202011.pdf

48. Don Hinrichsen and HenrylitoTacio THE COMING FRESHWATER CRISIS IS ALREADY HERE. http://www.wilsoncenter.org/sites/ default/files/popwawa2.pdfhttp://www.wilsoncenter.org/sites/default/ files/popwawa2.pdf

49. Dr Parajuli U et al; Water Sharing Conflicts Between Countries, and Approaches to Resolving Them , Water and Security in South Asia (WASSA) Projects, Volume III, p42

50. Dr. Crow-Miller Britt, Portland State University, United States,Diverted opportunity: Inequality and what the South-North Water Transfer Project really means for China. Posted On March 4, 2014 , Global Water Forum, Water Security

51. Draft: Indus Water Treaty and Managing Shared Water Resources for the Benefit of Basin States – policy issues and Options" IUCN, 2010.

http://cmsdata.iucn.org/downloads/pk_ulr_d1_2.pdf.

52. Durai Suchitra, "Issue of Utilisation, Development and Conservation of Common Water Resources between India and China", NDC, September 2008, http://www.ndc.in, accessed on 14 June 2014.

53. Dutta Arnab Pratim, "State pulse : Arunachal Pradesh : Reservoir of dams", Published in "Central Chronicle" on 12 May 2008, http://environmentportal.in/news/state-pulse-arunachal-pradesh-reservoir-dams, accessed on 01 August 2014.

54. Eastham et al., pp.23-24; Asif Inam et al., "The Geographic, Geological and Oceanographic Setting of the Indus River," in Large Rivers: Geomorphology and Management, Avijit Gupta ed. (Chichester, UK: John Wiley & Sons, 2007).

55. Erik Assadourian Lori Brown Alexander Carius Richard Cincotta Ken Conca Geoffrey Dabelko Christopher Flavin Hilary French Gary Gardner Brian Halweil Annika Kramer Lisa Mastny Danielle Nierenberg Dennis Pirages Thomas Prugh Michael Renner Janet Sawin Linda Starke Aaron Wolf State of the World,2005: Redefining Global Security, http://www.transboundarywaters.orst.edu/publications/abst_docs/wolf_sow_2005.pdf

56. Fan, C. Cindy and Mingjie Sun. "Regional inequality in China, 1978-2006." Eurasian Geography and Economics, 49.1, 2008: 1-20.

57. FAO, "Indus River Basin," in Irrigation in Southern and Eastern Asia in Figures: AQUASTAT Survey 2011, Karen Frenken ed. (Rome: FAO, 2012), http://www.fao.org/docrep/016/i2809e/i2809e.pdf. Note that some other studies cited in this report furnish slightly different figures for the total basin area and its distribution between the riparian states.

58. FAO, Aquastat online database; http://www.fao.org/nr/water/aquastat/countries_regions/IND/index.stm

59. FAO, Aquastat, Water resources and MDG Water Indicators, March 2013

60. FAOhttp://www.fao.org/nr/water/aquastat/water_use/index.stm

61. Final Settlement: Restructuring India-Pakistan Relations' Strategic Foresight Group, 2005. , http://www.strategicforesight.com/finalsettlement/lifeline.pdf

62. Fleischer, Torsten and Grunwald, Armin. "Making nanotechnology

developments sustainable.A role for technology assessment?"Journal of Cleaner Production. 2007.

63. Food and Agriculture Organization, Country Profile: Bangladesh, 2010, Aquastat database.

64. Foster W, Exploring alternative futures of the World Water System., Building a second generation of World Water Scenarios , Driving force: Technology, 2010pg 1-2

65. Free Flow , Reaching Water Security Through Cooperation, Tudor Rose, UNESCO Publishing

66. Fresh Water Futures: Imagining Responses to Demand Growth, Climate Change, and the Politics of Water Resource Management by 2040, Prepared by- The Stimson Center, www.stimson.org/images/uploads/.../StimsonCenterConfWaterReport.pdf

67. Garg and Hassan; 2030 Water Resources Group, Charting Our Water Future: Economic Frameworks to Inform Decision-Making (McKinsey & Company, 2009), http://www.mckinsey.com/App_Media/Reports/Water/Charting_Our_Water_Future_Full_Report_001.pdf.

68. General Assembly resolution 56/83 of 12 December 2001.

69. Global Risks 2015; 10th Edition, World Economic Forum Insight Report

70. Global Trends 2030 Alternative Worlds, NIC 2012-001; National Intelligence Council, http://www.dni.gov/files/documents/GlobalTrends_2030.pdf

71. Global Water Security, International Community Assessment, Dept of National Intelligence,USA,2012 . http://www.transboundarywaters.orst.edu/publications/publications/ICA_Global%20Water%20Security[1]%20(1).pdf)

72. Goswami Dulal C, Gauhati University, "Towards Sustainable Use of the Brahmaputra", Published in International Centre for Integrated Mountain Development (ICIMOD) Newsletter : Sustainable Mountain Development in the Greater Himalayan Region, No.50, Summer 2006

73. Government of India (2010), Groundwater Scenario of India 2009–10, Central Ground Water Board, Ministry of Water Resources: http://www.cgwb.gov.in/documents/Ground Water Year Book%2 02009-10.pdf

74. Hasan, Munawar "India Gives Go Ahead to another Dam on Chenab IHK" International The News, 14 March 2010. http://thenews.jang.com.pk/TodaysPrintDetail.aspx?ID=27783&Cat=13&dt=3/14/2010

75. Hayato Kobayashi, Exploring Alternative Futures Of The World Water System. Building A Second Generation Of World Water Scenarios. Driving Force: Agriculture, , 2010; United Nations World Water Assessment Programme.

76. Heather Cooley, Newsha Ajami, Mai-Lan Ha, Veena Srinivasan, Jason Morrison, Kristina Donnelly, and Juliet Christian-Smith ,Global Water Governance in the Twenty-First Century, pg 1

77. Hegde Narayan G. , WATER SCARCITY AND SECURITY IN INDIA

78. Himalaya Initiative-News.7 January 2011, http://chimalaya.org/2011/01/07/climate-change-can-stir-indo-pak-conflict/

79. Himalayan Glaciers: Climate Change, Water Resources, and Water Security. Committee on Himalayan Glaciers, Hydrology, Climate Change, and Implications for Water Security; Board on Atmospheric Studies and Climate; Division on Earth and Life Studies; National Research Council

http://www.nap.edu/catalog.php?record_id=13449)

80. Himalayas : Himalayan Facts : Main Himalayan Rivers,

http://www.himalaya2000.com/himalayan-facts/himalayan-rivers.html, accessed on 22 Febuary 2014 .

81. ICIMOD, Climate Change Impacts on the Water Resources of the Indus Basin (Kathmandu: ICIMOD, March 2010),

http://books.icimod.org/uploads/tmp/icimod-climate_change_impacts_on_the_water_resources_of_the_indus_basin:_.pdf.

82. ICIMOD, Climate Change in the Hindu Kush-Himalayas: The State of Knowledge (Kathmandu: ICIMOD, 2011),

http://lib.icimod.org/record/9417/files/icimod-climate_change_in_the_hindu_kush-himalayas.pdf;

83. ICIMOD, Status of Glaciers in the Indus Basin (Kathmandu: ICIMOD, March 2012), http://geoportal.icimod.org/MENRISFactSheets/

Sheets/2icimod-snow_cover_status_and_trends_in_the_indus_basin. pdf.

84. Igor A. Shiklomanov, State Hydrological Institute (SHL. St. Petersburg) and United Nations Educational,

85. Imtiaz Ahmed, Global Climate Change and Pakistan's Water Resources, Pakistan Council of Research in Water Resources (PCRWR), Jun 1999.

86. India allowed to go ahead with J&K's Kishanganga project. The Times of India, 21 Dec 13

87. India's National Water Policy, 2012; Government of India, Ministry of Water Resources India, Pages 3 and 5 http://wrmin.nic.in/ writereaddata/NationalWaterPolicy/NWP2012Eng6495132651.pdf

88. India's Water Woes Sunday, 16 March 2014 | Uttam Kumar Sinha | in Agenda http://www.dailypioneer.com/sunday-edition/agenda/cover-story/indias-water-woes.html)

89. India's Water Wealth .Water Resource Information system of India ,http://india-wris.nrsc.gov.in/wrpinfo/index.php?title=India%27s_ Water_Wealth

90. Indo-Bhutan hydropower initiative increase installation capacity", Economic Times, March 26, 2009, .

91. Indus River, Geography of India, Indianetzone, http://www. indianetzone.com/14/indus_river.htm, accessed on 31 October 2013.

92. Indus Waters : Kishenganga Arbitration (Pakistan v. India)

93. International Commission on Large Dams, "Intranet," online data; and World Commission on Dams, "Dams and Water: Global Statistics," online data.

94. International River Basins of the World International Journal of Water Resources Development, Vol. 15 No. 4, December 1999. http://www. transboundarywaters.orst.edu/publications/register/

95. International Rivers, 2013. Available at: www.internationalrivers.org/

96. International Water Law Project (IWLP),Status of the Watercourses Convention,

97. Interview of Kirit S. Parikh, in India's water crisis: causes and cures, Produced by The National Bureau of Asian Research for the Senate

India Caucus, August 2013

98. IPCC, 2014: Summary for policymakers. In: Climate Change 2014: Impacts, Adaptation, and Vulnerability. Part A: Global and Sectoral Aspects. Contribution of Working Group II to the Fifth Assessment Report of the Intergovernmental Panel on Climate Change [Field, C.B., V.R. Barros, D.J. Dokken, K.J. Mach, .

99. Iram Khalid, Trans-Boundary Water Sharing Issues: A Case of South Asia , Journal of Political Studies, Vol. 1, Issue 2, 79-96; pu.edu.pk/ images/journal/pols/Currentissue-pdf/Iram5.pdf

100. Ismail Serageldin, Roshni Chakraborty, Sharing of River Waters among India and its Neighbors in the 21st century: War or Peace?

101. Iyer, Ramaswamy. "Arbitration & Kishanganga Project" The Hindu, 25 June 2010. http://www.thehindu.com/opinion/ lead/article485555. ece

102. Iyer, Ramaswamy. "Baglihar: Resolving the Differences" The Hindu, 1 March 2007. http://www.hindu.com/2007/03/01/ stories/2007030101861000.htm

103. Iyer, Ramaswamy. "Briscoe on the Indus Treaty: A Response" EPW Research Foundation, 15 January 2011. http://epw.in/epw/user/ loginArticleError.jsp?hid_artid=15616

104. Jian Xie et al. (2009). Addressing China's Water Scarcity:Recommendations for Selected Water Resource Management Issues. TheWorld Bank: xx-xxi.

105. Jianchu Xu et al., "The Melting Himalayas: Cascading Effects of Climate Change on Water, Biodiversity, and Livelihoods," Conservation Biology 23, no.3 (2009), http://academic.regis.edu/ ckleier/conservation%20biology/melting_himalaya.pdf;

106. Jill Boberg, Liquid Assets: How Demographic Changes and Water Development Policies Affect Freshwater Resources (Santa Monica, CA: RAND, 2005)

107. Joseph Anil K, "No Plans to Divert the Brahmaputra: China", Posted in Rediff News on 22 November 2006 from Beijing, http://www.rediff. com/news/2006/nov/22china.htm, accessed on 10 August 2014.

108. Kao, H. M., Ren, H., Lee, C. S., Chang, C. P., Yen, J. Y., and Lin, T. H. "Determination of shallow water depth using optical satellite images."

International Journal of Remote Sensing.2009,

109. Kishanganga Water Dispute: Pakistan on Strong Wicket" South Asia Monitor. 18 June, 2010. http://www.southasiamonitor.org/index. php?option=com_content&view=article&id=273&catid=36&Item id=75

110. Krishnan Ananth, "India China and Water Security", Published in 'The Hindu" on 20 October 2009, http://www.thehindu.com/opinion/op-ed/article36468.ece, accessed on 30 July 2013

111. L. Berga. (2006). Dams and Reservoirs, Societies and Environment in the21st Century, Vol.1. (London: Taylor and Francis): 27.

112. Laghari et al. p.1069; Sharma et al., "Indo-Gangetic River Basins," p.4.

113. Leslie Hook, "China: High and Dry," Financial Times, May 14, 2013.

114. Lima climate accord: positive steps on the road to Paris, IISS Strategic Comments

115. Ling Li, "Save China Through Water From Tibet", Beijing, November 2005.

116. Liviu Giosan et al., "Fluvial landscapes of the Harappan civilization," Proceedings of the National Academy of Sciences, Early Edition on-line, forthcoming 2013, http://www.pnas.org/content/early/2012/05/24/1112743109.full.pdf.

117. Mckinsey Report, ' Chartingour Water Future', November 2009. http://www.mckinsey.com/App_Media/Reports/Water/Charting_Our_Water_Future_Exec%20Summary_001.pdf

118. M.M. Mekonnen and A.Y. Hoekstra, "The green, blue and grey water footprint of crops and derived crop products," Hydrology and Earth System Sciences 15, no.5 (2011), http://www.waterfootprint.org/Reports/Mekonnen-Hoekstra-2011-WaterFootprintCrops.pdf; Mesfin M. Mekonnen and Arjen Y. Hoekstra, "A Global Assessment of the Water Footprint of Farm Animal Products," Ecosystems 15, no.3 (2012), http://www.waterfootprint.org/Reports/Mekonnen-Hoekstra-2012-WaterFootprintFarmAnimalProducts.pdf

119. Mahanta Chandan, "Water Resources in the North East : State of the Knowledge Base", Background Paper No.2, August 2006, for World Bank Study "Development and Growth in Northeast India: The Natural Resources, Water, and Environment Nexus

120. Maj A Sharma , Dissertation , DSSC, 2010

121. Maj Gen AK Chaturvedi, (Retd) AVSM, VSM Water - A Source for Future Conflicts,

122. Maj General MKS Yadav, SM, Thesis submitted at National Defence College, New Delhi, 2011 on" Indo-China Trans-Border Rivers and Their Management"

123. Maj Rajiv Ahlawat, Dissertation Water Resource Management And Study Of It's Potential As A Source Of Future Conflict In South Asia. Need For A Comprehensive Strategy To Avert Such Regional Crisis, DSSC, 2010

124. Mallik, Priyanka. "Tulbul: The Politics of Water between India and Pakistan". Institute of Peace and Conflict Studies. 30 June 2006. http://www.ipcs.org/article_details. php?articleNo=2055

125. Mandhana Niharika, Water Wars: Why India and Pakistan Are Squaring Off Over Their Rivers, Time, Monday, Apr. 16, 2012

126. Mangla Dam Raising Afectees to Get Compesation by Year End' Dawn. 25 February 2011. http://www.dawn. com/2011/02/25/mangla-dam-raising-affectees-to-getcompensation-

127. Mark Giordano & Tushaar Shah (2014) From IWRM back to integrated water

128. Mark Giordano, Alena Drieschova, James A. Duncan, Yoshiko Sayama, Lucia De Stefano & Aaron T. Wolf, A review of the evolution and state of transboundary freshwater treaties, 2013 ,.http://www.transboundarywaters.orst.edu/publications/publications/Giordano%20et%20al.%20Treaty%20Update%204-13.pdf

129. Mats Eriksson et al., The Changing Himalayas: Impact of Climate Change on Water Resources and Livelihoods in the Greater Himalayas (Kathmandu: ICIMOD, 2009), p.2, http://books.icimod.org/index. php/search/publication/593.

130. Mazid Nizami, The Water Bomb, www.zimbio.com, 29 May 08.

131. Meador, Michael R." Inter-basin Water Transfer: Ecological Concerns." Fisheries, Vol. 17.2, 1992: 17-22.

132. Mekong River Commission Strategic Environmental Assessment 2010 that examines what would happen if the eleven proposed Lower

Mekong Dams were built. The study was conducted with input from many of the region's leading scientists, government officials, and the public. Before this study, the Mekong governments had limited understanding of the environmental and social costs of building the dams.

133. Ministry for Water Resources, River Development and Ganga Rejuvenation, Government of India.

134. Mukand S. Babel and Shahriar M. Wahid, Freshwater Under Threat: South Asia (Bangkok/Nairobi: Asian Institute of Technology/UNEP, 2008), p.14, http://www.unep.org/pdf/southasia_report.pdf;

135. Mustafa, Khalid. "India to help Afghanistan Build 12 Dams on the Kabul River." The News, 12 May 2011. http://www.thenews.com.pk/TodaysPrintDetail.aspx?ID=5933&Cat=13&dt=5/12/2011

136. National Group of China, ISRM, and National Society for Rock Mechanics and Engineering. (2009, December 3). "South-to-North Water Transfer Project."[Online]. Available: http://www.csrme.com/EN/News/2009-12/EnableSite_ReadNews713509261259769600.html.

137. Natural Resources Journal 2003, http://www.transboundarywaters.orst.edu/publications/abst_docs/giordano_mer_2003.pdf

138. Natural sciences ,UNESCO

139. Neelam-Jhelum Hydropower project Cost increases on Delays" PML-N Website, 30 March, 2011. http://www.pmln.org.pk/featured/report_1361_neelum-jhelumhydropower-project-cost-increases-on-delays.pmln

140. Nepali Times, 30 August - 5 September 2000,

141. Nitin Pai, Climate Change and National Security ; Preparing India for New Conflict Scenarios, Indian National Interest Policy Brief No. 1, Apr 2008.

142. Official Website of Central Water Commission, Government of India, http://www.cwc.nic.in/, accessed on 31 August 2014.

143. Official Website of Brahmaputra Board, http://brahmaputraboard.gov.in/, accessed on 01 August 2013.

144. Official Website of Central Water Commission, Government of India,

http://www.cwc.nic.in/http://www.cwc.nic.in/main/downloads/Water_Data_Complete_Book_2005.pdf, accessed on 31 July 2014.

145. Origin of Brahmaputra River', Geography of India, Indianetzone, http://www.indianetzone.com/29/origin_brahmaputra_river.htm, accessed on 31 July 2014.

146. Pahuja, Sanjay. "Planning and Prioritizing Water Resources Investments: The Example of the Kabul River Basin, Afghanistan" The World Bank, South Asia Region. http://www.carecinstitute.org/uploads/events/2009/8th-ESCC/Kabul-River-Basin-Example.pdf

147. Pakistan Water and Power Development Authority(WAPDA), History of Irrigation in Indus Basin, Volume I, Lahore, 1987.

148. Paul Wyrwoll, India's Groundwater Crisis. Posted On July 30 ,2012 In Development , Water Security, , Australian National University, Australia

149. Pomeranz, Kenneth, et al. "Himalayan Water Security: The Challenges for South and Southeast Asia." asia policy 16 (2013): 1-50.Himalayan Water Security: The Challenges for South and Southeast Asia; Asia Policy, number 16(july 2013), .

150. Quenching the Dragon's Thirst The South-North Water Transfer Project—Old Plumbing for New China? By Carla Freeman

151. Rafik Hirji and Richard Davis, Environmental Flows in Water Resources Policies, Plans, and Projects: Findings and Recommendations (Washington, DC: World Bank, 2009), p.48, http://siteresources.worldbank.org/INTWAT/Resources/Env_Flows_Water_v1.pdf.

152. Rahaman, M.M.: "The Ganges Water Conflict",p.196.

153. Report on Hydroelectric Projects in Himachal Pradesh, Chapter 2.3, http://sjvn.nic.in/projects/rampurpdf/chap2_revised_4.pdf, accessed on 25 August 2014

154. Resources management, International Journal of Water Resources Development,

155. Rodell, M., Velicogna, I. and J. Famiglietti (2009), 'Satellite-based estimates of groundwater depletion in India', Nature, Vol. 460, pp. 999-1002.

156. Roznama Jang, Pakistan, 27Jun 2009.

157. S. Puri and A. Aureli eds., Atlas of Transboundary Aquifers (Paris: UNESCO, 2009), http://www.isarm.org/publications/324.

158. Saxena, N.C. (2010) Personal Communication with Uma Lele.

159. Scientific and Cultural Organisation (UNESCO, Paris), 1999.

160. Seckler D, Barker R,Upali A et al, Water Scarcity in The Twenty first Century, 2010,Pg 40.

161. Shah, T. (2011), 'Innovations in Groundwater Management: Examples from India', International Water Management Institute: http://rosenberg.ucanr.org/documents/argentina/Tushar Shah Final.pdf.

162. Shaheen, Dr. Akhtar. "Emerging Challenges to Indus Water Treaty: Issues Of Compliance & Transboundary Impacts Of Indian Hydroprojects On The Western Rivers" Institute Of Regional Studies, Islamabad. Volume XXVIII, No. 3, 2010. http://www.irs.org.pk/PublFocus.htm

163. Sharma Vishal, "Lakes Pose Threat to North India", Published in "Chandigarh Tribune" on 19 August 2006, http://www.tribuneindia.com/2006/20060820/cth1.htm#7, accessed on 18 August 2013.

164. Shemin Ge, Mian Liu, Ning Lu, Jonathan W. Godt, and Gang Luo, "Did the Zipingpu Reservoir Trigger the 2008 Wenchuan Earthquake?" Geophysical Research Letters 36 (2009). Also see Richard Kerr and Richard Stone, "A Human Trigger for the Great Quake of Sichuan," Science, 323, no. 5912 (January 16, 2009); Sharon La Franiere, "Possible Link Between Dam and China Quake," New York Times, February 6, 2009; and Jordan Lite, "Great China Earthquake May Have Been Man-Made," Scientific American, February 3, 2009.

165. Singh Dhruv Vijay, erstwhile Secretary, Minister for Water Resources, River Development and Ganga Rejuvenation, Government of India

166. Singh Vijay P & Others, Editor, "The Brahmaputra Basin Water Resources", Chapter 13 on "Water Resources Planning" by Phukan SS, Pages 299-301.

167. South-to-North Water Diversion Project, China", Website for the Water and Wastewater Industry, http://www.water-technology.net/projects/South_north/, accessed on 09 August 2014.

168. Status of Watercourses Convention as on 22 May 2014, International Water Law website.http://www.internationalwaterlaw.org/

documents/intldocs/watercourse_status.html Accessed on 26 January 2015.

169. Stimson Centre- http://www.stimson.org/research-pages/the-indus-waters-treaty-a-history/

170. Stimson Centre Water Conference Report , 2010- Fresh Water Futures: Imagining Responses to Demand Growth, Climate Change, and the Politics of Water Resource Management by 2040

171. Stimson Centre: Regional Voices- Troubled Waters: Climate Change, Hydropolitics & Transboundary Resources (http://www.globalpolicy.org/images/pdfs/troubled_waters-complete.pdf)

172. Subrahmanyam Sridhar, The Indus Water Treaty, Security Research Review, Volume 13, www.bharat-rakshak.com.

173. Sultan, Ghalib. "In Kashmir, water treaty means less power to the people". Zone Asia-Pk. 30 July 2010. http://www.zoneasia-pk.com/ZoneAsia-Pk/index.php?option=com_content&view=article&id=11 54:inkashmir-water-treaty-means-less-power-to-the-people&catid= 35:internationalpolitics&Itemid=60

174. T. P. Barnett, J. C. Adam, and D. P. Lettenmaier, "Potential Impacts of a Warming Climate on Water Availability in Snow- Dominated Regions," Nature, No. 438 (November 17, 2005), p. 306.

175. T.E. Bilir, M. Chatterjee, K.L. Ebi, Y.O. Estrada, R.C. Genova, B. Girma, E.S. Kissel, A.N. Levy, S. MacCracken, P.R. Mastrandrea, and L.L. White (eds.)]. Cambridge University Press, Cambridge, United Kingdom and New York, NY, USA, pp. 1-32.

176. The CPC Central Committee and the State Council's Number 1 Document for 2011 (unofficial translation), at http://gain.fas.usdo.gov/Recent%20GAIN%.

177. The Daily Star 16 June 2010

178. The Dawn, Pakistan, 14 February 2005.

179. The Economic Times, PTI Dec 16, 2014, 01.03PM IST. China commissions its $80 billion water-diversion-project .http://articles.economictimes.indiatimes.com/2014-12-16/news/57112541_1_yangtze-danjiangkou-reservoir-water-quality

180. The Indus Equation, Strategic Foresight Group. Strategic Foresight

Group, 2011

181. The Indus Waters Treaty: A History, Research Pages, Stimson Centre-http://www.stimson.org/research-pages/the-indus-waters-treaty-a-history/

182. The Planning Commission Approach to the 12th Plan :The Challenges of Urbanisation in India

183. The Subansiri River", Official Website of Dhemaji District, http://dhemaji.nic.in/floods/rivers.htm, accessed on 31 July 2014

184. The UN Watercourses Convention Enters Into Force, Fri, 08/22/2014 - By: Jace White, the 1997 UN Convention on the Law of Non-Navigational Uses of International Watercourses (UNWC)

185. The World Water Organization Website, http://www.theworldwater.org/world_water.php, accessed on 30 Nov 2014.

186. Theme Paper on Transboundary Waters, World Water Day 2009 , Central Water Commission , Government Of India Ministry Of Water Resources.

187. Transboundary Freshwater Dispute Database (TFDD) http://www.transboundarywaters.orst.edu/database/interfreshtreatdata.html

188. Tributaries of Brahmaputra River", Geography of India, Indianetzone, http://indianetzone.com/29/tributaries_brahmaputra_river.htm, accessed on 11 January 2014.

189. Tubilewicz Czeslaw, Editor, "Critical Issues in Contemporary China", Routledge – Taylor & Francis Group, August 2006, Chapter 5: "China's Environmental Problems" by Richard Louis Edmonds, page 134.

190. Tuteja Ravi, "Status and Security Implications of Rivers Emanating fron Tibet and Flowing through India ",Article No : 1019 posted at "Centre for Land Warfare Studies" website on 12 October 2007, http://www.claws.in/index.php, accessed on 01 August 2014.

191. UN Convention on the Law of the Non-Navigational Uses of International Watercourses-1997,http://www.internationalwaterlaw.org/documents/intldocs/watercourse_conv.html,accessed   on   02 January 2015 .

192. UN Economic and Social Commission for Asia and the Pacific, The State of the Environment in Asia and the Pacific 2005 (Bangkok: UN

Economic and Social Commission for Asia and the Pacific, 2006)

193. UN Food and Agriculture Organization, 'Freshwater Availability: Precipitation and Internal Renewable Water Resources (IRWR)', Aquastat online table, http://www.fao.org/nr/water/, 2011.

194. UN World Water Development Report, 2014.

195. Undala Z. Alam, Water Rationality: Mediating the Indus Water Treaty, September 1998, (unpublished PhD thesis from University of Durham, UK, 1998) (Accessed 22 March 2013).

196. United Nation Economic Commission for Europe;

197. United Nations Development Programme, Human Development Report 2006. Beyond Scarcity: Power, Poverty and the Global Water Crisis (New York: UNDP, 2006), http://hdr.undp.org/en/media/ HDR06-complete.pdf.

198. United Nations World Water Assessment Program, Water in a Changing World Report (Colombella: UN World Water Assessment Program, 2009);

199. Unpublished Ph D thesis from University of Durham, UK, 1998 According to the water rationality thesis, countries would prefer cooperation to conflict to promote long-term security of their water supplies (p. 24).

200. UN-Water Concept Note "Water Security – A Working Definition" [internal document, 4th Draft, 2011] and the Ministerial Declaration of The Hague on Water Security in the 21st Century, Second World Water Forum, 22 March, 2000

201. Upali Amarasinghe 2012, The National River Linking Project of India: Some Contentious Issues ,Water Policy Research,www.iwmi. org/iwmi-tata/apm

202. Uttam Kumar Sinha (2012) Examining China's Hydro- Behaviour: Peaceful or Assertive?, Strategic Analysis, 36:1, 41-56, DOI: 10.1080/09700161.2012. Abcdefgh4th from rthttp://dx.doi.org/10.10 80/09700161.2012.628487

203. Uttam Kumar Sinha , Arvind Gupta & Ashok Behuria (2012): Will the Indus Water Treaty Survive?, Strategic Analysis, 36:5, 735-752

204. Uttam Kumar Sinha ,China: Geopolitics of a Thirsty Nation , Indian

Foreign Affairs Journal Vol. 6, No. 4, October-December 2011, 422-436, http://www.associationdiplomats.org/publications/ifaj/Vol6/6.4/ARTICLE%202.pdf

205. V.I. Kravtsova et al., "Variations of the Hydrological Regime, Morphological Structure, and Landscapes of the Indus River Delta (Pakistan) under the Effect of Large-Scale Water Management Measures," Water Resources 36, no.4 (2009), pp.367, 369;

206. Verghese, B.G. "An Inconvenient Truth: Responding to Pakistan's Water Concerns and Challenges" Writings and Commentaries – BG Verghese, 8 June, 2010. http://www.bgverghese.com/PakistanWater. html .

207. Vladimir Smakhtin, "Basin Closure and Environmental Flow Requirements," International Journal of Water Resources Development 24, no.2 (2008); Sharma et al., "The Indus and the Ganges: river basins under extreme pressure," Water International 35, no.5 (2010.

208. Walter W. Immerzeel, Ludovicus P. H. van Beek, and Marc F. P. Bierkens, "Climate Change Will Affect the Asian Water Towers," Science, Vol. 328, No. 5983 (June 11, 2010), pp. 1384- 85.

209. Water And Related Statistics, Water Resources Information System Directorate Information System Organisation, Water Planning & Projects Wing Central Water Commission, December 2013.

210. Water and Security in South Asia (WASSA) Projects, Volume III, p42

211. Water not Stolen in India but Wasted in Pakistan: Qureshi' Outlook India, April 2010. http://news.outlookindia.com/ item.aspx?678581

212. Water Rationality :Mediating the Indus Waters Treaty . Undala Z. Alam.

213. Water Resources Group 2030 (Barilla Group, Coca-Cola Company, International Finance Corporation, McKinsey & Company, Nestlé S.A., New Holland Agriculture, SABMiller PLC, Standard Chartered Bank, and Syngenta AG), Charting Our Water Future (New York: 2030 Water Resources Group, 2009), p. 10.

214. Water Security & the Global Water Agenda, A UN-Water Analytical Brief, United Nations University Institute for Water, Environment & Health (UNU-INWEH),2013

215. Water Security for India: The External Dynamics; Institute for

Defence Studies and Analyses

216. Water Wars: Enduring Myth or Impending Reality, Africa Dialogue Monograph Series No.2, Edited by Hussein Solomon and Anthony Turton

217. Water: New Challenge for Pakistan. Special Report Water Crisis" Pakistan, courtesy Pakistan Observer. No date specified. http://www.pakissan.com/english/watercrisis/water.new.challenge.for.pakistan.shtml

218. Weiluo Wang, "Water Resources and the Sino-Indian Strategic Partnership", http://www.hrichina.org/sites/default/files/oldsite/PDFs/CRF.1.2006/CRF-2006-1_Water.pdf, accessed on 09 August 2013

219. World Bank (2010), Deep Wells and Prudence: Towards Pragmatic Action for Addressing Groundwater Overexploitation in India, World Bank.

220. World Bank, Pakistan's Water Economy: Running Dry (Washington, DC: World Bank, 2005).

221. World Climate Research Programme's Third Coupled Model Inter-comparison Project

222. Wullar Barrage: An Unresolved 'Question". Kashmir Life. http://www.kashmirlife.net/index.php?option=com_content&view=article&id=734:wullar-barrage-an-unresolvedquestion

223. WWAP (United Nations World Water Assessment Programme). 2014. The United Nations World Water Development Report 2014: Water and Energy. Paris, UNESCO. http://www.unesco.org/new/en/natural-sciences/environment/water/wwap/wwdr/wwdr3-2009/downloads-wwdr3/.

224. www.Pakistaninfo.com, article titled 'Water the Lifeline' by Abdul Majid dated 23 April 2001.

225. Xinhua News Agency, "Scientist finds new origin of Indus River", Published in "China Daily" on 21 October 2010, http://www2.chinadaily.com.cn/china/2010-10/21/content_11441098.htm, accessed on 30 April 2014

226. Y. Ding, S. Liu, J. Li, and D. Shangguan, "The Retreat of Glaciers in Response to Recent Climate Warming in Western China," Annals of

Glaciology Vol. 43, No. 1 (2006), pp. 97-105

227. Yoshihide Wada et al., "Non-sustainable groundwater sustaining irrigation: A global assessment," Water Resources Research 48, W00L06 (2012), p.11, http://onlinelibrary.wiley.com/doi/10.1029/2011WR010562/pdf.

228. Zhang, Quanfa. "The South-to-North Water Transfer Project of China: Environmental Implications and Monitoring Strategy." Journal of the American Water Resources Association, Vol. 45.5, 2009: 1238-1247.

229. Zhengyin Qian, "Water Resources Development in China", China Water and Power Press, Beijing, 1994, Chapter 2, "History of Water Conservancy", page 43-93.

LIST OF WEBSITES ACCESSED

1. http ://www. c e a . n i c. in / hydro/Cooperation%20with%20 Neighbouring%20Countries.pdf

2. http//www.lib.tkk.fi

3. http://12thplan.gov.in/12fyp_docs/17.pdf

4. Center For Climate Change and Energy Solutions. http://www.c2es. org/

5. Central Ground Water Board, http://www.cgwb.gov.in/

6. http://chellaney.net/2012/03/17/asias-worsening-water-crisis/

7. http://content.time.com/time/world/article/0,8599,2111601,00.html

8. http://dx.doi.org/10.1080/09700161.2012.712376

9. http://economictimes.indiatimes.com/News/News-By-Industry/Indo-Bhutan-hydropower-initiative-increase-installation-capacity/articleshow/4320446.cms.

10. http://himalaya.socanth.cam.ac.uk/collections/ journals/nepalitimes/pdf/Nepali_Times_007.pdf

11. http://lib.icimod.org/record/9417/files/icimod-climate_change_in_the_hindu_kush-himalayas.pdf

12. http://timesofindia.indiatimes.com/india/India-allowed-to-go-ahead-with-JKs-Kishanganga-project/articleshow/27738180.cms

13. http://untreaty.un.org/ilc/texts /instruments/english/ draft%20 articles/9_6_2001.pdf

14. http://worldwater.org/wp-content/uploads/sites/22/2013/07/ww8-ch1-us-water-policy.pdf

15. http://wrmin.nic.in/forms/list.aspx?lid=347&Id=4

16. http://www.bhutanpeoplesparty.org/lawtreaty/chukhahydro.htm

17. http://www.c2es.org/international/key-country-policies/india/climate-plan-summary

18. http://www.cwc.nic.in/main/downloads/Water%20and%20Related%20Statistics-2013.pdf

19. http://www.fox8.com/news/nationworld/sns-ap-as-kashmir-melting-glaciers,0,3853345.story

20. http://www.gee-21.org/publications/Water-Sharing-Conflicts-Between-Countries-and-Approaches-to-Resolving-Them.pdf

21. http://www.indiaenvironmentportal.org.in/files/book_WaterSecurity.pdf

22. http://www.internationalrivers.org/resources/the-lower-mekong-dams-factsheet-text-7908

23. http://www.internationalwaterlaw.org/documents/intldocs/watercourse_status.html

24. http://www.opfblog.com/7193/pakistan%E2%80%99shydropower-generation-agenda/

25. http://www.pca-cpa.org/formulier_members.asp?pag_id=1161

26. http://www.strategicforesight.com/finalsettlement/lifeline.pdf

27. http://www.strategicforesight.com/publication_pdf/10345110617.pdf

28. http://www.thedailystar.net/newDesign/news-details.php?nid=142804

29. http://www.unece.org/env/water/

30. http://www.unesco.org/water/news/transboundary_aquifers.shtml

31. http://www.wilsoncenter.org/article/us-china-cooperation-the-significance-the-joint-agreement-climate-change-and-clean-energy

Other References

Abramovitz, Janet. (1996, March). Imperiled waters, impoverished future: The decline of freshwater ecosystems (Worldwatch Paper No. 128). Washington, DC: Worldwatch Institute.

Agence France Presse. (2000, November 23). Sun Star Davao, page 5.

Asian Development Bank (1999). "Water in the 21st century."Asian Development Bank Annual Report 1999.Manila, Philippines: Asian Development Bank.

Brautigam, A. (1999). "The freshwater biodiversity crisis ."World Conservation 30 (2), 4-5.

Brown, L. &Halweil, B. (1998). "China's water shortage could shake world food security." Worldwatch11 (4), 10-21.

Carty, W. (1991)."Towards an urban world."Earthwatch 43, 2-4.

Clarke, R. (1991). Water: The international crisis. Cambridge, Massachusetts: MIT Press.

Darmon, A. (1996). "The makings of a water crisis."UNESCO Sources 84, 12-13.

Department of Environment and Natural Resources.(1998). Water watch. Manila: Department of Environmental and Natural Resources.

Engelman, Robert &LeRoy, P. (1993).Sustaining water: Population and the future of renewablewater supplies.Washington DC: Population Action International.

Engelman, Robert &LeRoy, P. (1995).Sustaining water: An update. Washington DC: Population Action International.

Environmental Management Bureau.(1996). Philippine environmental quality report (1990-1995). Manila: Department of Environment and Natural Resources.

Environmental Protection Agency. (1995). The quality of our nation's water: 1994. Washington DC: Environmental Protection Agency.

European Schoolbooks. (1994). The battle for water: Earth's most precious resource. Cheltenham, United Kingdom.

Facon, Thierry. (2000). Rice production and water management in Asia:

Some issues for the future. Food and Agriculture Organization, Bangkok, Thailand.

Falkenmark, Malin. (1990). "Population growth and water supplies: An emerging crisis." People 17 (1), 18-20.

Falkenmark, Malin. (1991). "Rapid population growth and water scarcity: The predicament of tomorrow's Africa." In K. Davis & M. Bernstam (Eds.), Resources, environment and population:Present knowledge and future options (pages 81-94). New York: Oxford University Press.

Falkenmark, Malin. (1994). "Population, environment and development: A water perspective." In

Population, environment and development: Proceedings of the United Nations Expert Group Meeting on Population, Environment and Development (pages 99-116). New York: UnitedNations.

Falkenmark, Malin&Lundqvist, Jan. (1997).Comprehensive assessment of the freshwater re-sources of the world: World freshwater problems call for a new realism. Stockholm: StockholmEnvironment Institute.

Gardner-Outlaw, Thomas &Engelman, Robert. (1997). Sustaining water, easing scarcity: A secondupdate. Washington DC: Population Action International.

Gleick, Peter. (1993). "An introduction to global fresh water issues." In Peter Gleick (Ed.), Water incrisis (pages 3-12). New York: Oxford University Press.

Gleick, Peter. (2000). The world's water 2000-2001. Washington, DC: Island Press.

Gorecho, Dennis. (1998, January 10). "Water: RP's future is dry and dirty." Today, A21.

Harrison, P. (1992). The third revolution: Environment, population and a sustainable world. Lon-don: I.B. Tauris.

Havas-Szilagyi, E. (1998). "National groundwater protection program in Hungary."Presented at the International Conference of Water and Sustainable Development, Paris, March 19-21.Authors.

Hinrichsen, D. (1998). Coastal waters of the world: Trends, threats and strategies. Washington, DC: Island Press.

Langit, Richel. (1996, April 29). "Rich, poor both cry out, 'Tubig!'" The

Manila Times, A4.

Lefort, R. (1996). "Down to the last drop."UNESCO Sources 84, 7.

Malaysian Water Partnership. (2000). Malaysia: National water vision to action—The way forward. Paper presented at the FAO-ESCAP Technical Cooperation Project on World Water Vision, Bangkok, Thailand. Authors.

Maniquis, Estrella. (1996). "Water policy in Manila."The IDRC Reports. Ontario, Canada: Interna-tional Development Research Center.

Marcoux, A. (1994). Population and water resources. Rome: FAO.

Mitchell,J.(1998,January-February). "Beforethenextdoubling."Worldwatch Magazine, 20-27.

"Most rivers in the world are polluted." (1999). Washington DC: Inter-Press Service Wire Service.

Nash, L. (1993). "Water quality and health."In Peter Gleick (Ed.), Water in crisis. New York: Oxford University Press.

National Water Resources Board.(2000). Case study on the formulation of national water vision. Paper presented at the FAO-ESCAP Technical Cooperation Project on World Water Vision, Bangkok, Thailand.

Niemczynowicz, J. (1996). "Wasted waters."UNESCO Sources, No. 84.

Patel, T. (1997, April 26). "India faces chaos over water rights." New Scientist, 12.

Pimentel, David; Houser, J.; Preiss, E.; White, O.; Fang, H.; Mesnick, L.; Barsky, T.; Tariche, S.; Schrick, J.; & Alpert, S. (1997). "Water resources: Agriculture, the environment and society."

BioScience 46 (2), 97-105.

Population Reference Bureau.(1998). Population and environment dynamics [Wall Chart]. Wash-ington, DC: Population Reference Bureau.

Postel, Sandra. (1996a). Dividing the waters: Food security, ecosystem health and the new politicsof scarcity (Worldwatch paper No. 132). Washington, DC: Worldwatch Institute.

Postel, Sandra. (1996b). "Sharing the rivers." People & the Planet 5 (3), 6-9.

Postel, Sandra. (1997). Last oasis: Facing water scarcity. New York: WW Norton & Co.

Postel, Sandra. (1999). Pillar of sand: Can the irrigation miracle last? New York: WW Norton & Co.

Postel, Sandra; Daily, G.; & Ehrlich, Paul.(1996). "Human appropriation of renewable freshwater."Science 271 (5250), 785-788.

Pullen, S. and Hurst, P. (1993).Marine pollution prevention.WWF background report. Gland, Swit-zerland: WWF.

Purdum, Todd. (1997, December 19). "U.S. acts to meet water needs in the West." New YorkTimes, A10.

Revkin, A. (1997, August 31). "Billion dollar plan to clean New York City water at its source."NewYork Times, A1, A28.

Robey, B.; Rutstein, S.O.; Morris, L.; and Blackburn, R. (1992). "The reproductive revolution: New survey findings." Population Reports Series M, No. 11. Baltimore: Johns Hopkins Univeristy School of Public Health.

Serageldin, I. (1995). Toward sustainable management of water resources. Washington, DC: World Bank.

Sharing of River Waters among India and its Neighbors in the 21st century: War or Peace?by Ismail Serageldin, RoshniChakraborty

Shikolomanov, I.A. (1997). Assessment of water resources and water availability in the world. Stockholm: Stockholm Environment Institute.

Tacio, Elena. (1994, March 27). "The great thirst." Manila Chronicle, A13.

Tyler, P. (1996, May 23). "China's fickle rivers: Dry farms, needy industry bring a water crisis." NewYork Times, A10.

UNCHS (Habitat). (2001). The state of the world's cities. Nairobi: UNCHS.

United Nations Children's Fund (UNICEF). (1997). Facts and figures.[On-line]. Available: http:// www.unicef.org/factx/facright.htm

United Nations Food and Agriculture Organization (FAO).(1990). Water for life. Rome: FAO.

United Nations Foundation. (2000, January 21). "Water: Manila meeting highlights Southeast Asian woes." [On-line]. Available: http://www.unfoundation.org/unwire/archives/UNWIRE000121.asp.

United Nations Population Fund (UNFPA). (1997). Population and sustainable development: Fiveyears after Rio. New York: UNFPA.

Vitousek, P.; Mooney, H.; Lubchenco, J.; &Melillo, J.M. (1997)."Human domination of the earth's ecosystems."Science 277, 494-499.

World Health Organization (WHO). (1992). Our planet, our health— Report of the WHO Commis-sion on Health and Environment. Geneva: WHO.

World Health Organization (WHO). (1997). Health and environment in sustainable development:Five years after the Earth Summit. Geneva:

Index

www.ingramcontent.com/pod-product-compliance
Lightning Source LLC
Chambersburg PA
CBHW021120270326
41929CB00009B/976